I0810305

IMAGES
of America

ISABELLA COUNTY
1859–2009

1859 2009

ISABELLA COUNTY

150

Sesquicentennial

The Isabella County Sesquicentennial Committee of the Isabella County Board of Commissioners selected the logo design of Mount Pleasant resident Earl R. Nitschke to symbolize the spirit of the county's 150-year celebration of August 9–16, 2009. As of May 2008, the committee consisted of Christine Alwood (chair), Loren Anderson, Kathy Beebe, Mary Ellen Brandell, Steve Davidson, Robert Denslow, Clair Lapham, Margaret Lapham, Judy Pamp, Ron Roby, Robyn Shepherd (intern), Keith Voeks, Nancy White, and Richard Young.

On the cover: Lumberjacks in Michigan eventually worked themselves out of a job. This photograph from Wise Township's Don and Sandy Methner Moore shows Will and Claud Moore of Coldwater Township in front of their makeshift lumber camp quarters on May 21, 1911, the eve of their departure for Alberta, Canada. (Courtesy of the Clarke Historical Library, Central Michigan University.)

IMAGES
of America

ISABELLA COUNTY
1859–2009

Jack R. Westbrook

ARCADIA
PUBLISHING

ISBN 978-0-7385-6154-7

Published by Arcadia Publishing
Charleston, South Carolina

Printed in the United States of America

Library of Congress Catalog Card Number: 2008928995

For all general information contact Arcadia Publishing at:
Telephone 843-853-2070
Fax 843-853-0044
E-mail sales@arcadiapublishing.com
For customer service and orders:
Toll-Free 1-888-313-2665

Visit us on the Internet at www.arcadiapublishing.com

Dedicated to Isabella County pioneers, early, present, and future. Also to Bernadette "Bernie" Sunderman and her daughter Betsy Stonerock of Beal City, who insisted I expand my historical "looksees" beyond Mount Pleasant.

CONTENTS

ACKNOWLEDGMENTS

Unless otherwise indicated, photographs herein are from the files of the Clarke Historical Library, Central Michigan University, Mount Pleasant. Thanks to Isabella County residents who responded to the Isabella County Sesquicentennial Committee plea for vintage pictures, which are individually identified in captions if used. Some were unusable for this book, but all images are going into an Isabella County searchable pictorial index to be ready for the county's 150th year, 2009. Thanks to Arcadia Publishing acquisitions editor Anna Wilson and publisher John Pearson for their advice and help. Thanks to Frank Boles, director; Marian Matlyn and Tanya Fox, archivists; John Fierst, reference librarian; Pat Thelan, scanning/digitizing specialist; and Samantha Minnis, reference assistant, all of the Clarke Historical Library, for their patience and aid. Thanks to Donna Hoff-Grambau, whose body of local historical data online is commendable. When I started this project, I knew that in each county segment there was a history guru with an encyclopedic memory and photographs to match that memory. I found Joyce McClain of Mount Pleasant, an astounding woman who speaks of pioneer and current northwest Isabella County residents like friends and brought them alive for me; the Walter Rau family of Beal City; Wise Township's Sandy Methner-Moore, who was invaluable in assembling northeast Isabella County pictures from not only her own but neighbors' collections for scanning; and in the southwest quadrant of the county thanks to Wayne Barrett, whose antique shop in Winn and museum just outside town is a local-history treasure trove, brought to life by his amazing sense of his area's history. The southeast area of the county is my most familiar, but I still need Hudson Keenan; John Cumming; and Rosemary Reid of Mount Pleasant, all local historical gurus to the extreme, to bail me out occasionally; and Loren Anderson filled picture gaps of Rosebush, Blanchard, and the North Main Street Mount Pleasant depot with postcard images. Finally and most importantly, thanks to my best friend, wife, proofreader, and 50-year soul mate, Mary Lou, for her loving patience and countless saves on this and our lifetime projects.

INTRODUCTION

If you look at a map of the Lower Peninsula of Michigan you will see a right-hand mitten shaped peninsula. In the palm of that mitten is Isabella County, comprised of 16 townships, each six miles square with one-mile sections numbered 1 through 36 in a zigzag pattern beginning with the upper right corner and ending in the bottom right corner. On that canvas of flatland to gently rolling hills, people of multiple races and nationalities have come for centuries to make a new life in the land known since 1831 as Isabella County.

The area now known as Isabella County was home to abundant majestic pine and hardwood trees, one of the best such forests in the Great Lakes region. Known among the American Indians as Ojibiway Besse (the place of the Chippewa), part of the area of present-day Isabella County was their winter hunting grounds and may have been used by American Indians for more than 10,000 years. Europeans are comparatively recent arrivals. Fr. Jacques Marquette's successor, Fr. Henry Nouvel, spent a winter here in 1675 with the Beaver Clan of the Chippewa Indians. Nearly two centuries later, Europeans returned to the middle of Michigan and the area known as Isabella County.

The most commonly accepted theory is that the county, when carved out of surrounding territory and named by legislative action in 1831, was named for Queen Isabella of Spain, patroness of Christopher Columbus.

In 1855, Isabella County's first township, Coe, was established, and John Hursh settled in the area near what would become present-day Mount Pleasant. In 1859, Act No. 118 of the Michigan legislature officially established and organized Isabella County.

The story of Isabella County is not just a story of lumbering, then clearing the land, planting seeds, and growing things while pockets of population created villages, towns, and cities. Those things happened practically anywhere in the upper eastern portion of Midwest America. Isabella County's unique story is of triumph. This slender volume can only give glimpses of the millions of stories of triumphs contained in Isabella County's 576 square miles, 150 years, 89 named villages, and would-be settlements (with 30 additional "otherwise known as" names). Some named post offices existed less than a year, established at a lumber camp and discontinued at that location when timber operations moved elsewhere. In my previous Arcadia Publishing books, *Michigan Oil and Gas*, *Mount Pleasant* in the Then & Now series, and *Central Michigan University*, I focused on some facets of Isabella County life. All those, with different pictures from previous Arcadia volumes, are touched upon herein.

A brief word about content: the Isabella County Sesquicentennial Committee has been of aid gathering photographs and plans to use this book as a fund-raiser. However, decisions on the contents of this book were made solely by me, based on photographs made available to me by formal reference venues and through the generosity of Isabella County residents who opened family albums to help make this book possible. Many pictures in this book are previously unpublished, thanks to all the foregoing. There was no attempt to favor or ignore any place, family, business, or aspect of Isabella County life. This pictorial footnote is designed only to encourage the reader to seek more details about the place we live. I am sure the list of "left out" is going to exceed the "I was glad to see" comments about this effort. An old saying goes, "When you try to be all things to all people, you end up being nothing to anyone," so I did not try to write the omnibus history. Instead I subscribed to Ricky Nelson's thought expressed in an old song lyric, "If you can't please everybody, then you've got to please yourself," and I have with this, the latest of my middle Michigan photographic histories.

One

Northwestern Isabella County

The northwestern quadrant of Isabella County consists of four relatively flat and sparsely populated townships slightly more wooded than townships to the east in the county. This quadrant is not traversed by any major highway. Some light industry dots the landscape, but primarily the area is inhabited by part-time farmers and those who commute to nearby Mount Pleasant and other more populous places for employment. Three of the county's four major water recreation lakes lie in the northwestern group of Isabella County townships: Coldwater Lake (pages 26 and 27), Lake Isabella, and Littlefield Lake.

Townships and settlements in northwest Isabella County include Coldwater Township, the northwesternmost Isabella County township, which was established on March 3, 1868, on the petition of a group of 36 people to organize a village named Coldwater, after the lake in the area. The village of Coldwater never came to be, possibly because another Coldwater, Michigan, community already existed in southwestern Michigan, but the Coldwater Township name remained.

Coldwater Township had only two named towns that started but no longer exist. They are Brinton (see pages 21–25) and Nero, a post office with no known surrounding businesses that existed from 1871 until 1877 in section 24, apparently to accommodate a nearby lumber camp.

Gilmore Township, in the northern tier of the county's townships at the northeast corner of the northwest county quadrant, was organized in 1870 and named Gilmore in honor of Civil War general Quincy A. Gilmore by Rufus Glass, the first township supervisor. The only town, now defunct, ever formed in Gilmore Township was named Gilmore, settled in the 1860s, and given a post office in 1891 that operated until 1906. Littlefield Lake, a primarily residential lake, lies in Gilmore Township.

Nottawa Township, established in 1875, was originally called Nottaway, after a Chippewa Indian chief who had taken up residence in the area. The first Nottawa Township supervisor was 1870s pioneer Michael McGreehan, and the next supervisor was former Michigan senator Alonozo T. Frisbee. Nottawa Township is home to Coldwater Lake County Park, the oldest park in the county, and to the Coldwater Lake 4-H Camp.

Nottawa Township settlements include the present-day Beal City (see pages 12–20). In 1911, Isaac A. Fancher said of the village, "It is in the center of one of the very best of farming communities. It is settled largely with Germans, a thrifty, prosperous and intelligent class. This is one of the places in the county that you can stand on a raise of ground and count from one spot nine large oval roofed farm barns, a sight that is seldom witnessed anywhere in the state or in any other state." Nottawa, also known as Nottawa Center, was a faded-to-history 1872 settlement that never reached a size to warrant a post office and had no major railroad. Van Decar, later known as Vandecar, was a small settlement named for general store owner Levi B. Van Decar, who was the first postmaster in 1880 of a post office that operated until 1905.

Sherman Township, the southwestern corner township of the northwestern county quadrant, was established in 1868 and is the most populous of the quadrant's townships. The township is named in honor of the famous Civil War Union general William Tecumseh Sherman.

Included in Sherman Township settlements was Drew, a station on the Pere Marquette Railroad with two establishments: a store owned by Edward W. Benn, postmaster from 1899 until the 1904 closing, and a grist- and sawmill owned by Millard Pennington. Horr changed to Woodins Mills in 1886, then changed back to Horr in 1890 (see page 44). Lake Isabella began as commercial home development on a man-made impoundment and was incorporated in 1998 as Michigan's newest Home Rule Village and the first such incorporation in more than half a century. Sherman City (see pages 29–35) was a defunct village that thrived from its 1871 founding but began to fade by the dawn of the 20th century. Weidman, the oldest remaining community in Sherman Township, was a station on the Detroit, Grand Rapids and Western Railroad and is where a community was established in 1894 (see pages 36–43).

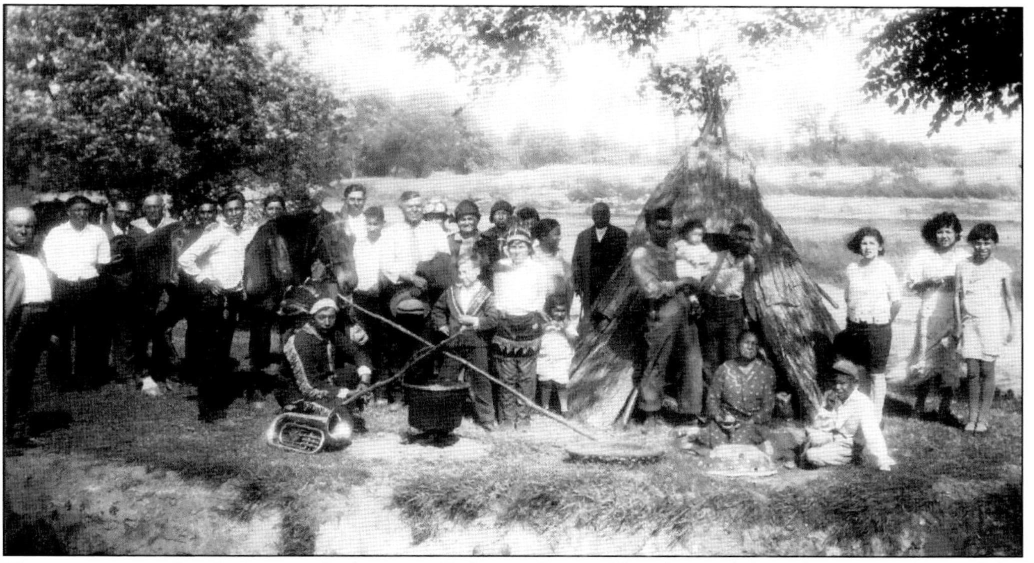

Known among the American Indians as Ojibiway Besse (the place of the Chippewa), part of the area of present-day Isabella County was their winter hunting grounds, as depicted in the 1931 re-creation above, and may have been used by American Indians for more than 10,000 years. Following missionary visits to the area in 1675, the Isabella County region saw its first European visitors in more than 200 years, when the verdant pines and hardwoods brought timbermen, like those below, anxious to harvest the forests to satisfy a growing hunger for lumber as settlements throughout the nation grew with abandon. New York lumberman David Ward, who ultimately became "father" of the Isabella County seat at Mount Pleasant, was Michigan's first lumber millionaire from his property holdings in central Michigan.

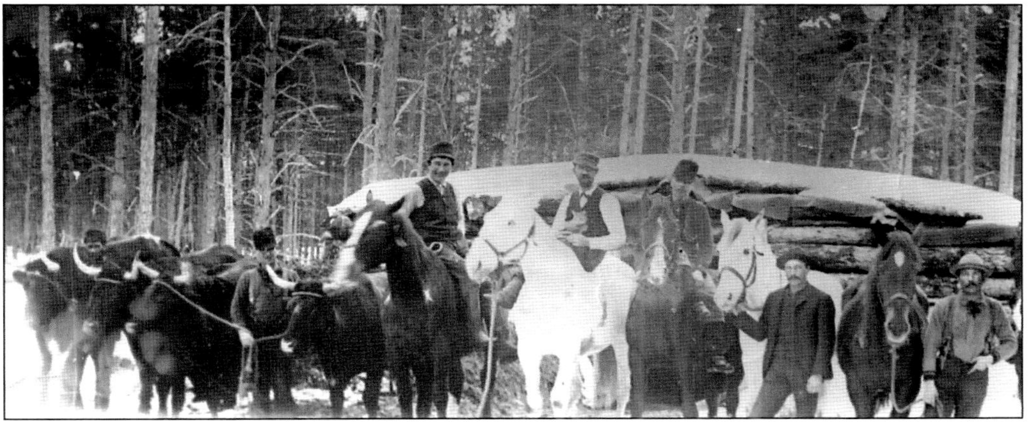

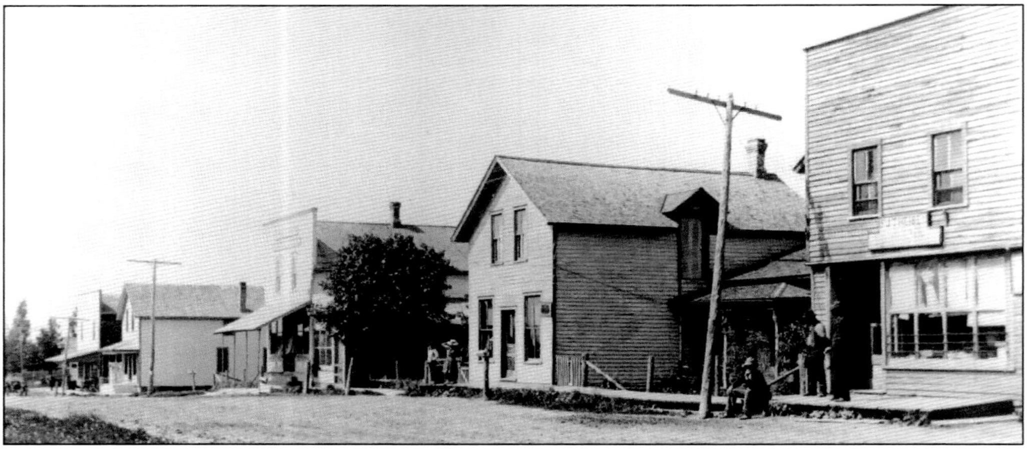

A settlement around a lumber camp starting in 1875, Beal City was unnamed for many years. In 1881, Nicholas Beal built the first general store and the first Beal City post office in the southeast corner of section 21, Nottawa Township, the second building from the left above. Frank Vogel built the second store in Beal City in 1882, which evolved into the Tilmann Hardware. The original Beal store was purchased in 1905 by Edward N. Smith, who added an annex for a meat market and built a tavern alongside the store in 1934. Smith ran the store for 40 years, then sold to Walter Rau. Below, the same area of modern Beal City is shown.

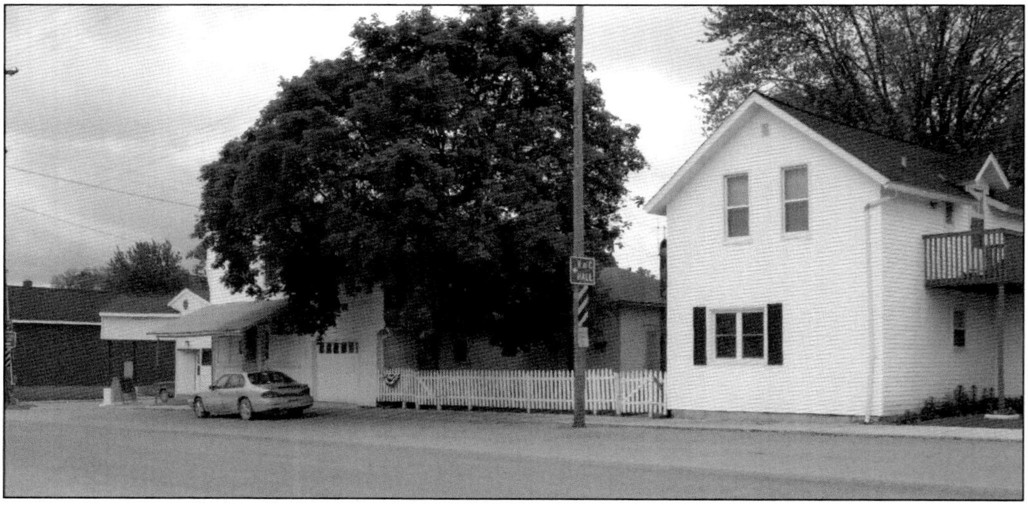

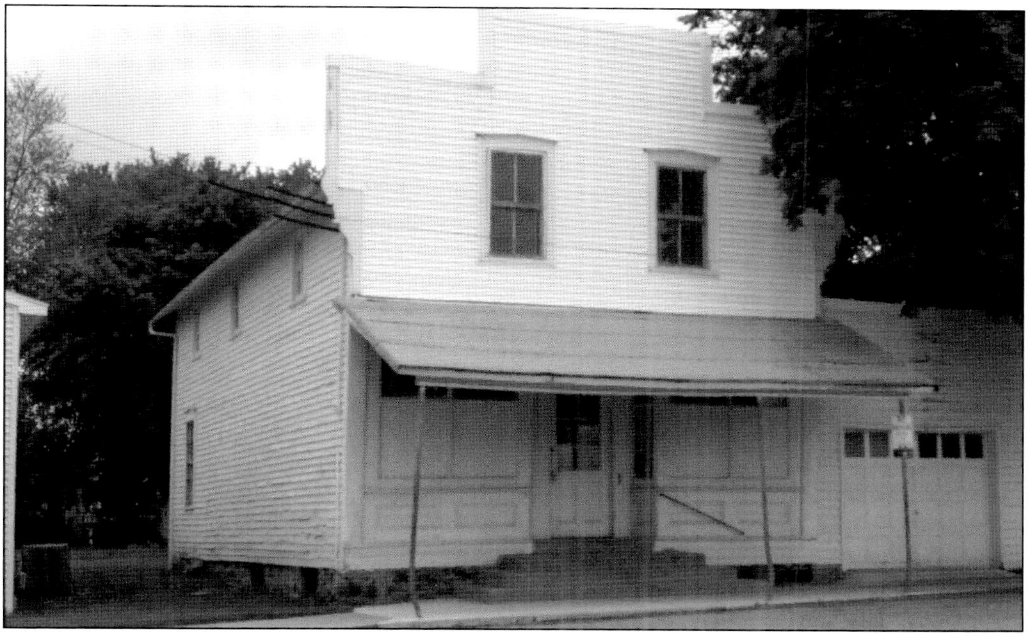

In 1945, Walter Rau bought the original Beal store from Smith, who had operated the business for 40 years. In 1961, Rau moved the business to a more modern building across the street and renamed the business Rau's Foodland. Above, the now-abandoned original Nicholas Beal store was a local gathering place, where Beal City citizens in pioneer costumes watched the village centennial parade in 1975. Below, behind the counter in the meat department in the early 1950s, Rau keeps an eye on his daughters Ginny and Delores Rau. The Rau family continues to live in Beal City.

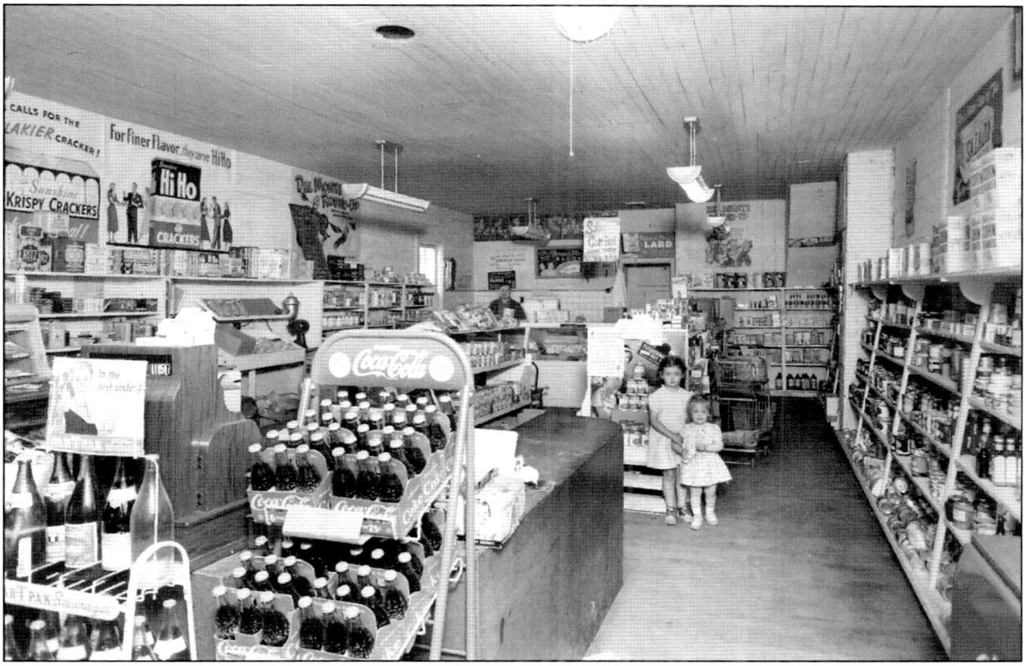

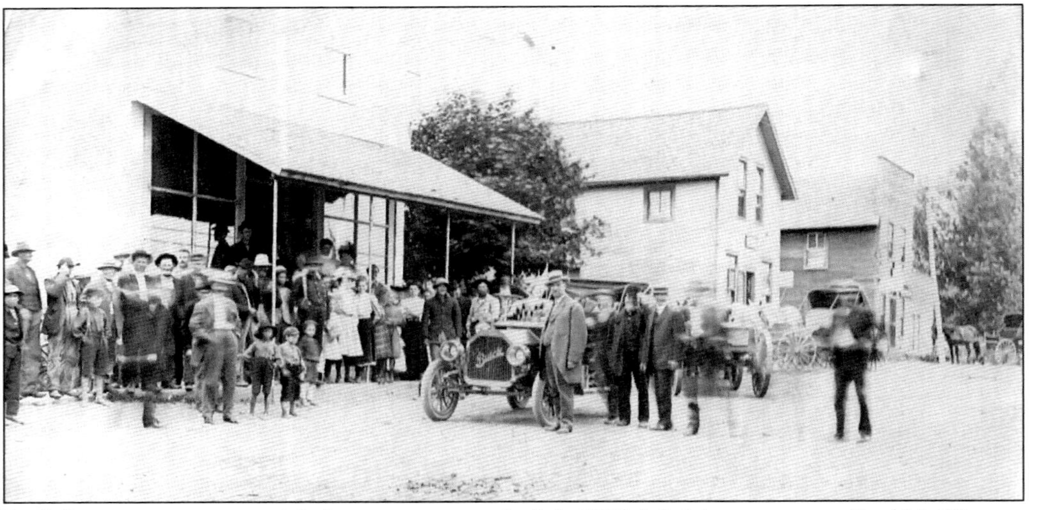

Beal City is no stranger to Michigan governors. In July 1908, Michigan governor Fred M. Warner, above at driver's fender of the car, paused in front of Edward N. Smith's store campaigning in Beal City for reelection. Beal City High School graduate John Engler was elected a Michigan state representative in 1971 and served 20 years in the Michigan legislature before his 1991 election to the first of three terms as Michigan governor. Senator Engler is at the far right, below, in 1977 with U.S. senator Don Riegle, Michigan Oil and Gas Association executive vice president Frank Mortl, and president Clyde E. "Gene" Miller.

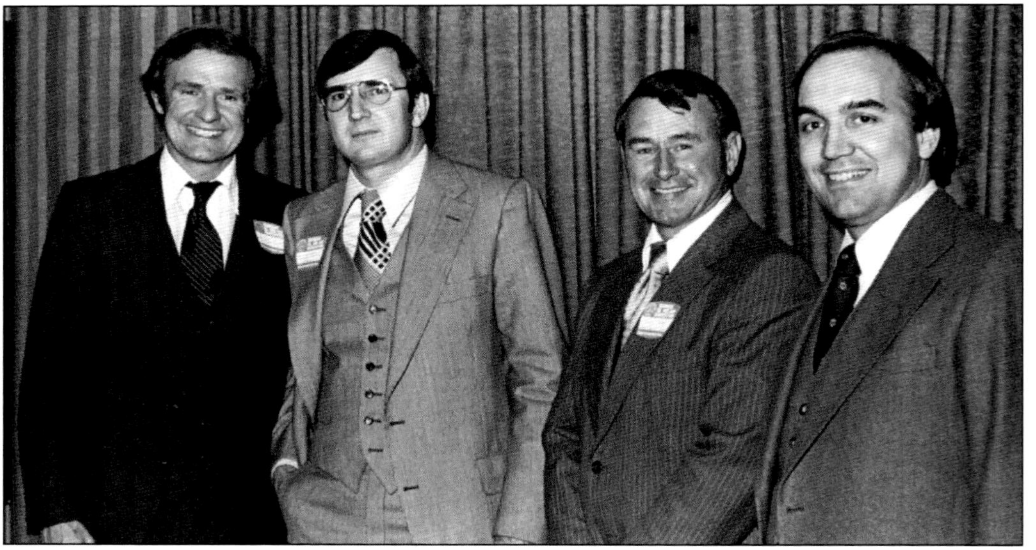

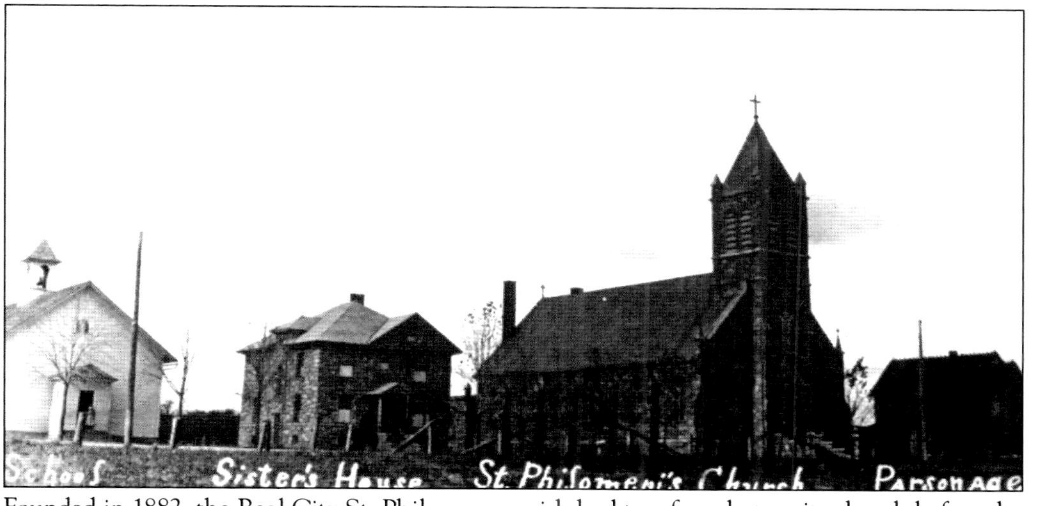

Founded in 1882, the Beal City St. Philomena parish had two fires destroy its church before the present structure was completed and consecrated in 1907. Above, the St. Philomena grounds are seen in about 1910. In 1961, the name of the parish was changed to St. Joseph the Worker. Below, with the commercial center of Beal City just a couple of blocks away (left center), St. Philomena/ St. Joseph the Worker Catholic Church has remained an integral part of community. A modern school has replaced the sisters home building depicted in the photograph above.

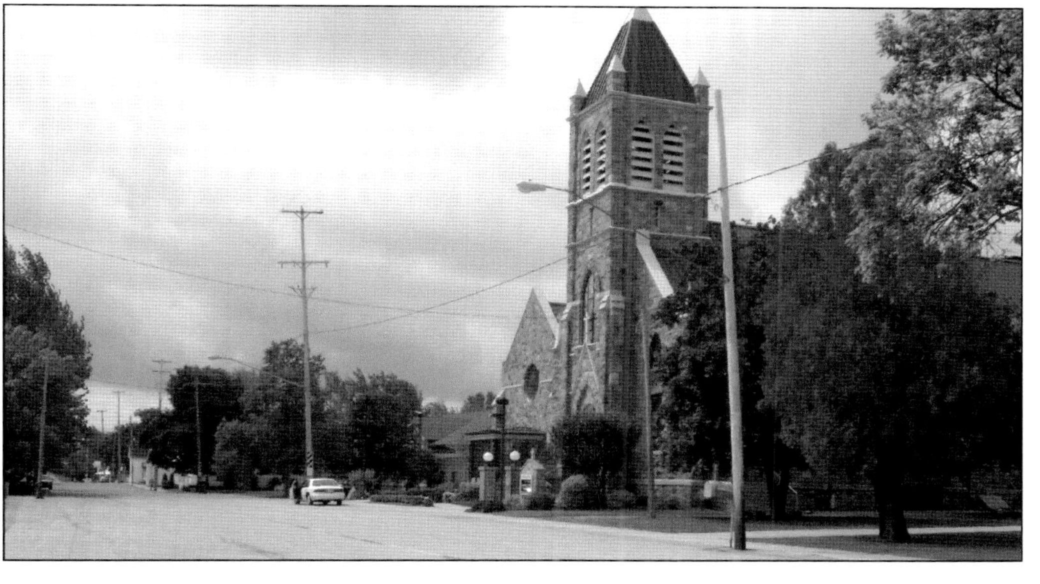

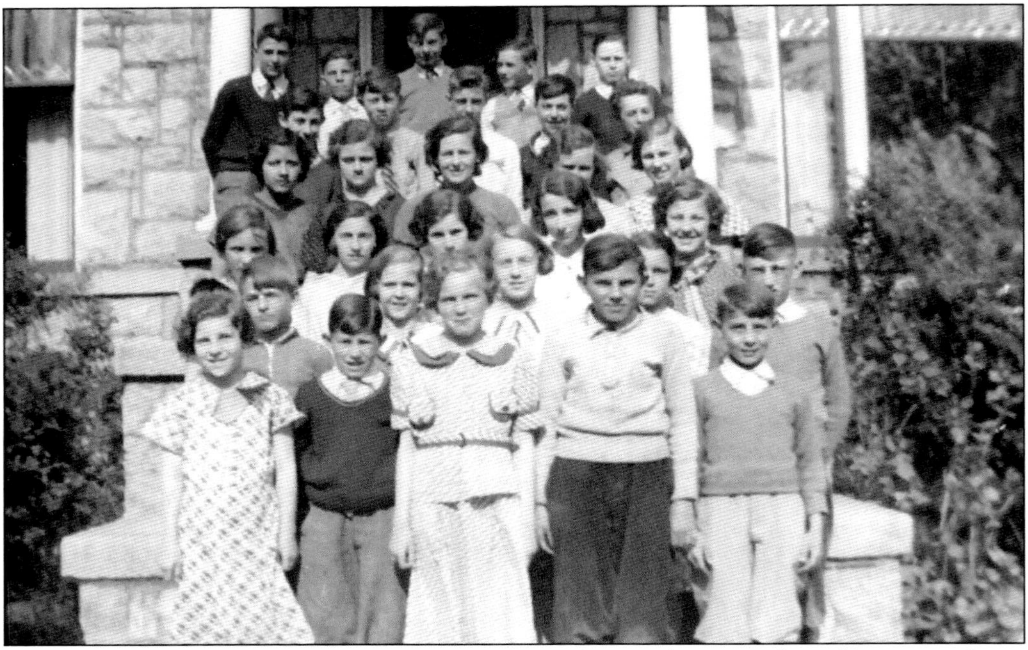

In 1936, St. Philomena school seventh and eight graders on the steps of parish's nun residence are, from left to right above, (first row) Helen Reihl, Jack Sheahan, Marie Reihl, Bob Bliese, and Bill Tilmann; (second row) Vic Boge, Agnes Ahlers, Gladys Sebenick, Kathleen Schafer, and Howard Martin; (third row) Edna Kremsreiter, Rita Weber, Aileen Tilmann, Harriet Lawrence, and Dorothy Grinzinger; (fourth row) Josephine Gurrero, Edman Smith, Agnes Tilmann, Vada Pung, and Agnes Bliese; (fifth row) Herman Kremsrieter, Ray Zuker, Albert Tilmann, Norman Tilmann, and Ray Blaren; (sixth row) Pete Thielen, Ed Reihl, Steve Rau, John Reihl, and John Forest. The St. Philomena grade school, in service since 1886, was moved slightly west to make room for construction of a brick school. A few months later the school burned, below, causing grade-school students to move into the new building (still in use) before it was completed.

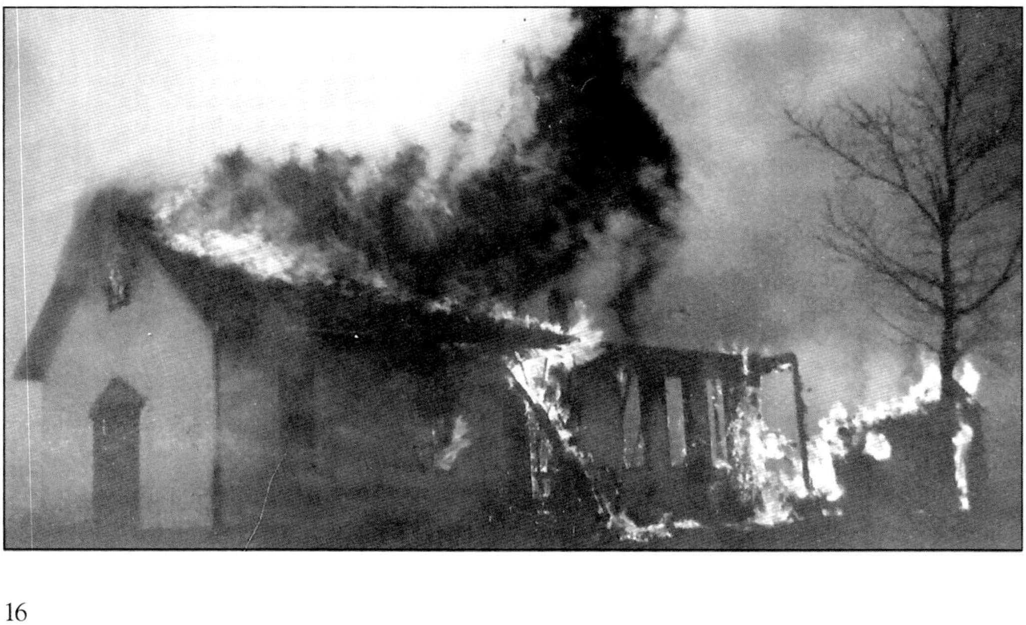

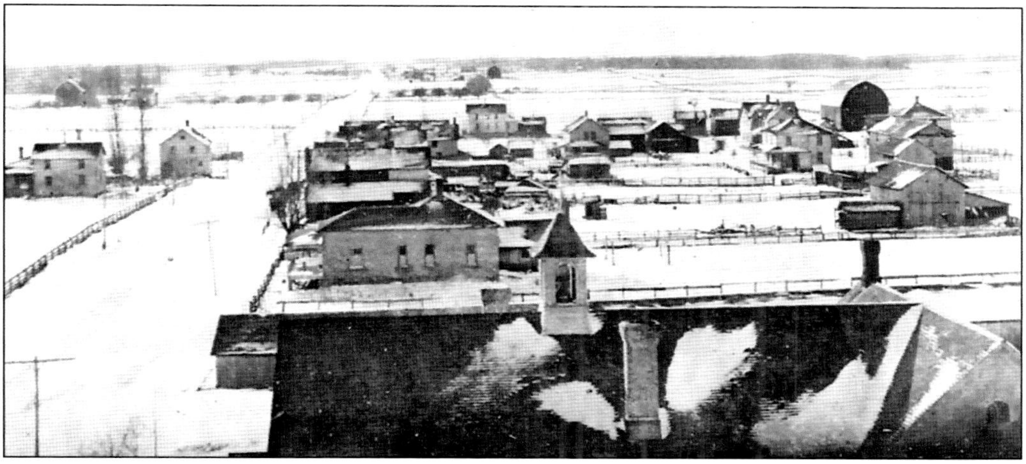

Above, this bird's-eye view of Beal City was shot from the belfry of the second St. Philomena Catholic Church, built of brick in 1890 on the site of the present St. Joseph the Worker Catholic Church after the original wooden church burned and was replaced on the same foundation with a schoolhouse (see facing page). The 1890 church was 60 feet deep and 112 feet long with no basement. The Beal City St. Philomena men's choir competed in a 1950s competition in Big Rapids. From left to right below are Chum Schafer, Ray Gross, Art Faber, Marvin Pasch, Lavern Schafer, Ben Weber, organist Geraldine Horn, and Dick Smith.

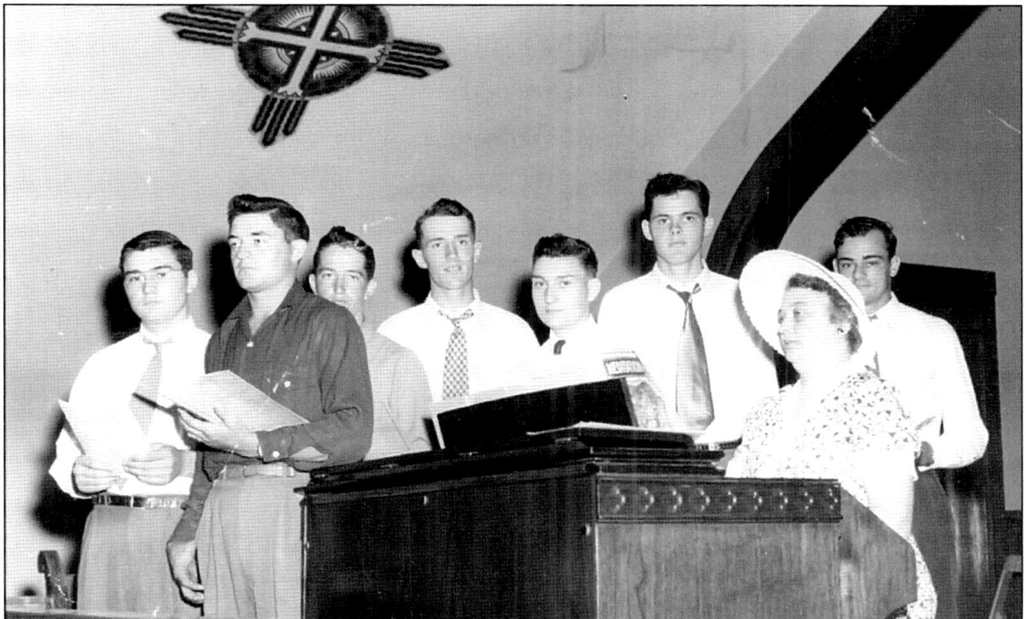

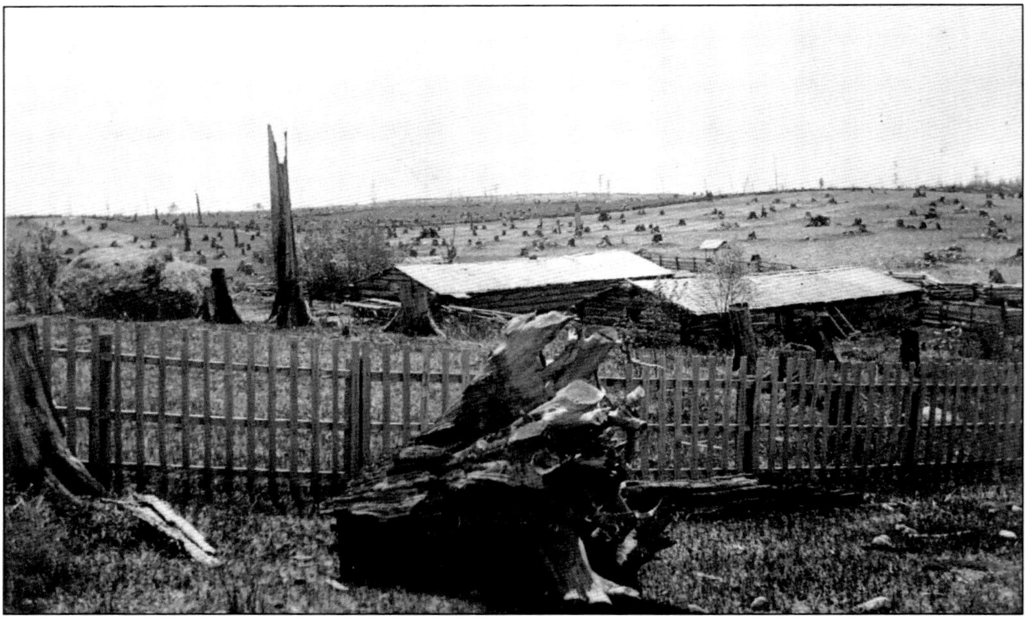

The denuded landscape above lends insight to the colossal task that faced the farmer/settlers who came to the "timbered out" sections of late-19th-century Isabella County. The John Gross farm, below, on Weidman Road just north of Beal City, above, housed the family of John and Gertrude Gross. John was born in the Eifel region of Germany in 1847, sailed to America, and arrived in New York in 1868. He and his family lived in Westphalia before settling in the Michigan Upper Peninsula's Keewenaw Peninsula, where he worked with his father and brothers in copper mines. He and his brother settled, with their families, in Nottawa Township during the late 1880s.

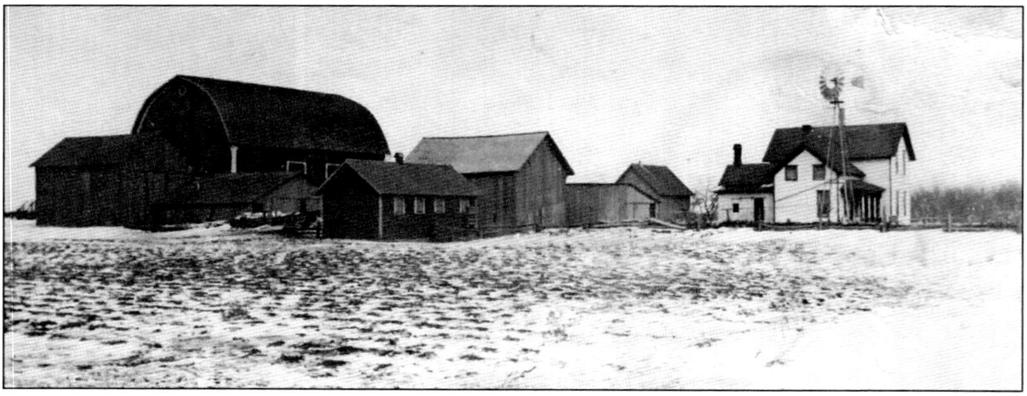

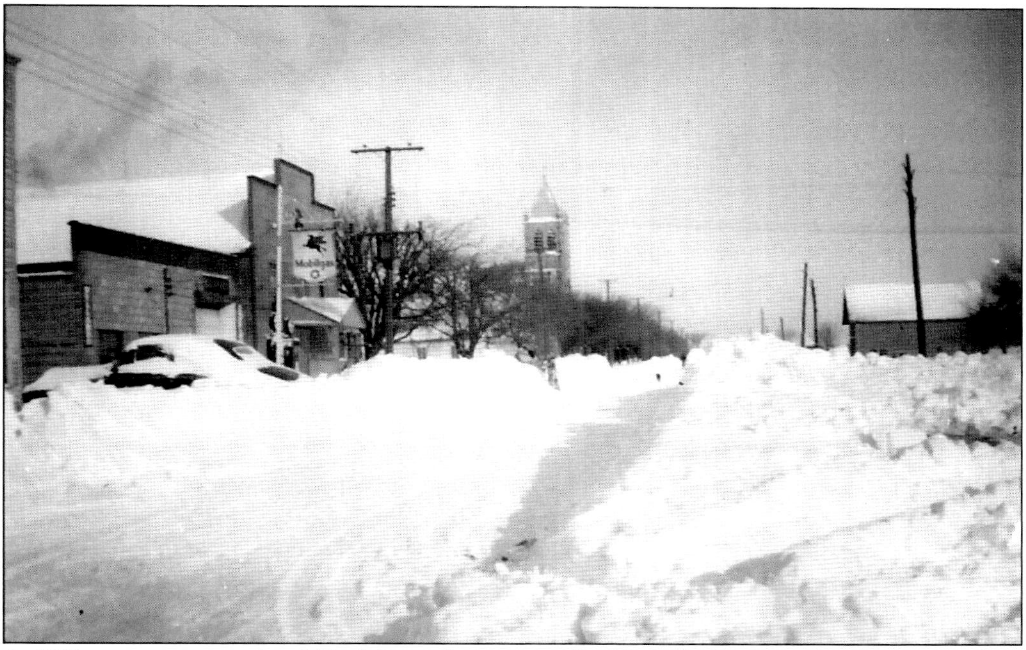

A 1937 snowstorm paralyzed Beal City, along with all of Isabella County, above. Again, when compared with the photograph at the bottom of page 15, the proximity of St. Philomena/ St. Joseph Catholic church to the commerce center of Beal City is clear. Note the drive-up proximity to the street of the gasoline pumps underneath the Mobil sign. Below, Lake Isabella began as a private real estate development around a man-made lake created in the late 1960s by damming the Chippewa River. In 1998, after nearly a decade of work by devoted residents, Lake Isabella became the state of Michigan's newest incorporated Home Rule Village. Lake Isabella became the first new village in the state in nearly half a century.

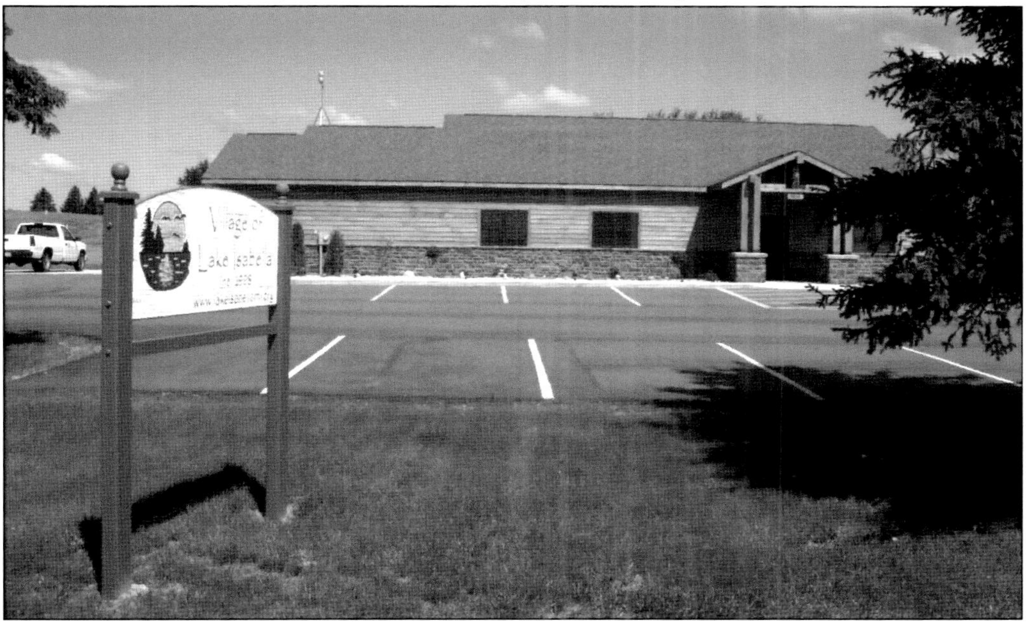

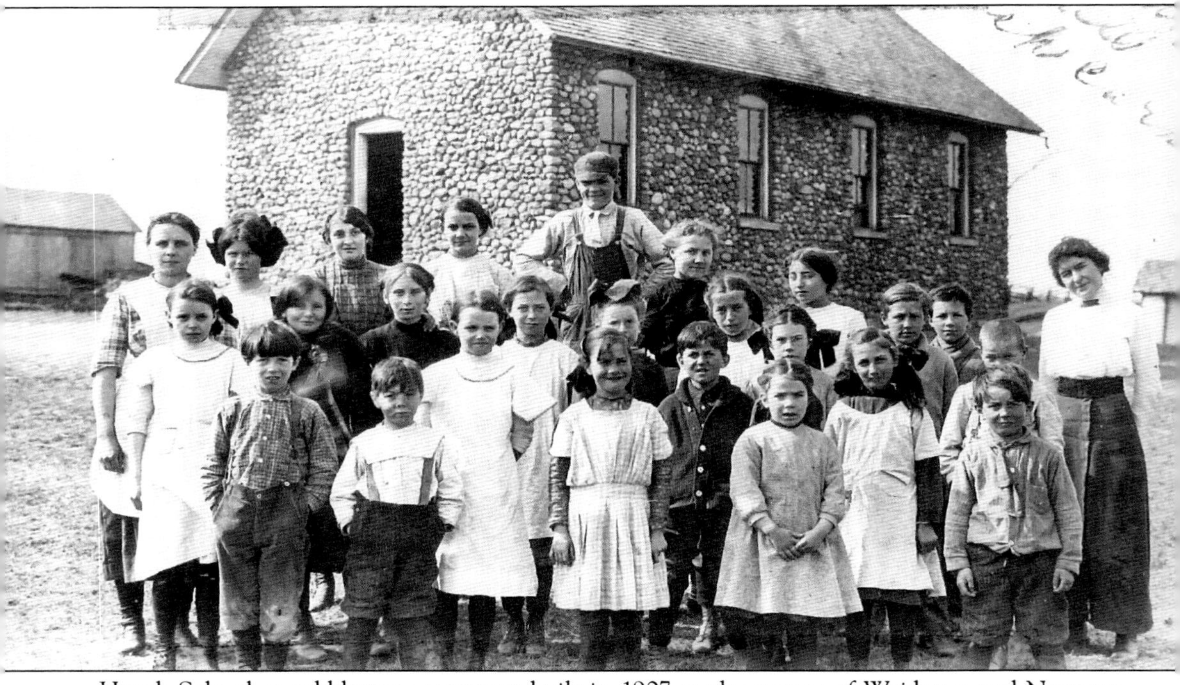

Hauck School, a cobblestone structure built in 1907 at the corner of Weidman and Nottawa Roads on the Nottawa/Isabella Township border northeast of Beal City, had Mae Young (far right) as a teacher in 1914 when this photograph was taken. The pupils from left to right are (first row) Erwin Hartman, Jerome Bichnau, Irene McCollum, Edward Zeien, Helen Hauck, Edna Hartman, and Vernon Bichnau; (second row) Margaret Funnel, Martha McGuirk, Bessie Myers, Bertha Funnel, Anna Martin, Frances Martin, Lillian Hauck, Frank Berg, Jacob Nixon, and James McGuirk; (third row) Gladys Funnel, Minnie McGuirk, Helen Zeien, Margaret Berg, Maxwell Love, Mathilda Berg, and Mamie Martin.

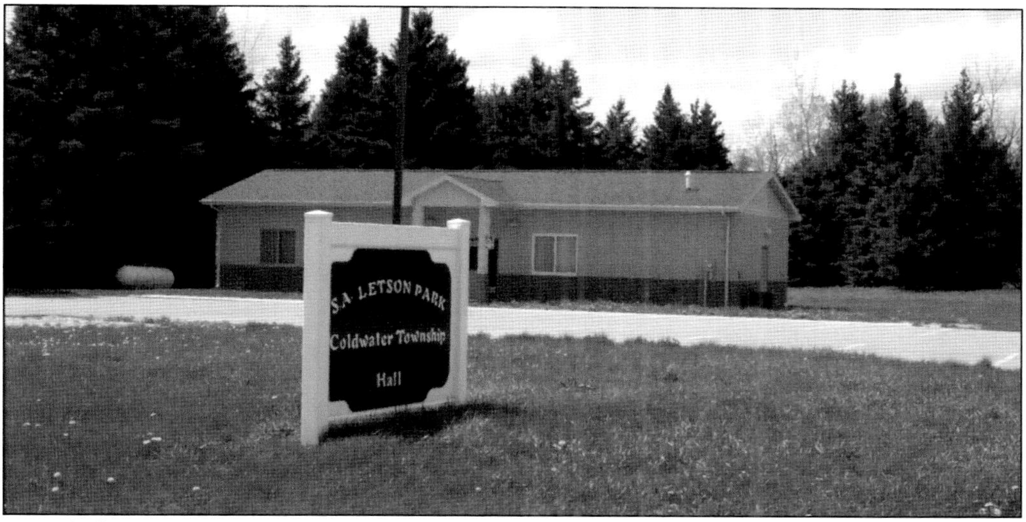

Long before Europeans came to Coldwater Township, American Indians were drawn to the boiling springs in section 22, considering them sacred. Settlers began gathering in the area in 1862. Among them was S. A. Letson, for whom the township park above is named at the site of his 1886 post office, a mile south of Brinton in the southern part of section 22. In 1888, the post office was moved a mile north, to a village platted in 1887 by E. F. Coburn at the juncture of sections 15 and 22, and renamed Brinton, for early settler and father of the charcoal kilns that made the village a famous early industrial town, Oscar T. Brinton.

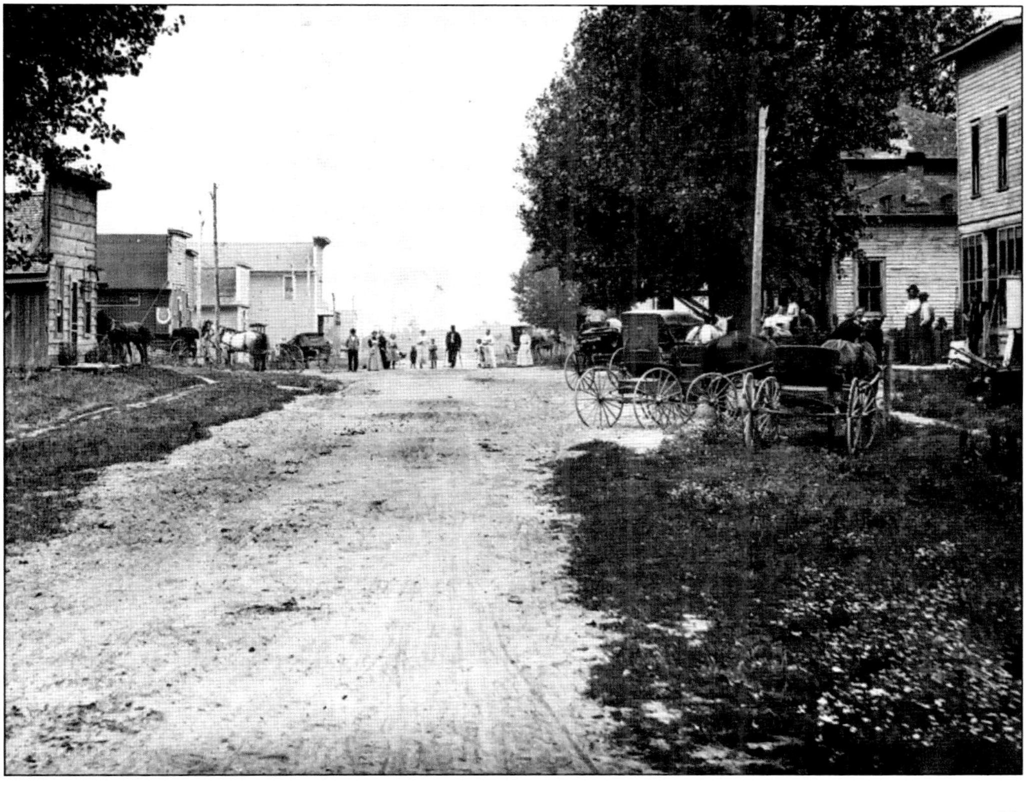

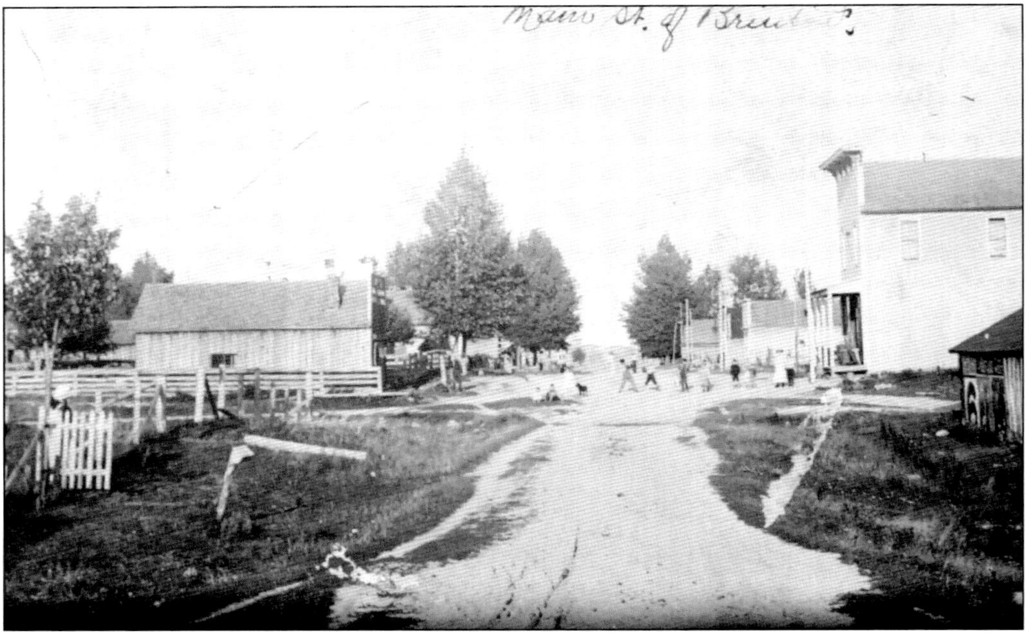

Seen in the right foreground above and the close-up below, the Brinton International Order of Odd Fellows Lodge was established in 1889 and at peak had 130 members. The village flourished after Oscar T. Brinton got the idea to build kilns to convert timber to charcoal 1887, causing the village to be labeled "Coal Town" and "Charcoal Town" by locals. The Flint and Pere Marquette Railroad built a spur line into the town to haul the charcoal to market the same year. The kilns operated from 1888 to 1896. As timber in the area grew sparse and the railroad discontinued, the town faded to a cluster of residences with no business center.

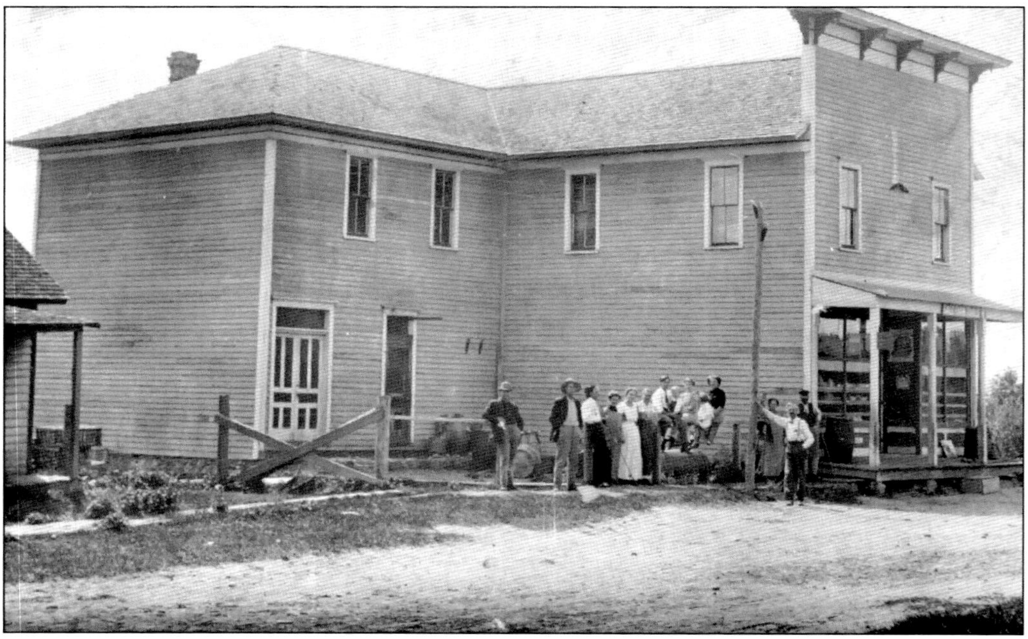

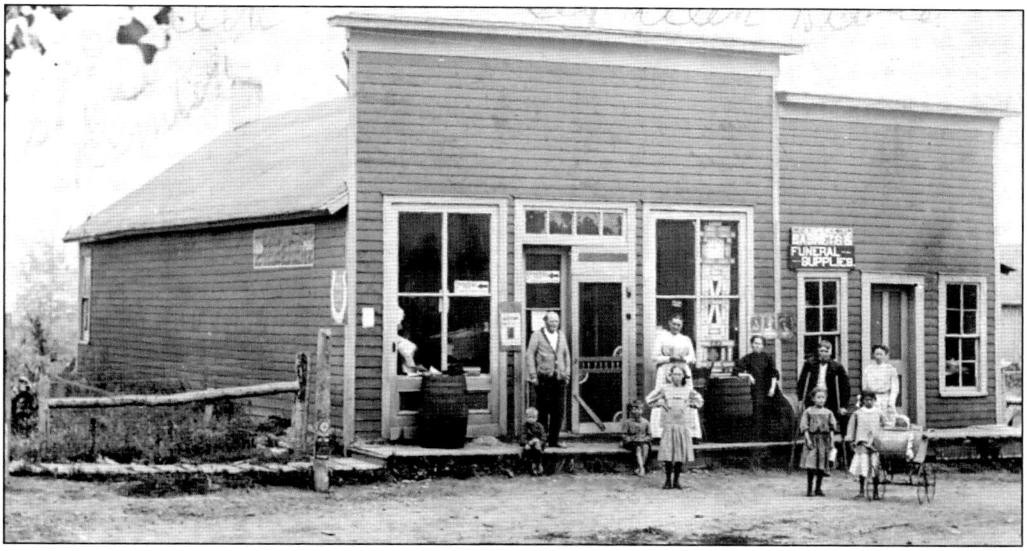

Soloman F. Frye came from Pennsylvania and, following the Civil War and injuries making it difficult to endure hard work, had a number of jobs in central Michigan, finally moving to Brinton to open a drugstore in 1889. Frye's store at Main and Bartlett Streets in Brinton, above, drew a crowd of customers to pose for this picture, including Judson Herbert Clark, left, teacher, veterinarian, hotelier, and merchant. George H. Allen worked cutting wood in Coldwater Township, and in July 1896, he started a general store in Brinton, below, doing a lively mercantile business. Allen served three terms as treasurer of his township, one term as superintendent, and for a time was Brinton's postmaster. The last store closed in Brinton in 1970.

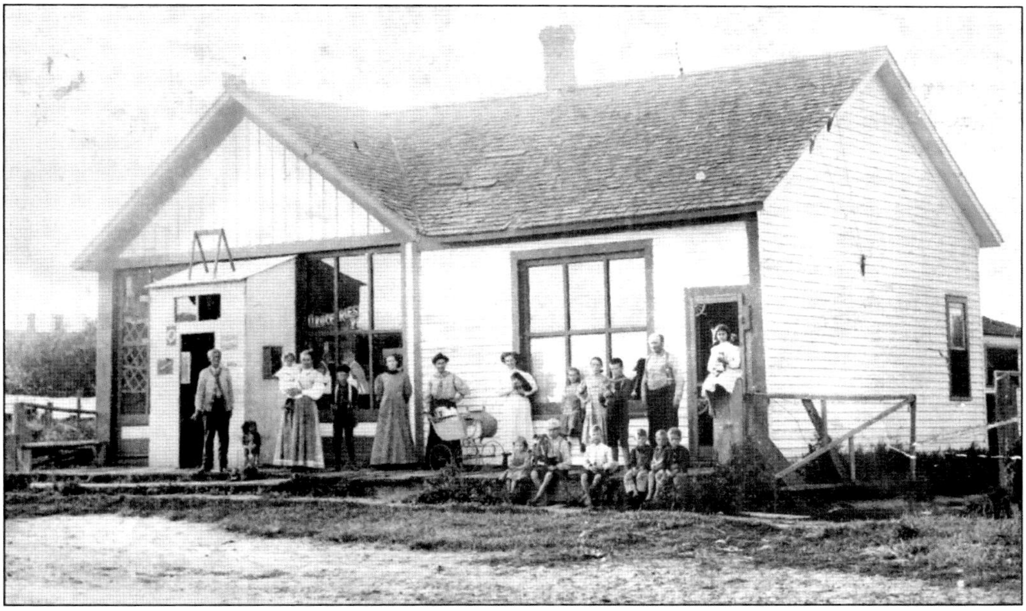

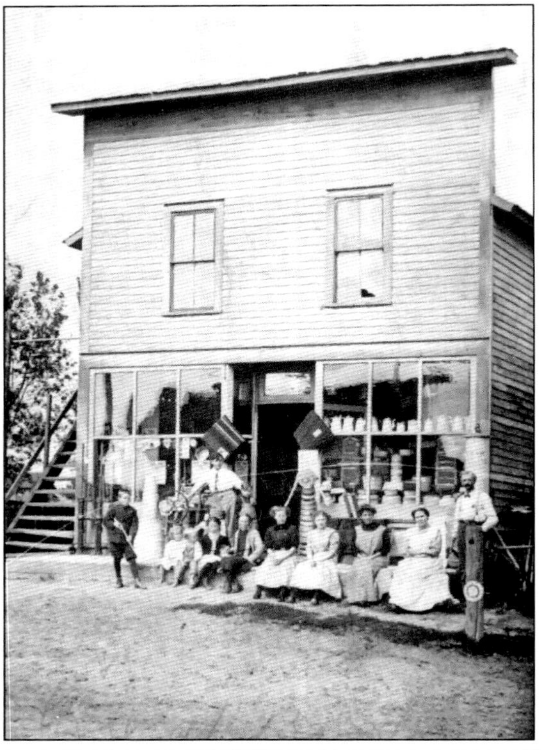

Judson Herbert (Bert) Clark's general store, with Clark at the right, housed the first Odd Fellows lodge upstairs, which burned on April 9, 1892, and was rebuilt that same year as the building with a wing shown on page 22. Clark, a Brinton local who had earned a teacher's certificate at Central Normal School in Mount Pleasant and taught for three years, opened Clark's Hotel in 1893, and the ubiquitous J. H. Clark, below holding the horse, operated that for awhile before leaving for Grand Rapids in the second decade of the 20th century to become a veterinarian. Returning in about 1914 as Dr. Clark, he served the area as a veterinarian after moving to Weidman to be near his children and grandchildren.

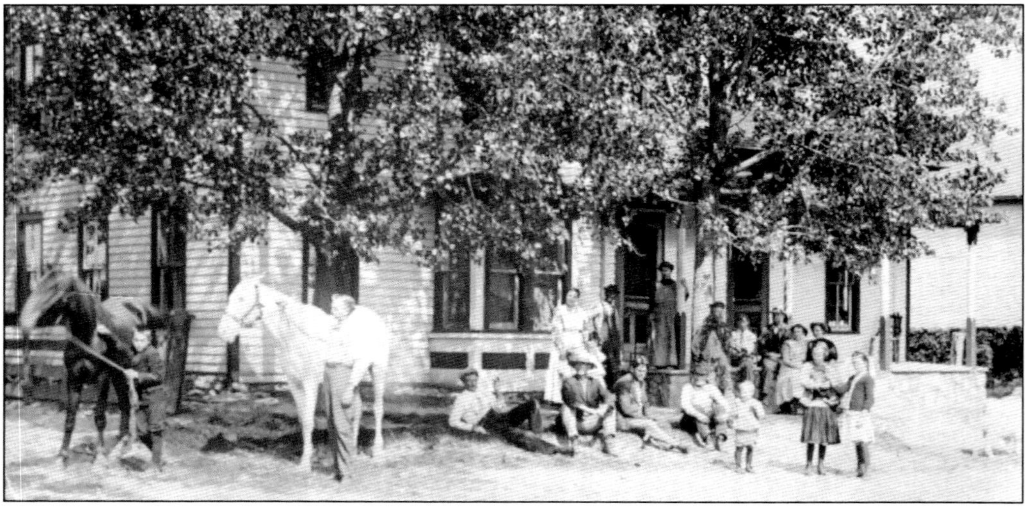

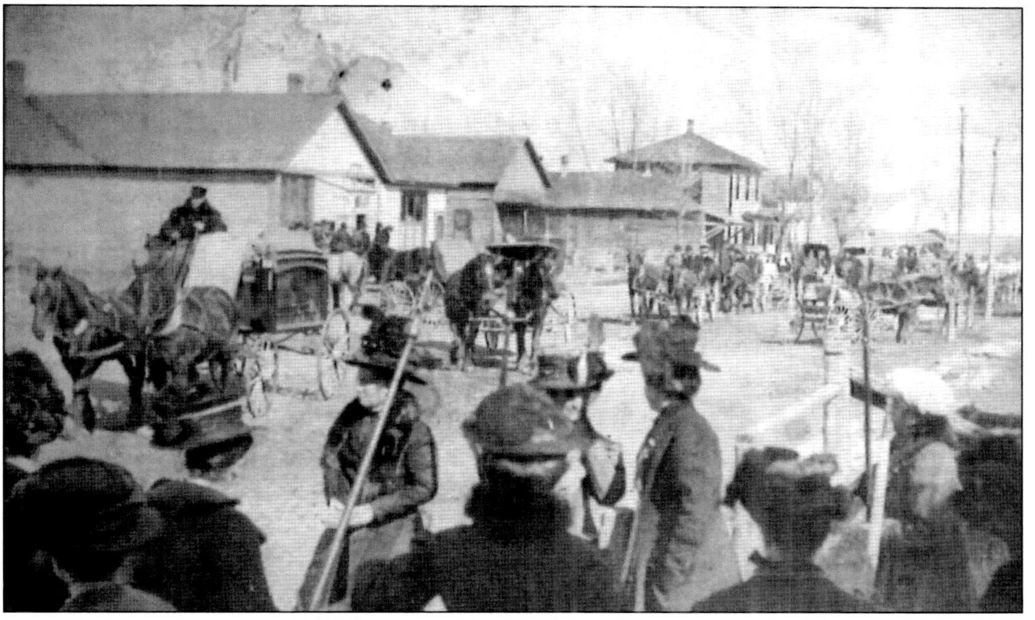

Benjamin B. Stevens, originally from Bay City, Michigan, was among Brinton's most prominent citizens, having come to the area in 1904 after disposing of his Dakota ranching interests. He cleared 160 acres for cultivation and raised more than 300 sheep and bred hogs there, while serving in the leadership of the Grange and the Odd Fellows. Benjamin's wife since 1885, Ida (Parmenter) Stevens was equally respected and beloved as a teacher and neighbor, as evidenced by her March 1911 funeral procession, above, and ceremonies at the Odd Fellows lodge with a salute by the Sisters of Rebekah, below.

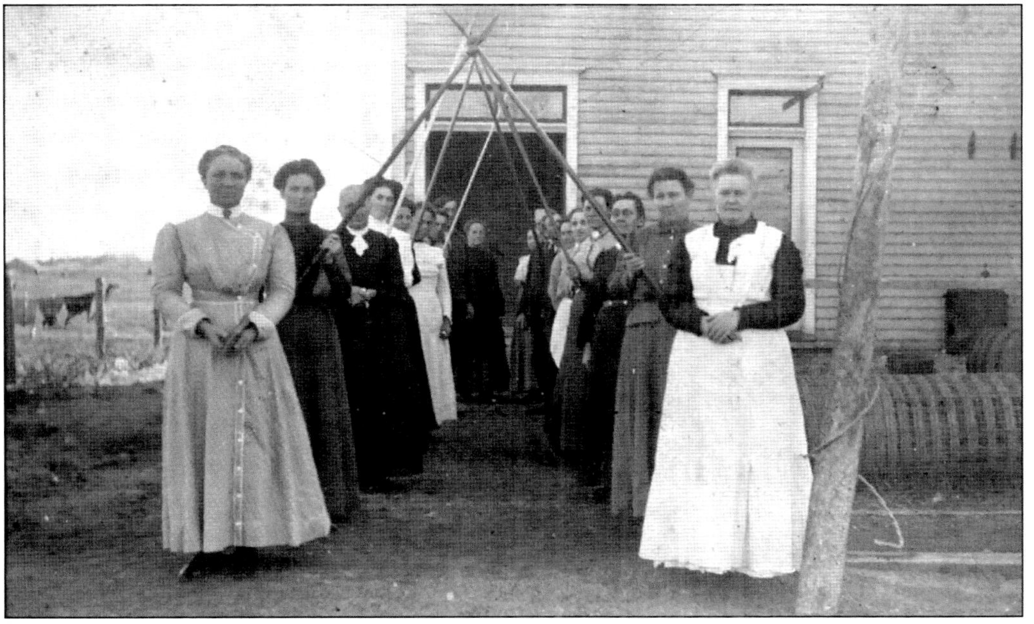

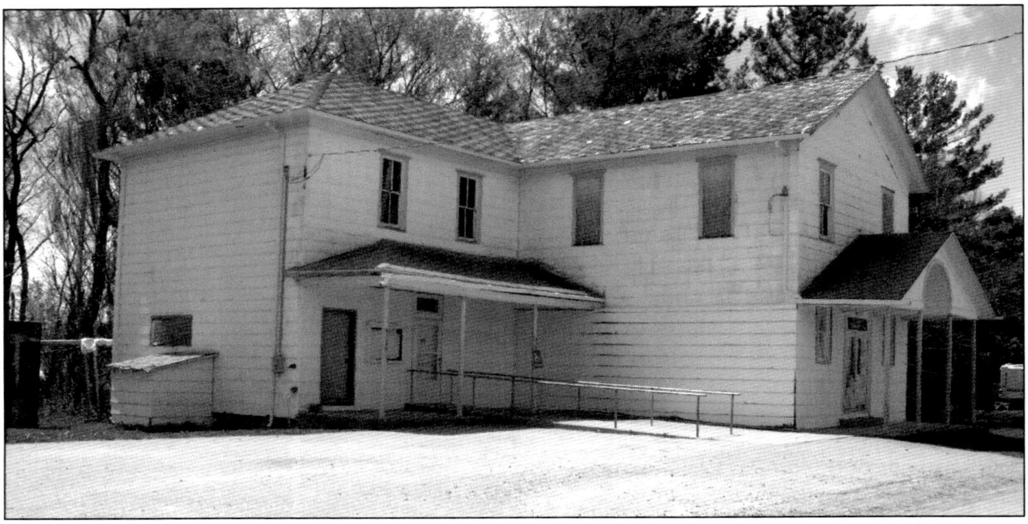

Standing at the edge of a primarily residential area as a sentinel to the memory of the once thriving village is the last remaining original building of the once prominent downtown Brinton. It served as a store, an Odd Fellows hall, and more recently as the Coldwater Township offices, until those offices moved to Letson Park (see page 21).

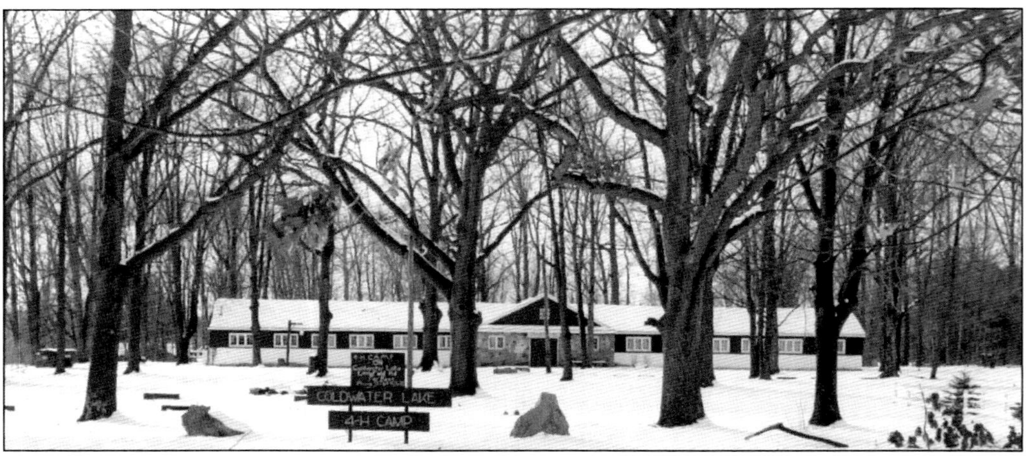

In 1947, 45 acres with 208 feet of lake frontage at the north end of Coldwater Lake were purchased by the Isabella County 4-H club for a camp. The main lodge was built in 1948 with the kitchen, dormitories, dining hall, and recreation hall added later. Owned by the Isabella County 4-H, the camp is devoted to the young people in surrounding communities and is available for rental by outside groups.

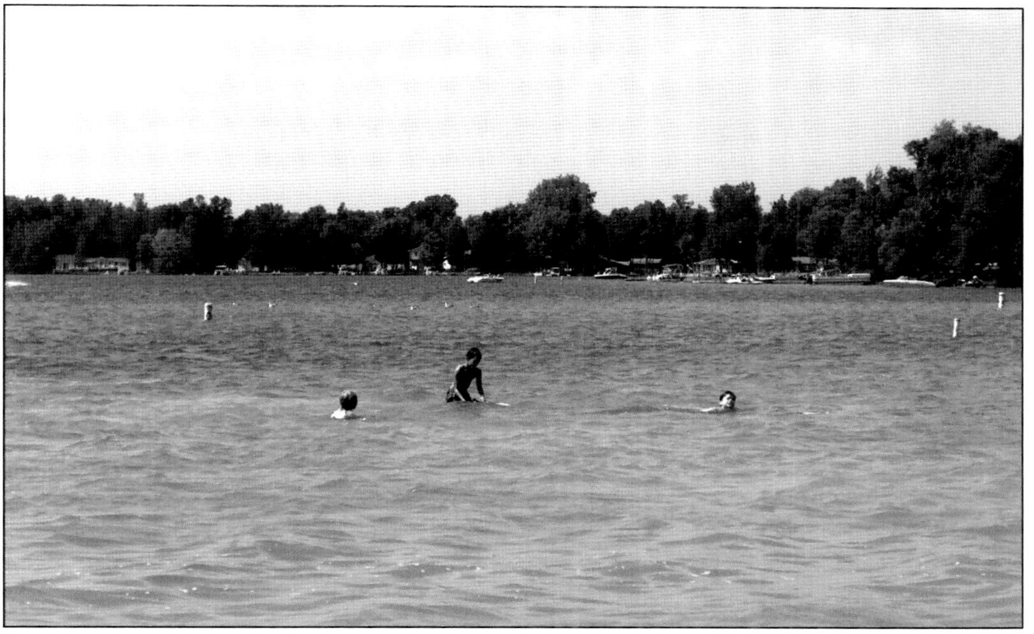

Established in 1945, Isabella County Coldwater Lake Family Park encompasses 28 acres with a boat launch, small mooring area, fishing access, and sandy beach, as well as a ball field, volleyball court, picnic areas, pavilion, Old West playground, and campground containing 95 campsites and five rustic cabins.

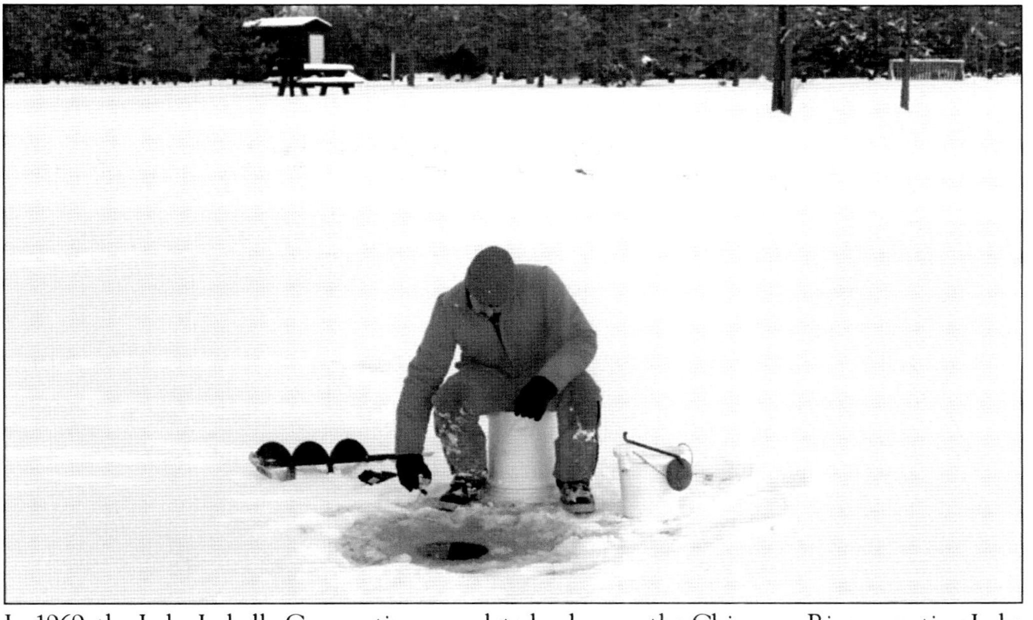

In 1969, the Lake Isabella Corporation completed a dam on the Chippewa River, creating Lake Isabella. In 1970, the corporation gave seven acres to Isabella County for a day-use park to be named Maynard S. Gilmore Park, in exchange for county property flooded in the Lake Isabella impoundment. The Maynard S. Gilmore Park has trails, a parking area, a fishing platform, and winter access to ice fishing.

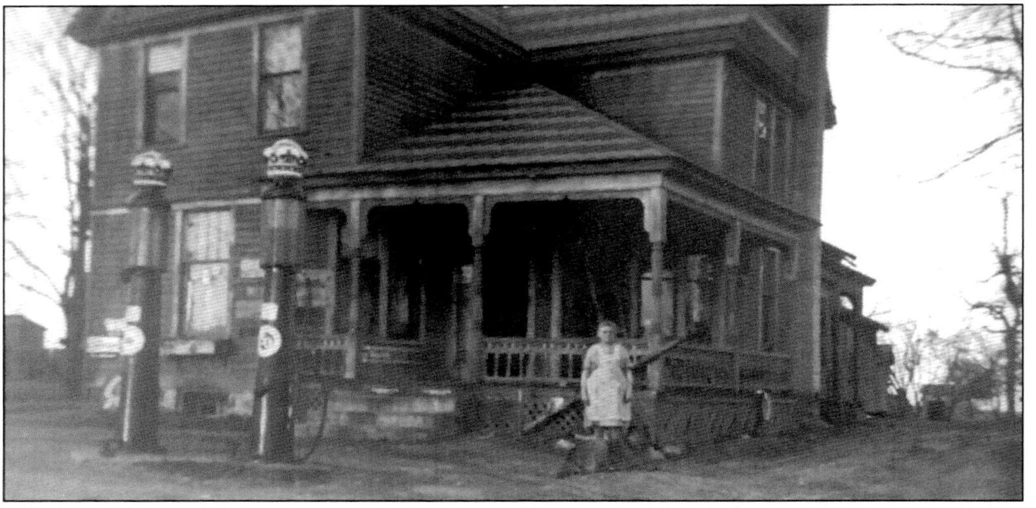

Typical of "at home" stores that grew up in isolated areas of Isabella County, this home was built in 1893 by Gilbert Johnson, who had a Sherman City store built in 1879. In 1925, Ervin and Nellie Herman bought Johnson's home and store. After Ervin's 1927 death, Nellie (above) moved the store to the Johnson house, where she operated it until being the last Sherman City business to close in 1943. Frank Chase and his two sons pose (below) in front of the home of his mother, Welthy Chase, in a 1910 photograph taken by Barryton photographer Floyd L. Lyon. Emery Chase, a Coldwater Township pioneer, moved to this home a half-mile south of Sherman City, where his wife Welthy is said to have told fortunes by tea leaf reading.

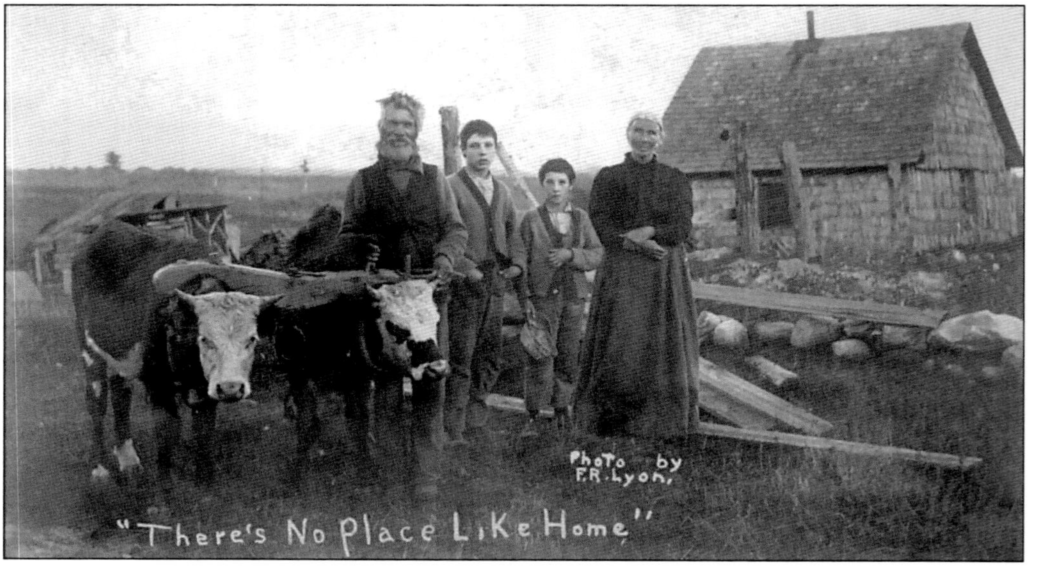

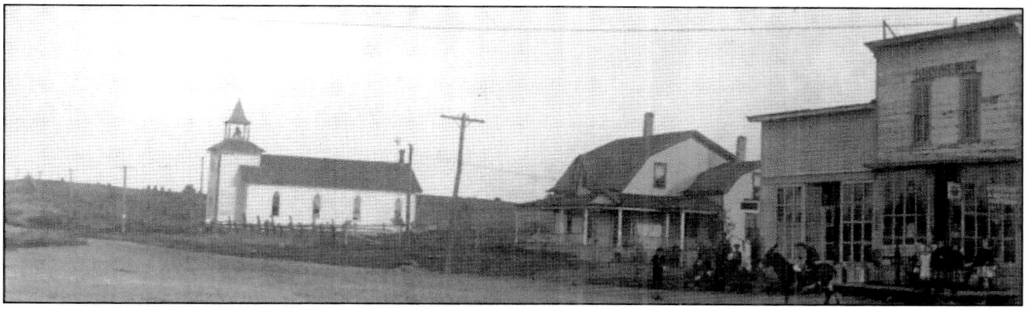

Sherman City, above looking south, is one of many places named for Civil War generals. It was given a post office in 1871, which closed in 1913. The town was platted by John Cohoon in 1873, embracing the lower part of Sherman Township section 31 and the upper part of Sherman Township section 6, with a population of 150 that year. Sherman City's growth in the timber-boom years was so spectacular that it once rivaled Mount Pleasant as a commercial center. The Crusaders, a Sherman City evangelical Christian movement active in the late 19th century, held a baptism in the Chippewa River in the early days of the village.

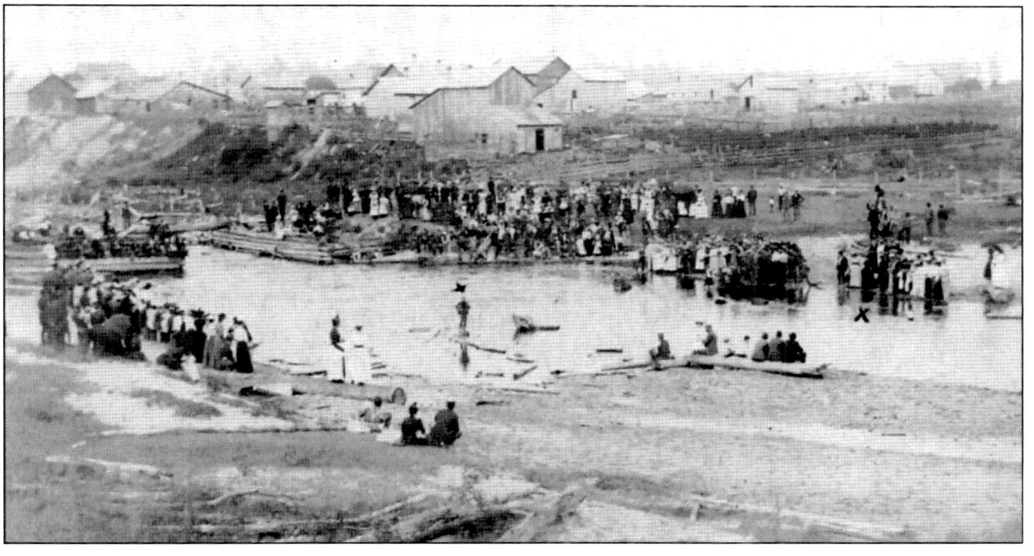

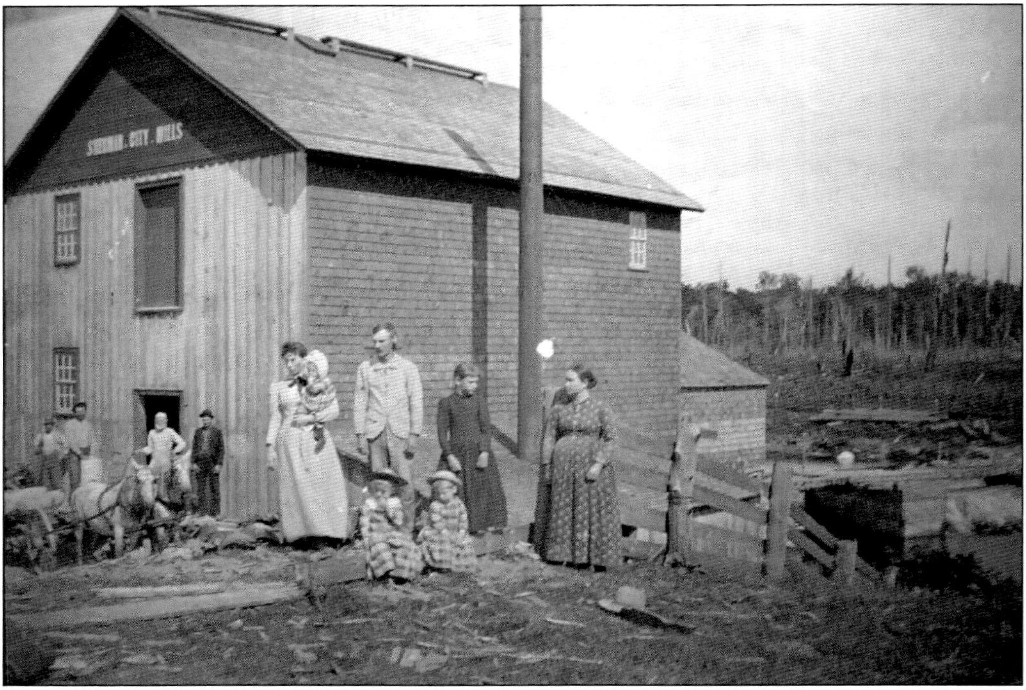

Above is a front view of the Daniel Estes gristmill in about 1892, and below is the rear view of the mill about 1903. Grist- and sawmills were prevalent along the millpond, created by damming the Chippewa River at the thriving town of Sherman City in the last quarter of the 1800s. With stores, mills, hotels, and doctors, Sherman City, a boomtown in its heyday and another rival to Mount Pleasant in terms of growth for a while, is now a collection of retirees' homes. The sawmill and gristmill site is now an open field on the south bank of the Chippewa River.

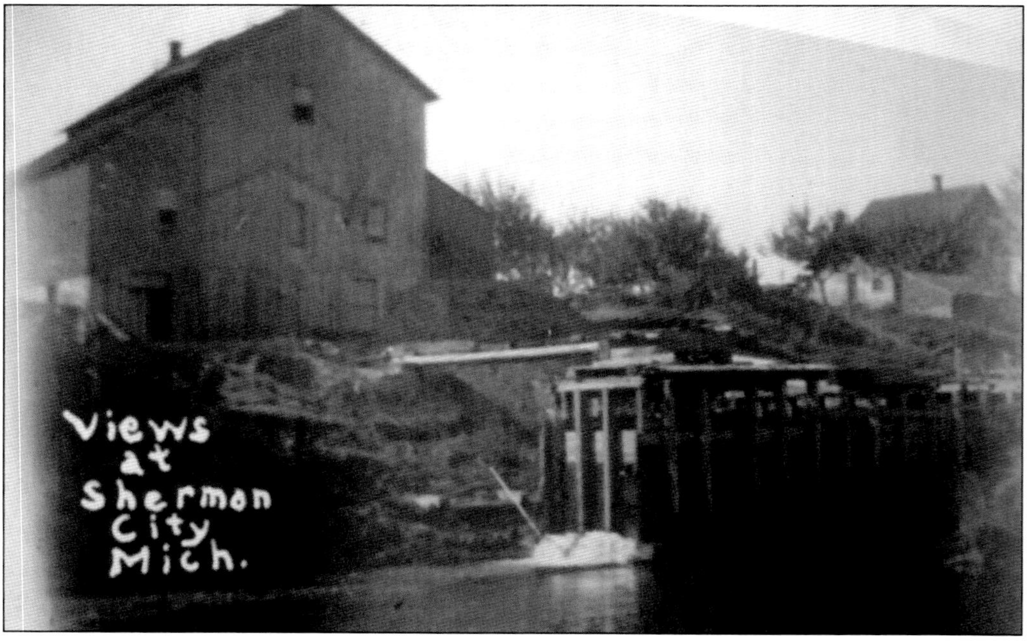

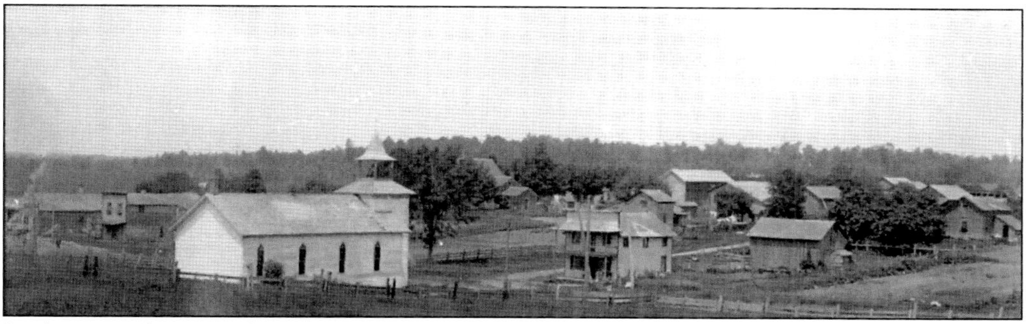

Looking northeast at Sherman City in its infancy from a hillock southwest of the village, above, the Sherman City Union Church dominates the skyline, the Mindel home next door to the church has not yet been constructed, and trees are sparse. A tornado hit Sherman City in September 1878, destroying most of the north side of town. Below, besides the Sherman City Union Church and the Mindel house, only a Michigan historical marker notes the long-departed downtown Sherman City, where a few homes dot the roadside, with no trace of the once bustling village.

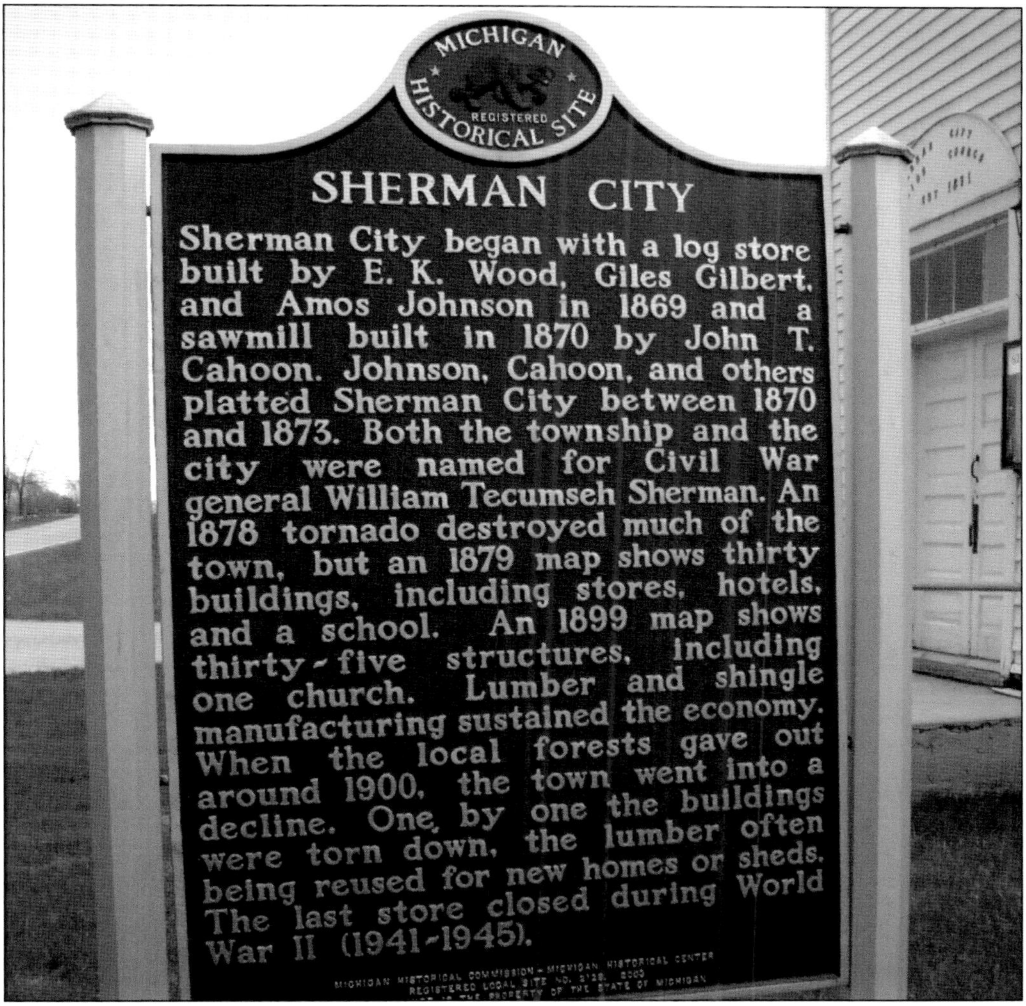

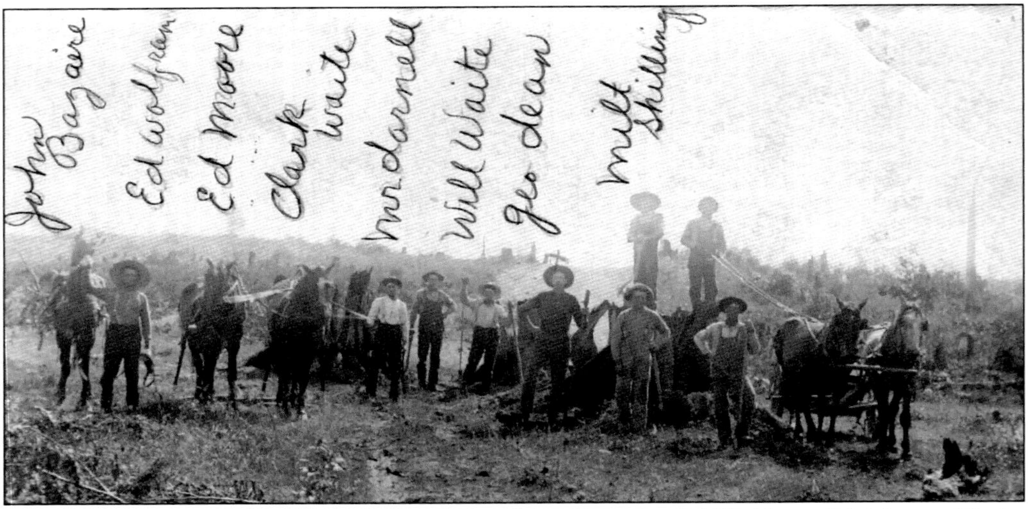

Sherman City men, above from left to right, John Barzaire, Ed Wolfram, Ed Moore, Clarke Waite, William Darnell, Will Waite, George Dean, and Milt Shilling, are working off their taxes by working on the roads in their area in this late-1800s view. In September 1908, the area was plagued by nearby forest fires, and in November that same year, the Chippewa River and regional lakes were at the lowest levels in memory. Grace Johnson's grandchildren, below, enjoy a ride in Guy Myer's "not exactly road legal" goat cart in 1907 while an unidentified dog is greatly unimpressed by the novel mode of transportation.

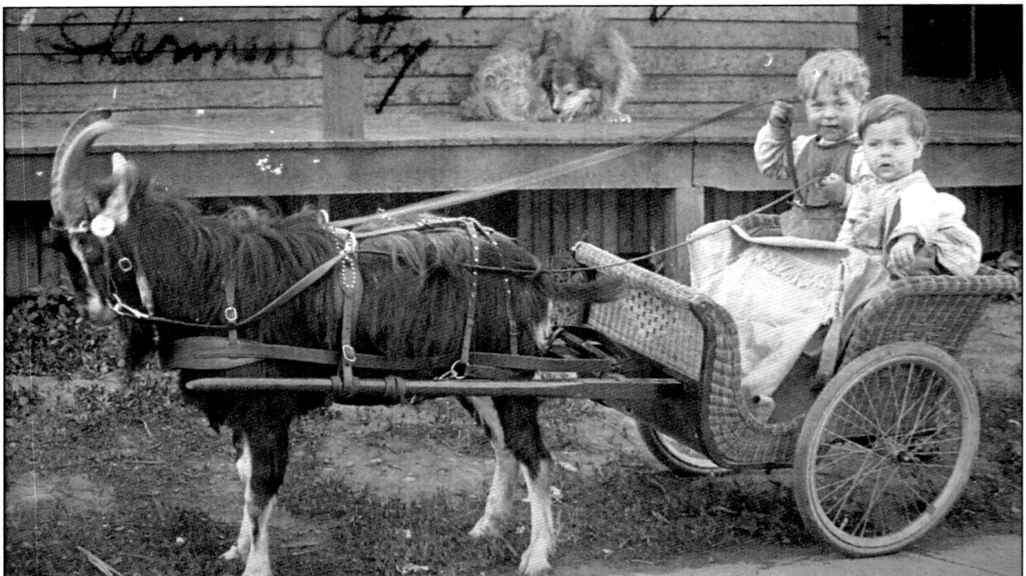

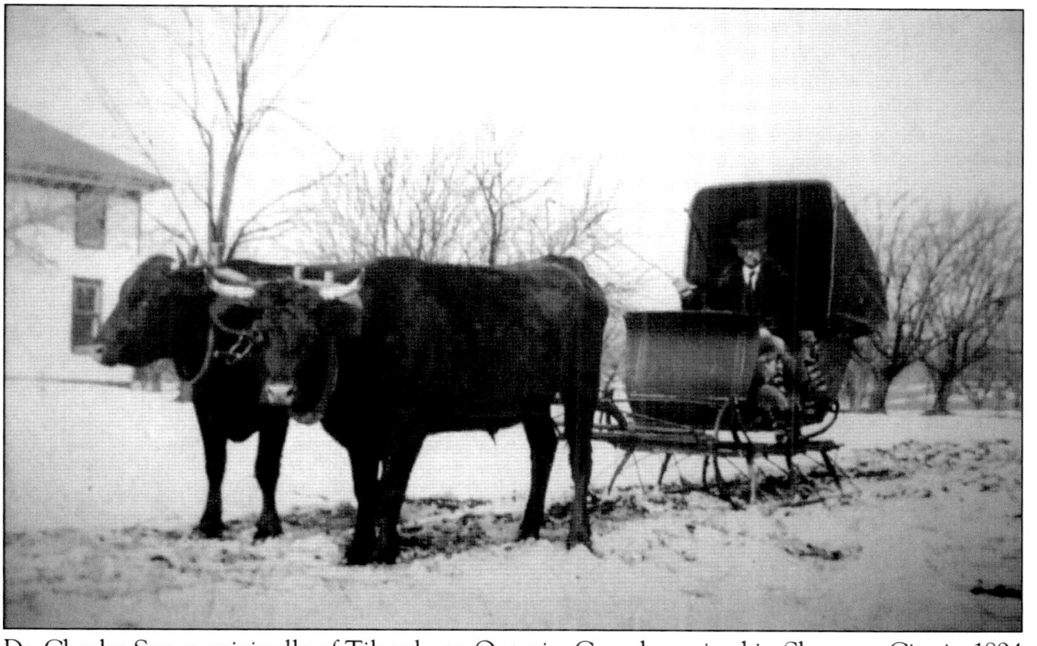

Dr. Charles Soper, originally of Tilsonburg, Ontario, Canada, arrived in Sherman City in 1894 with his wife Grace, small son James, and his brother Dr. Henry Soper. The Soper brothers took up medical practice in Sherman City. Charles, above heading out for a winter house call, served the town until 1912, when he and his wife moved to Barryton to be near James and his family. Dr. Ernest F. Rondot, below in a horse-drawn wagon for a house call, came to Sherman City in 1907 and established offices in a drugstore he bought from J. R. Cameron. In 1910, he built an office near the river and practiced there until the 1950s, when he moved to Windsor, Ontario, Canada, where he died in 1977.

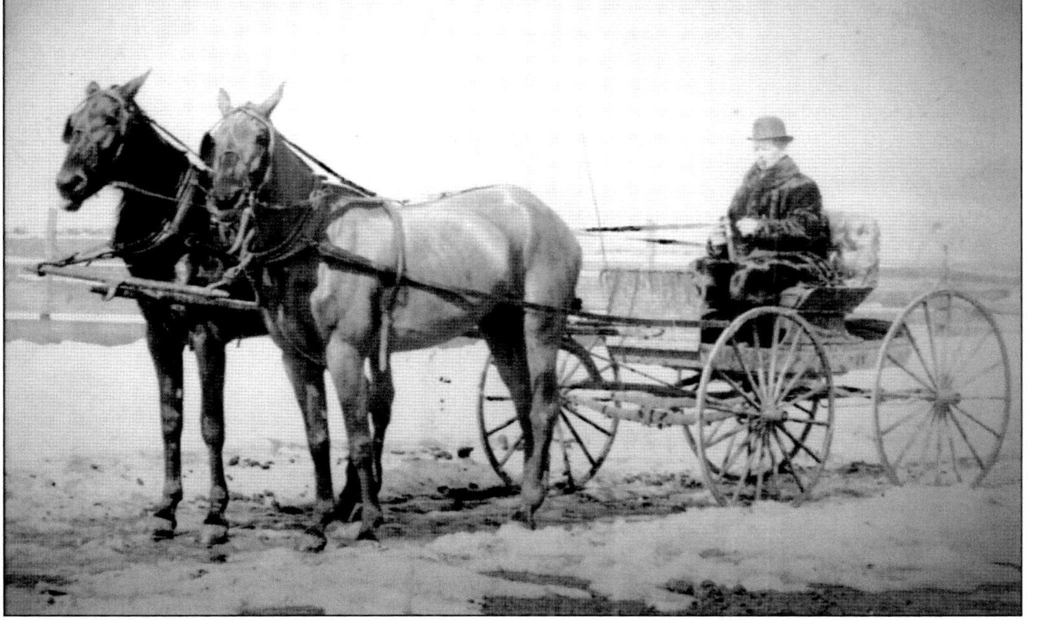

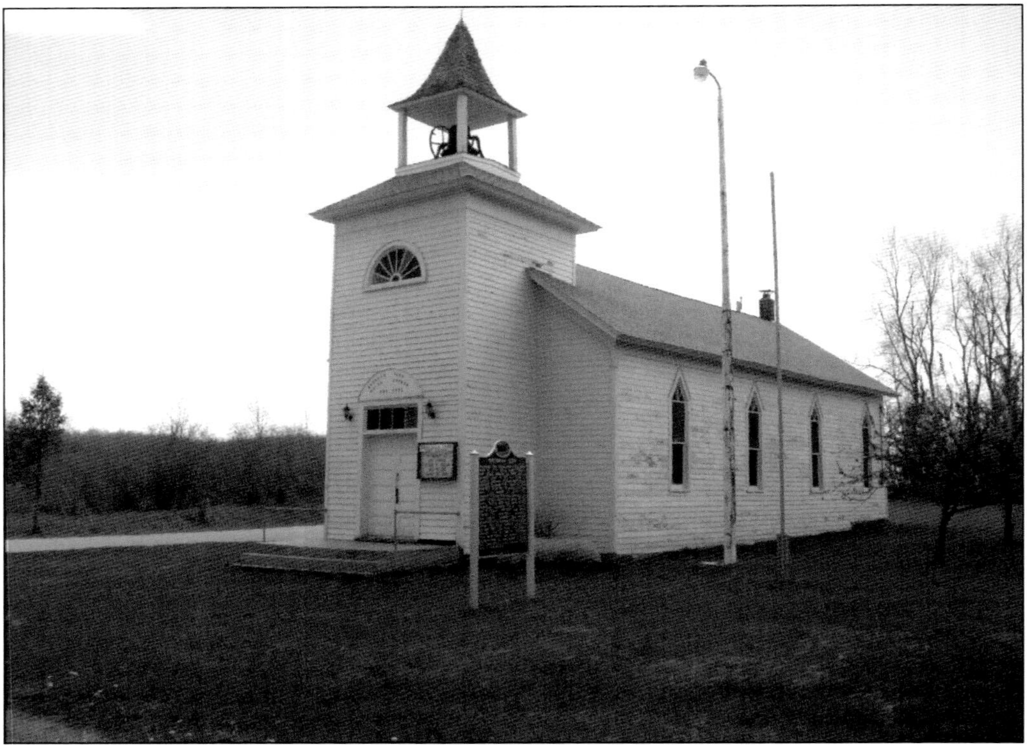

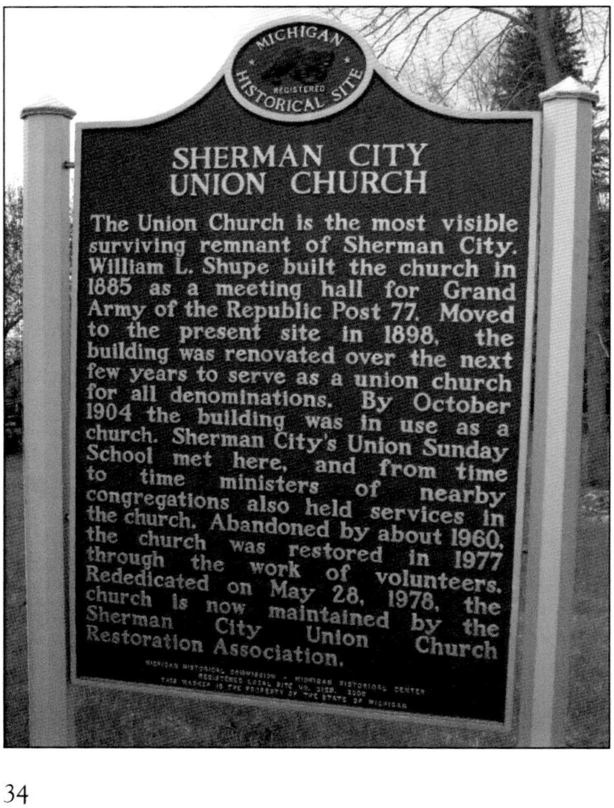

The last remaining landmark of the once thriving Sherman City is the Sherman City Union Church, built in 1871 as the Guard of American Revolution Hall. In 1898, the building was fitted out as a church and served as a nondenominational gathering place for all faiths, including the Ku Klux Klan (meeting to oppose the Catholic Church in Beal City), as well as a social gathering place for box socials, ice-cream socials, quilting bees, and bazaars. The church fell into a state of disrepair after abandonment in the 1950s but was rescued from obscurity when Elwood and Iola Miller organized a group of neighbors from nearby Beal City and Weidman to overhaul and redo the inside of the church, which was rededicated in 1978.

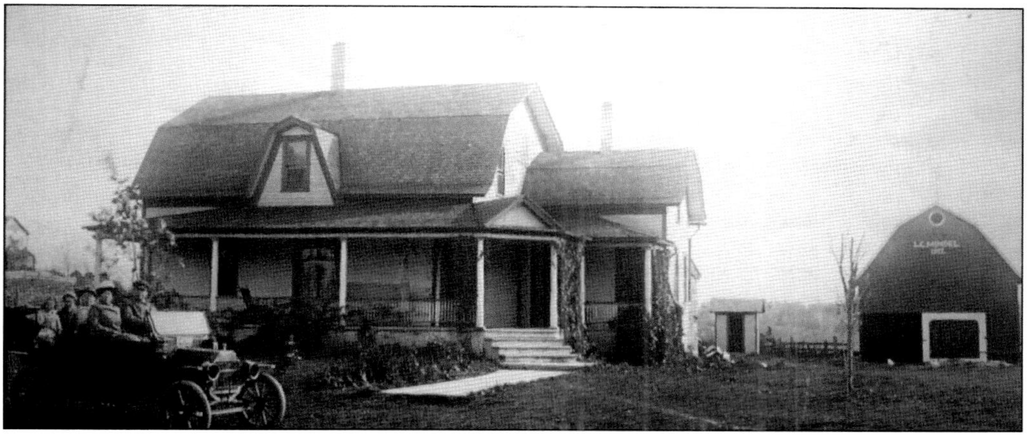

Louis Mindel of Sherman City bought a five-passenger Ford automobile, above, in June 1913. Apparently the new car owner had trouble adapting to traffic patterns, because the June 11, 1915, *Isabella County Enterprise* reported "L.C. Mindel of Sherman City was accosted by an officer for driving his auto on the wrong side of the street, but Mr. Mindel did not take it kindly. He 'riled' the officer's dander and was arrested. He paid a fine of $7.00." The Mindel home, below, next to the Sherman City church was later to become the home of George McClain, whose automobile repair business in his barn grew to become McClain Motors of Weidman.

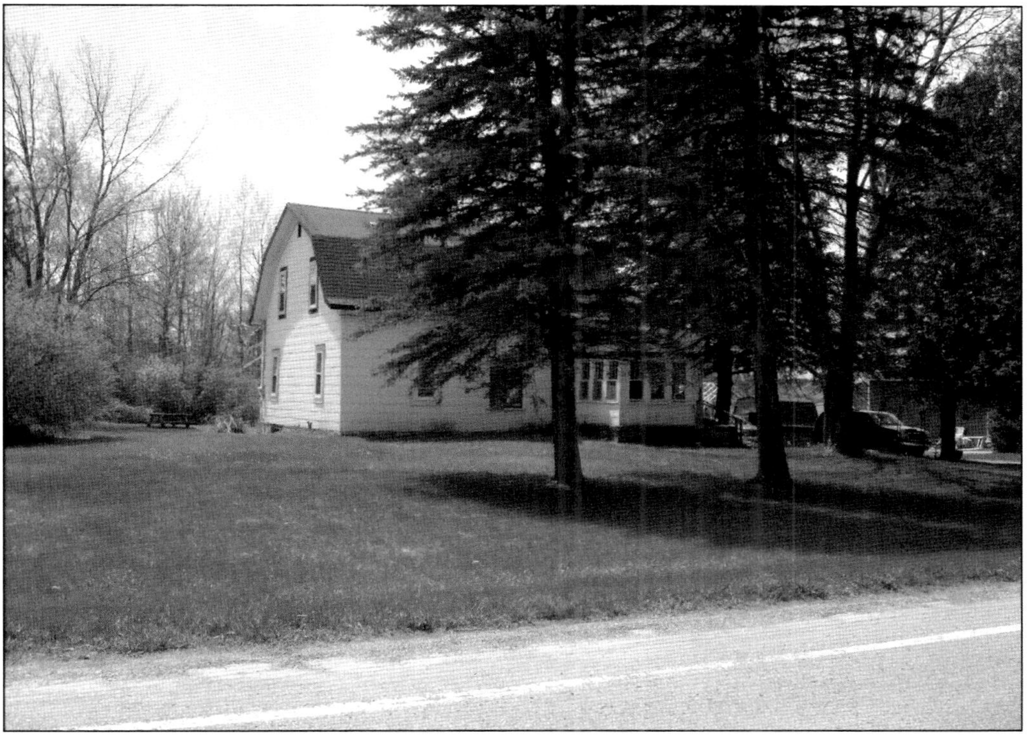

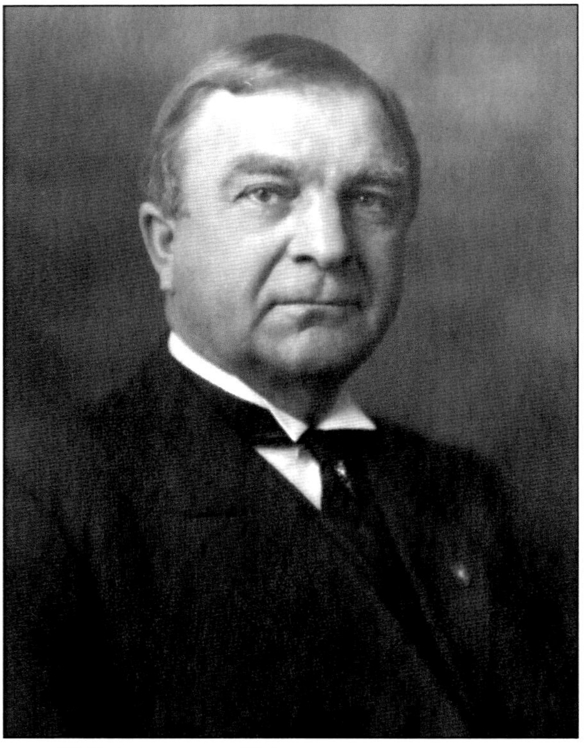

In 1894, John S. Weidman came from his boyhood family farm in Mecosta County and bought timberlands in the Nottawa/Sherman area to follow his father into the lumber business. He dammed the Coldwater River to float logs to his planing, saw, and shingle mills and on July 4, 1894, signed the plat establishing the village of Weidman's perimeters and streets. At the sawmill, John built a men's shanty and cookhouse for his mostly local workers. For the first year, his wife Margaret Weidman cooked for the workers, but as the operation grew, a men's cookhouse was constructed. John erected several businesses and donated lumber for a school to be built. He operated his mills for 16 years before selling out his interests in 1911.

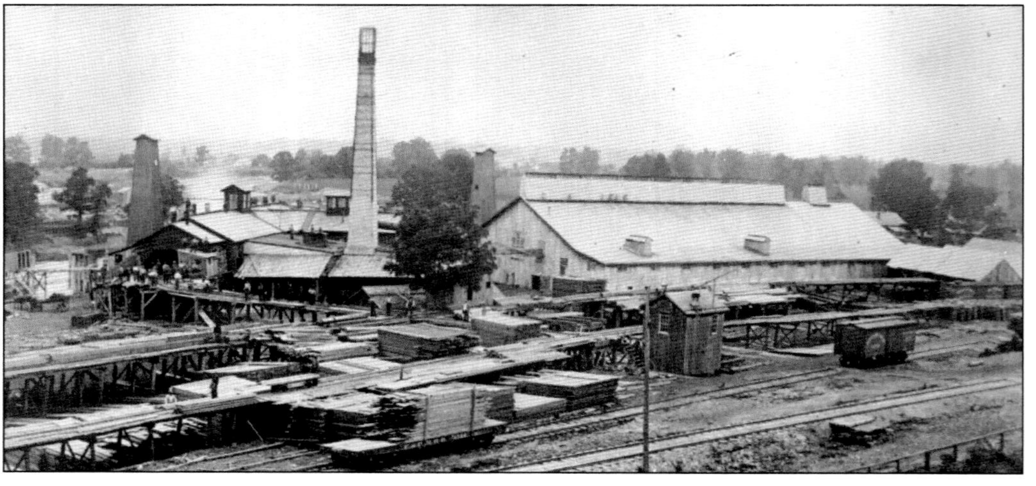

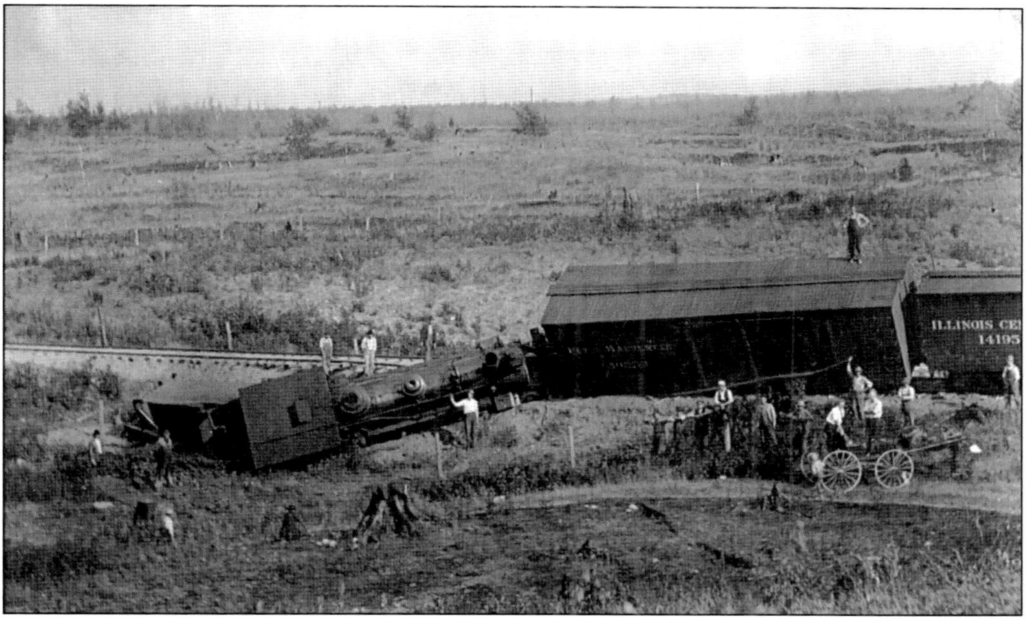

The village of Weidman, present population of 886, on the Sherman Township section 13 and Nottawa Township section 18 line, grew and prospered around the dawn of the 20th century. For several years after 1894, John S. Weidman's mills, above, produced about 10 million board feet of lumber annually, prompting Weidman to persuade the Pere Marquette Railroad to come to the village to ship lumber, which experienced a derailment in 1900, above, and is shown below in 1908. Expanding his interests, Weidman started the Weidman Banking Company around 1900 in Weidman and was also founder of the Isabella County State Bank in Mount Pleasant in 1902.

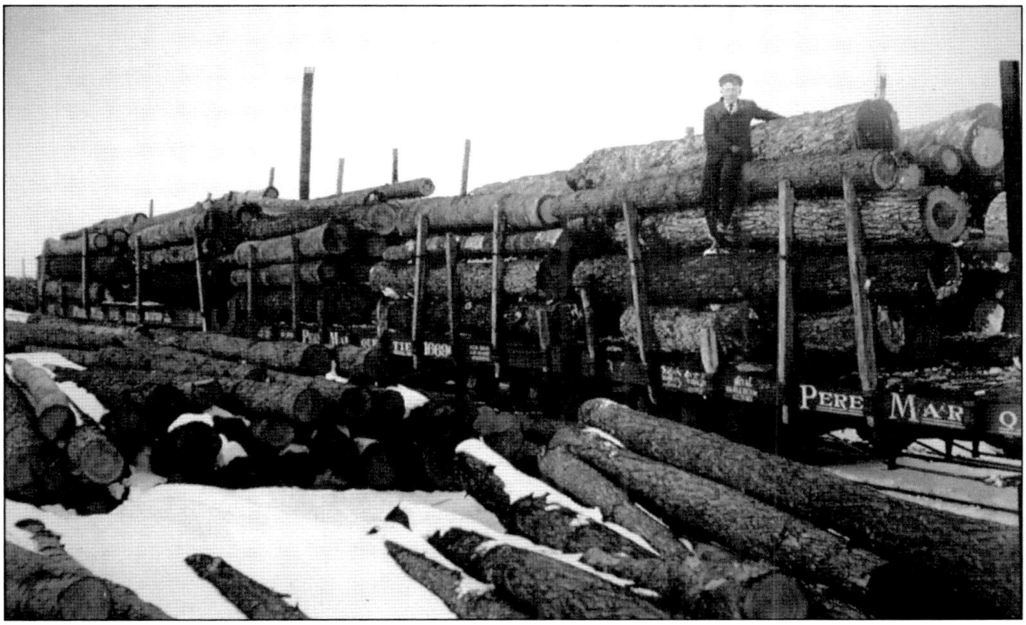

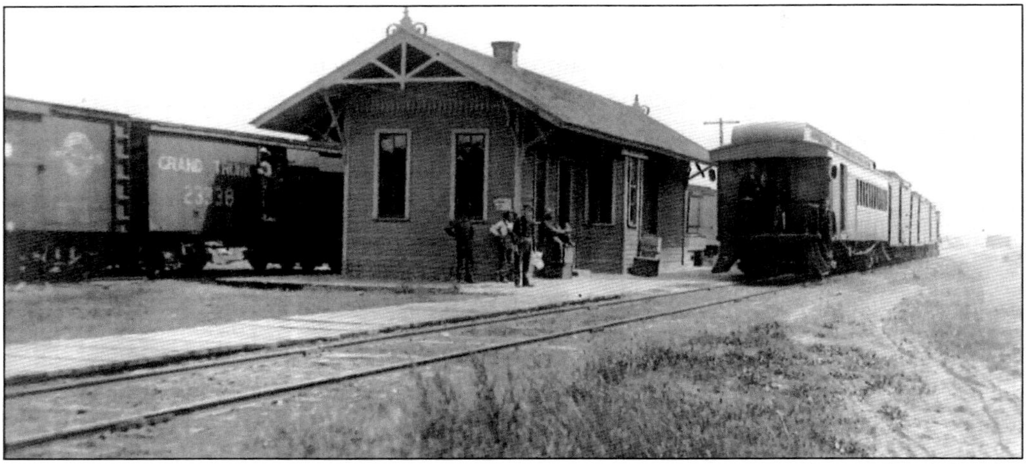

Rail service to and from the Weidman railroad depot, above, primarily involved freight, although a passenger car was generally included as a convenience when freight and lumber hauling allowed. Weidman became the largest community in Sherman Township, with a busy commercial district, drawing customers and workers from miles around with ease during summer months. Wintertime brought transportation problems for freight and folks, with howling winds and heavy snows clogging rails and roadways. The Pere Marquette Railroad snowplow, below, cleared the tracks between Weidman and Remus in Mecosta County, never failing to draw a crowd when it chugged up to the depot run by George Bollinger. Rail service to Weidman continued until the 1930s.

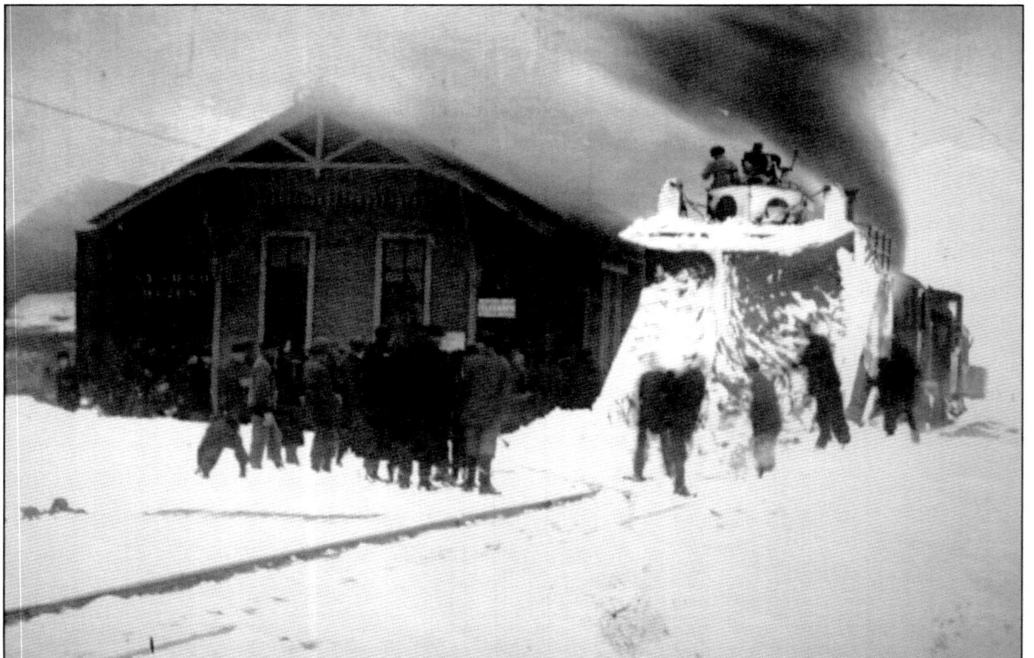

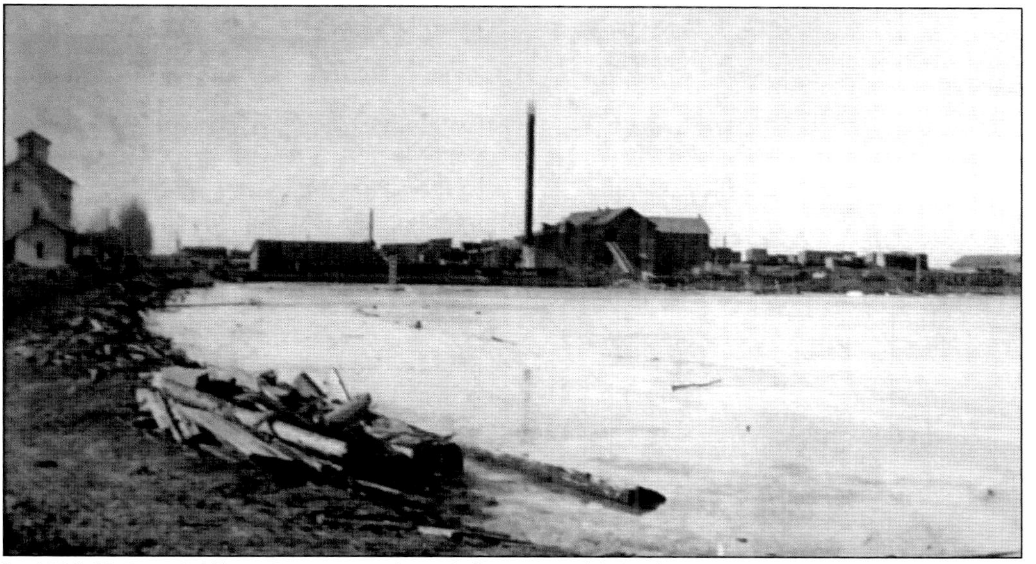

In 1905, Holmes Milling Company, above left, was established in Weidman, building an elevator and mill powered by water shared from the millpond constructed by John S. Weidman. During World War I, 1914–1918, a shortage of able-bodied men saw an increase of female employees at the mill. Holmes Milling Company employed ladies to hand-sort gravel and other impurities from seed and bean on the second floor of the mill. The "bean pickers" Bloomer Girls basketball team in the 1915–1916 season includes, from left to right, (first row) Harriet McArthur; (second row) Ruth Taylor, Evalena Taylor, and Hazel Parks; (third row) Izora Wright, Hattie Dutcher, and Theresa Kavanaugh.

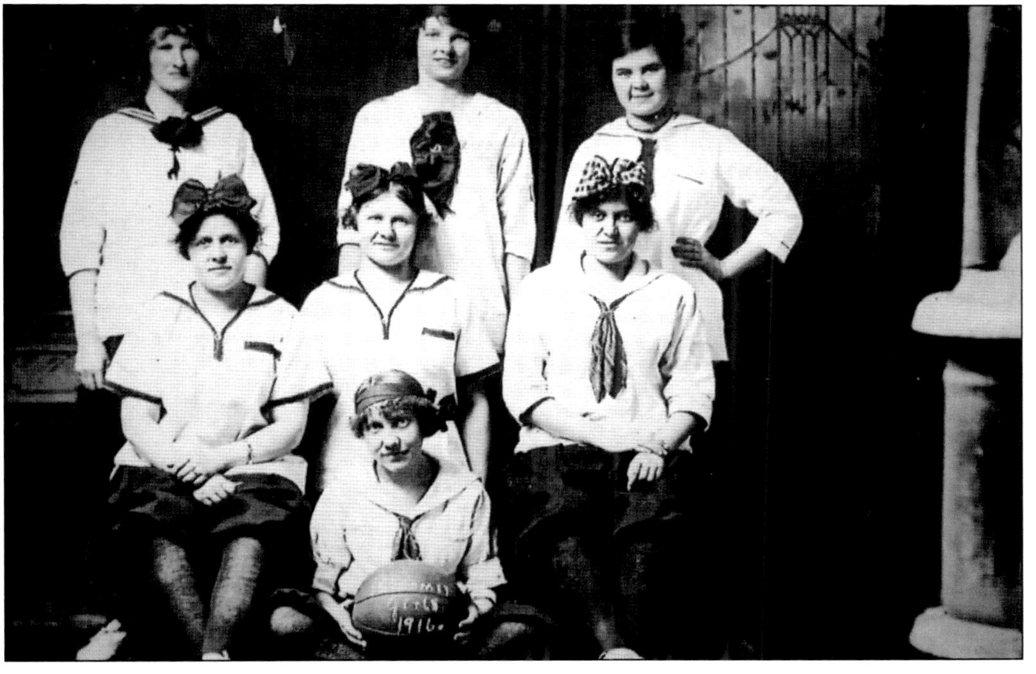

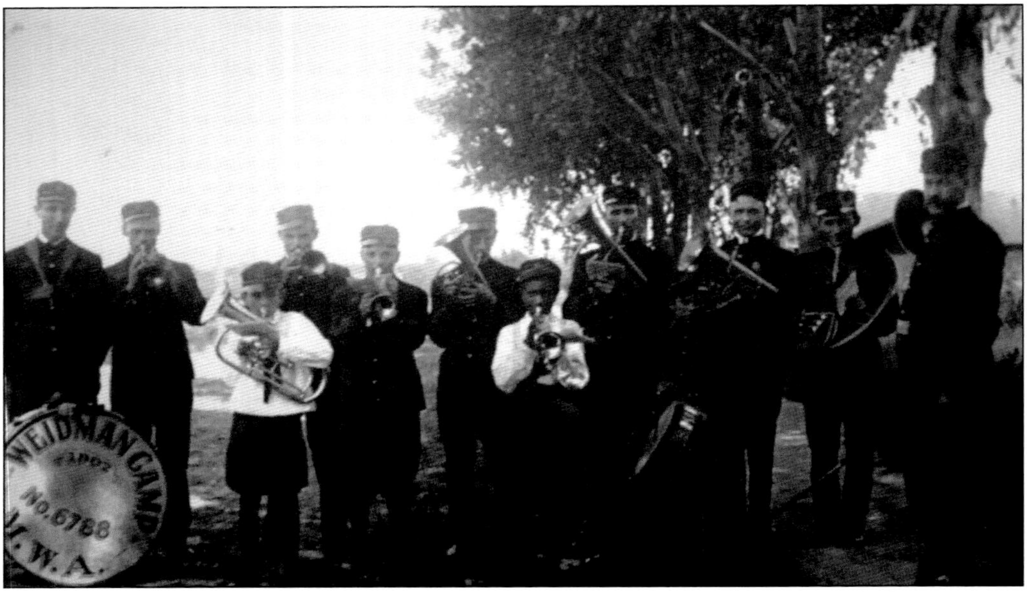

The 12-member Modern Woodmen of America Weidman Camp No. 6788 band, above, was an important source of entertainment at parades and concerts after formation in 1902. Note the multiethnic makeup of the band, reflecting the influence of former slaves who made their way north along the Underground Railroad to homestead in Michigan. The Weidman baseball team was another source of local entertainment, shown here at a game played against Riverdale on June 9, 1911, to an enthusiastic crowd. Below, from left to right are Miles Drallette, Henry Doll, Orthel Beutler, mascot Harold Clark, Howard Kennedy, Floyd Darnell, Alvin Wood, John J. Middlesworth, Lee Otto, Charles Losey, George Van Suckle, Leon McArthur, and John Ritchie (manager). Weidman won the game 17-0.

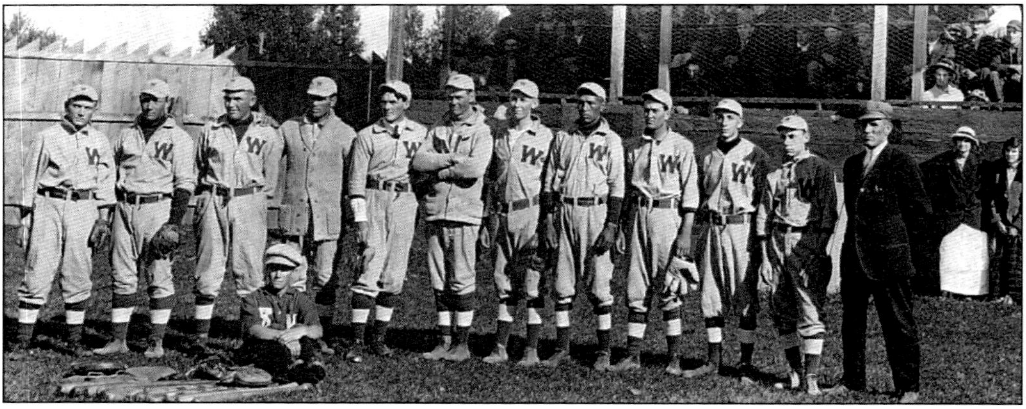

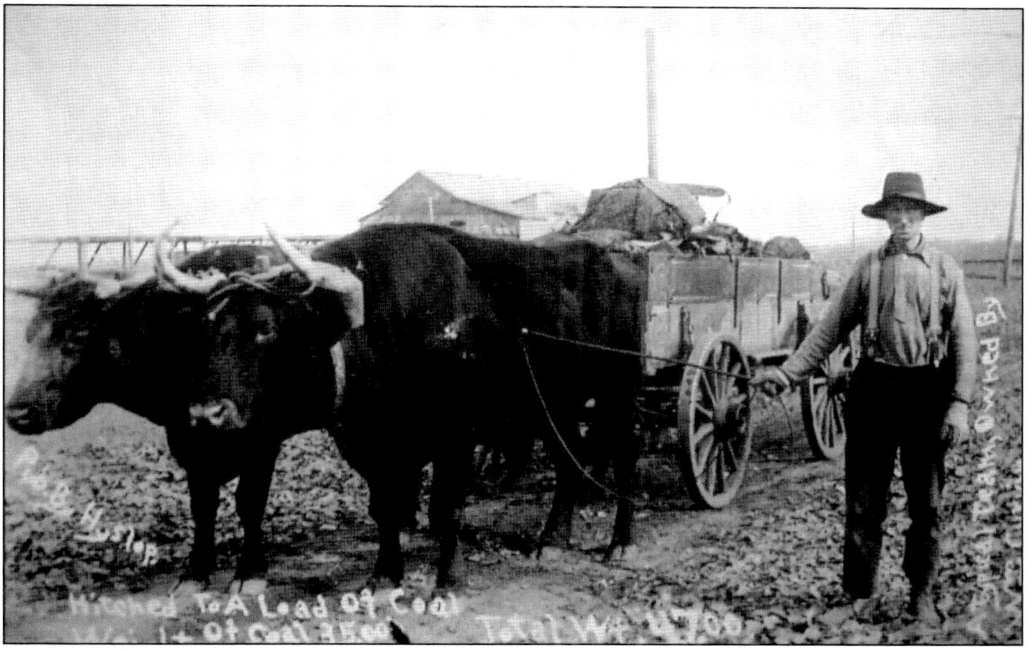

Four-legged critters, used for work and play, were the chief means for carrying in early Weidman life. Above, an oxen team owned by William Currie carries 3,500 pounds of coal in a wagon weighing 1,200 pounds for a total weight of 4,700 pounds, according to notations on this photograph by Robert Hyslop, owner of the Hyslop Hotel on Coldwater Lake and an accomplished photographer whose classic images of northwestern Isabella County life are invaluable to researchers. Charles H. Woolworth, in the driver's seat below, sold several different makes of automobiles in Weidman during the 1914–1919 era. In the back seat of this demonstration drive are William Rickett and his father-in-law Thomas Houck.

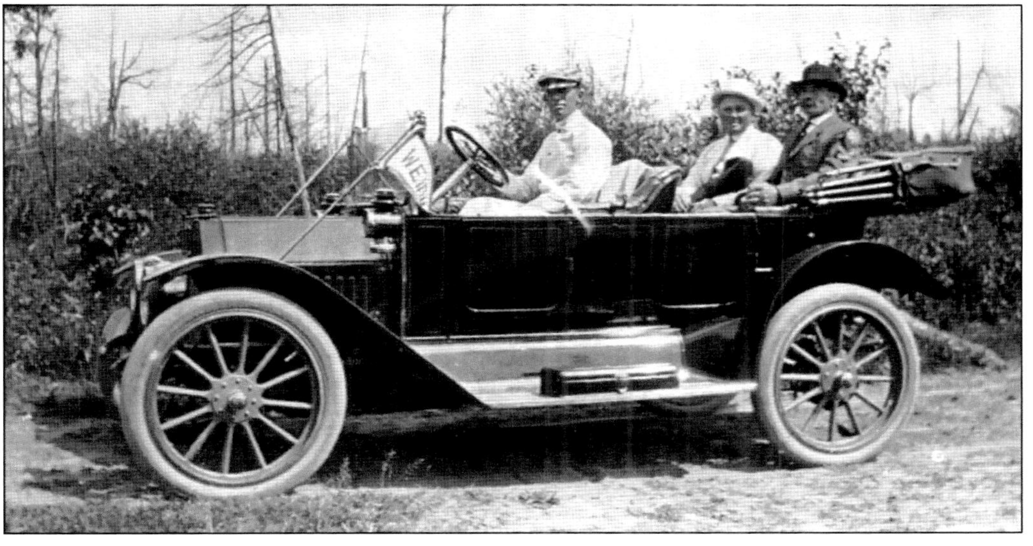

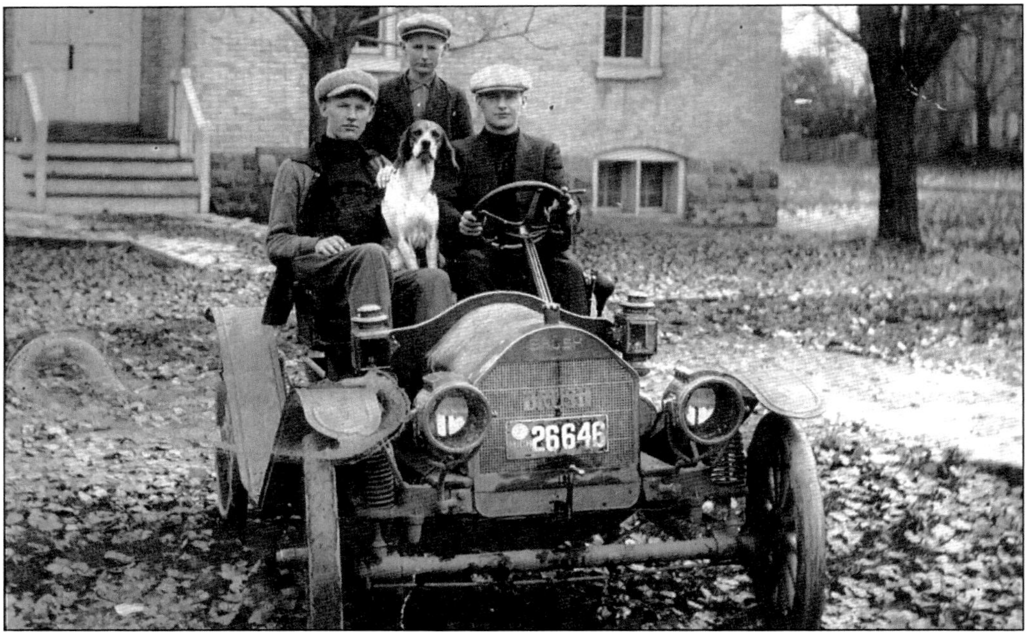

In 1911, the automobile was beginning to be the preferred mode of transport, and while still rare enough to cause a stir, Weidman residents showed off their rides in style. Above, Silas Wright, rural Weidman mail carrier, allowed sons, from left to right, George, Charlie, and Gilbert to take a spin in his new automobile. Cattle buyer Louis LaPearl, in the driver's seat below, shows off his new Ford to teacher Mae Wolfe (front seat), along with students, from left to right, Sadie Richardson, Florence Dawson, Nora Coffin, and Rosalia Dale, many of whom, it is said, were employees of the Weidman Banking Company, opened in 1908 by John S. Weidman.

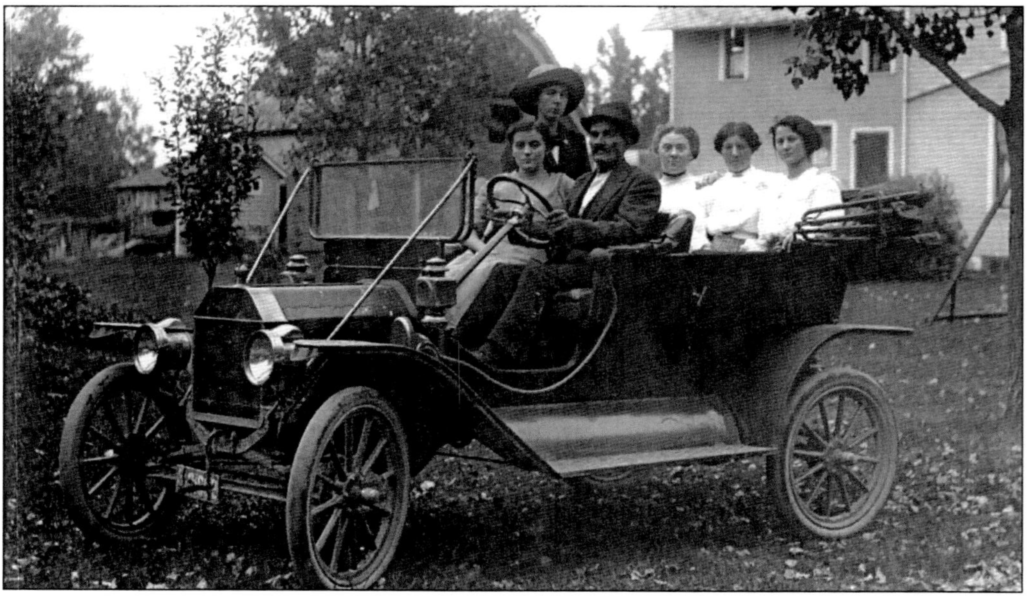

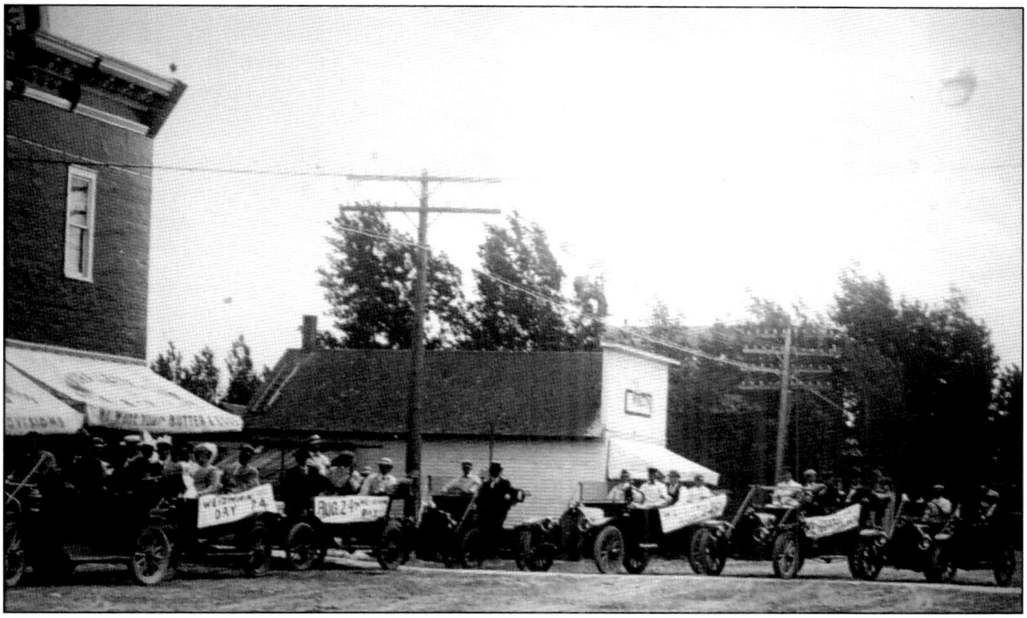

On August 28, 1909, the 11th annual Weidman Field Days, sponsored by Klondike brand flour from local Holmes Milling Company, feted townsfolk to a day of entertainment, festivities, and scoping out the wares of vendors in street booths. Three years later, the event morphed into Weidman Days, as the August 24, 1912, opening parade of now-common automobiles wends its way down Main Street in front of Drallette's store. For several years, a highlight of Weidman life was the annual John Deere Days, sponsored by Charles Woolworth. In 1951, Weidman Business Association members, below from left to right, George McClain Jr., Mitchell McArthur, Leo Neubecker, and Clarence Wiley plan more celebrations for the community's entertainment.

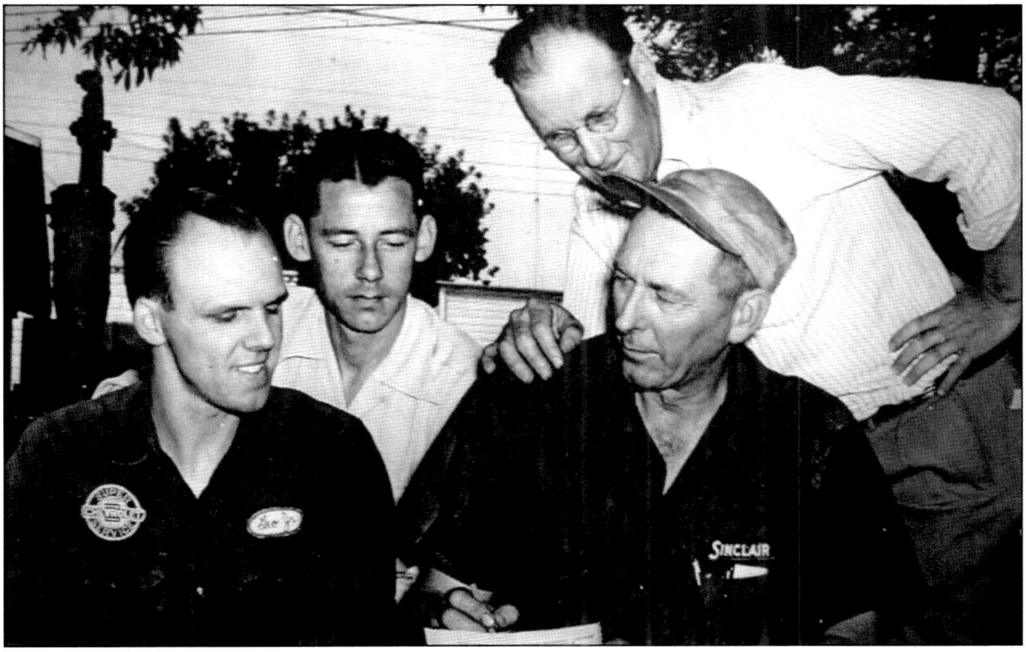

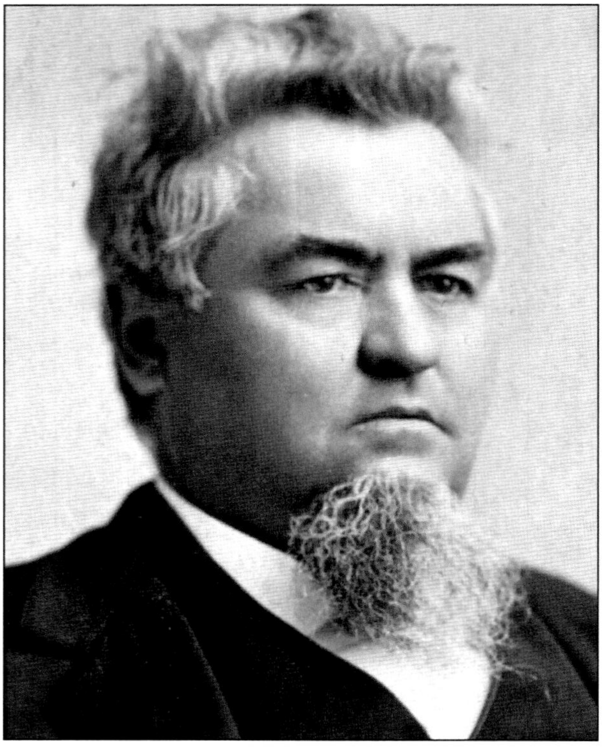

Attorney Roswell Gilbert Horr, at left, was engaged in mining for six years in Missouri before moving to Saginaw in 1872. Horr was elected congressman for Michigan's Eighth Congressional District and served in the U.S. Congress from 1879 to 1885. In 1884, a post office was established at the settlement near Woodins Mills in Sherman Township and named Horr in honor of Congressman Horr. The post office name was changed from Horr to Woodins Mills, from 1886 to 1890, as a nod to the importance of farmer, lumberman, and township supervisor Henry Woodin's sawmill and the lumber industry. It changed back to Horr until 1904, closing when lumber waned in importance in the area. The Horr store, below, continues to the modern day as an operating entity.

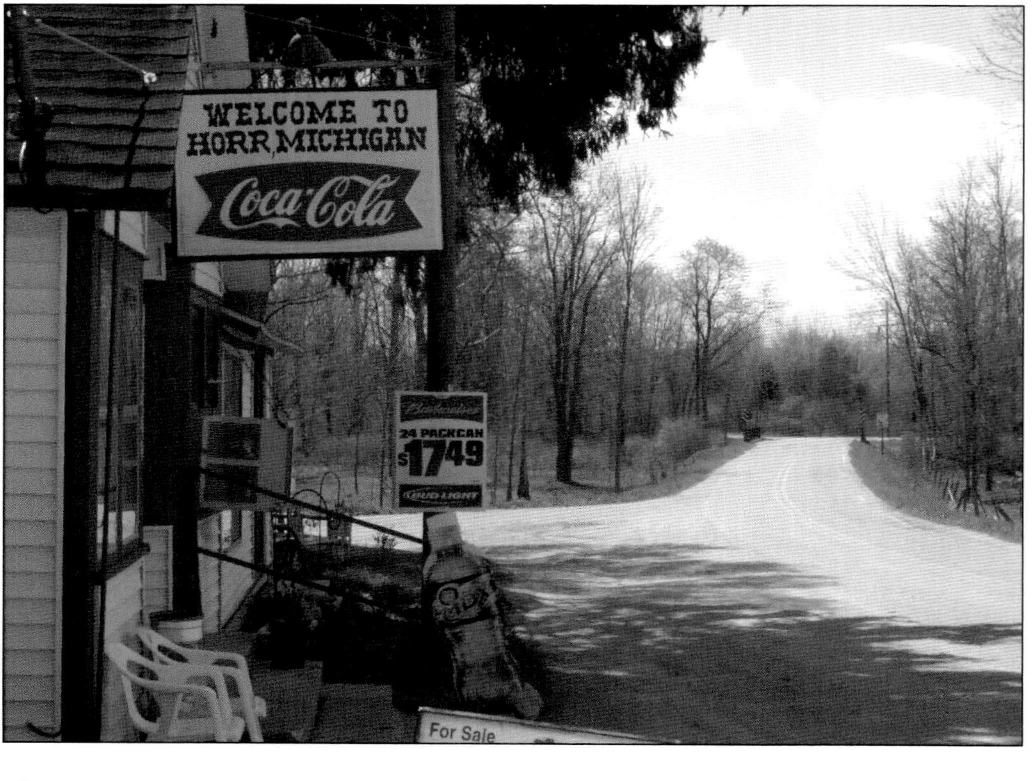

Two

Northeastern Isabella County

The northeastern quadrant of Isabella County consists of four relatively flatland townships in an agricultural area with little present industry.

Denver Township, in township 15 north, range 3 west, is the southeastern township of the quadrant. It was settled in 1875–1876 by Lewis Hawkins, John Collins, and Julius C. Jordan, created by the Isabella County Board of Supervisors in 1876, and named by a resident who had lived in Denver, Colorado.

Denver Township had several settlements. Delwin was in section 16 (see page 49). Jordan, a flag station with no post office that existed until about 1895, was on the Pere Marquette Railroad line, 4.3 miles northeast of Mount Pleasant. Leaton (see page 48) was named in 1880 for Mount Pleasant attorney John C. Leaton. Tomkinsville, in section 22, never had a post office or railroad and disappeared after appearing only on a 1900 map. Wise (Freeney's Mill) was a station on the Pere Marquette Railroad formed around a sawmill owned by John H. Freeney. A post office was established there in 1884 with the name Freeney's Mill until 1892. It was renamed Wise (see pages 61–64) in 1893 until its 1906 closing.

Isabella Township, in the southwest corner of the county's northeast quadrant, was established in 1857 and at first encompassed all of the area of the present Isabella County except Coe Township. The initial boundaries were the same as the county's, to be subdivided in the ensuing years. The only remaining community in the township is Rosebush, also known as Calkinsville and Halfway (see pages 56–59), with a present population of more than 300 and a post office.

There were other defunct Isabella Township settlements. Elm Grove was platted southwest of Rosebush, just down the railroad tracks from the depot, where speculators hoped to establish a housing development that never occurred. Isabella was three miles northeast of Mount Pleasant on the Pere Marquette Railroad, where the Blunt post office was transferred and renamed Isabella in 1865, then permanently transferred to Mount Pleasant in 1869. Nippessing was a settlement with an odd geological-era name, about two miles southwest of Rosebush, that was never platted, developed, or had a post office. Whiteville, in section 31, was where storekeeper Omer L. White was given a post office in 1884 that operated until 1902.

Vernon Township was established in 1866 and was named at the suggestion of someone who had settled there from a southern Michigan town named Vernon. Burnhan in section 16 (sometimes spelled as Burnham, also known as Burnham Crossing and Burnham Station) was a station on the Mount Pleasant-to-Clare railroad and had a sawmill, boardinghouse, and storage yard for logs in 1875. Cowdens was briefly, around 1900, a rail stop along the Ann Arbor Railroad about nine railroad miles north of Mount Pleasant. It disappeared from railroad records by 1910. Curriers Crossings was a small settlement about two miles southwest of Clare that appeared on railroad maps in the early 1900s and likewise was absent from them by 1910. Dinghams was one of 12 settlements on the Ann Arbor Railroad's 25 miles of track in Isabella County. Doherty was 4.7 railroad miles north of Dinghams. Both Dinghams and Doherty were too small for post offices. Ellaville had a post office for only a year in a hotel built by Alexander R. Bush. Russell was the post office six miles north of Rosebush at the railroad stop for Burnham, named for an early township settler, Edwin Russell. Vernon (Vernon City), just south of the Isabella–Clare county line, was platted in 1871 on the Little Tobacco Creek and is now within the city limits of Clare. Vernon Center, at the intersection of sections 14/15 and 22/23 never had a post office or railroad but was less than a mile from the Ann Arbor Railroad.

Wise Township was organized in 1872 and named for cofounder and early settler George W. Wise. Township settlements included Herrick (once known as Lansingville), a station on the Pere Marquette Railroad three and a half railroad miles southeast of Clare, which had a sawmill, blacksmith shop, charcoal kiln, church, and the Herrick Full Cheese Company when a post office was established in 1895 and operated until 1908. Loomis is where Erastus G. Loomis, Wise, and E. F. Gould built a general store and sawmill, then platted a village in 1871 with a post office named Buchtel, renamed Loomis a year later (see pages 53–55).

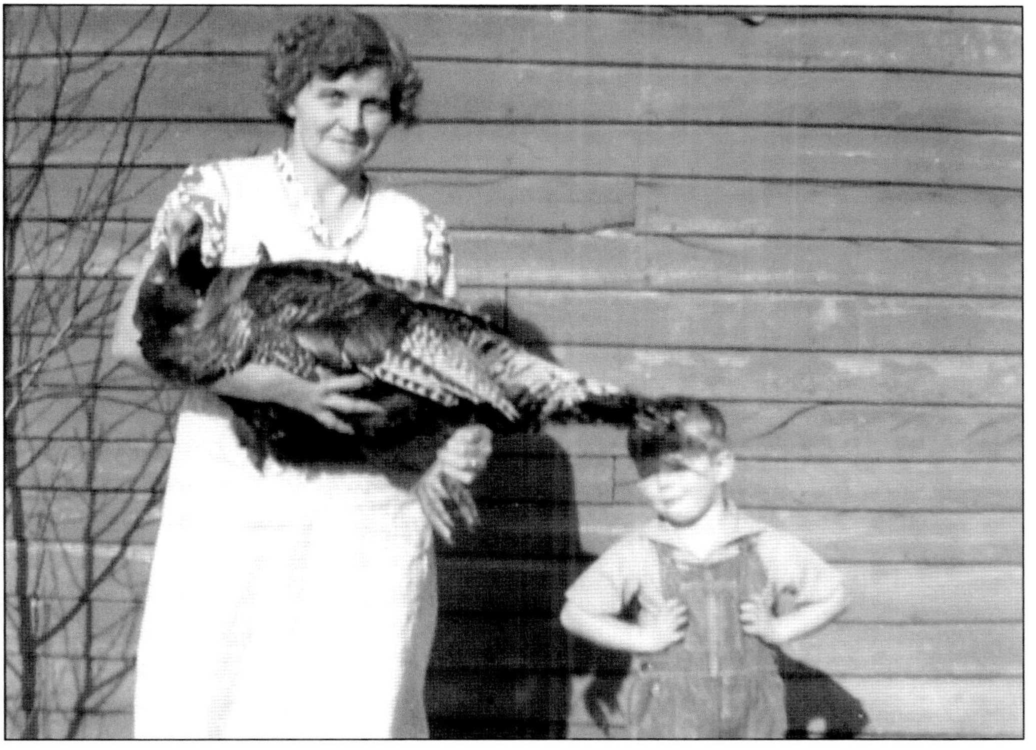

A hapless turkey wandered into the backyard of Verna Moore in the 1940s, just about the time she was wondering what to have for supper. Verna and the turkey came to an agreement heavily to the bird's disadvantage but nourishing for the family of seven sons and a daughter. Above, youngest son Don Moore, now of the southwest corner of section 27 in Wise Township, looks in awe at the newly arrived gobbler supper. Almost 50 years and two family generations later, Don's grandson Riley Andrews shows the same awe at the turkey his father shot while hunting in 1995.

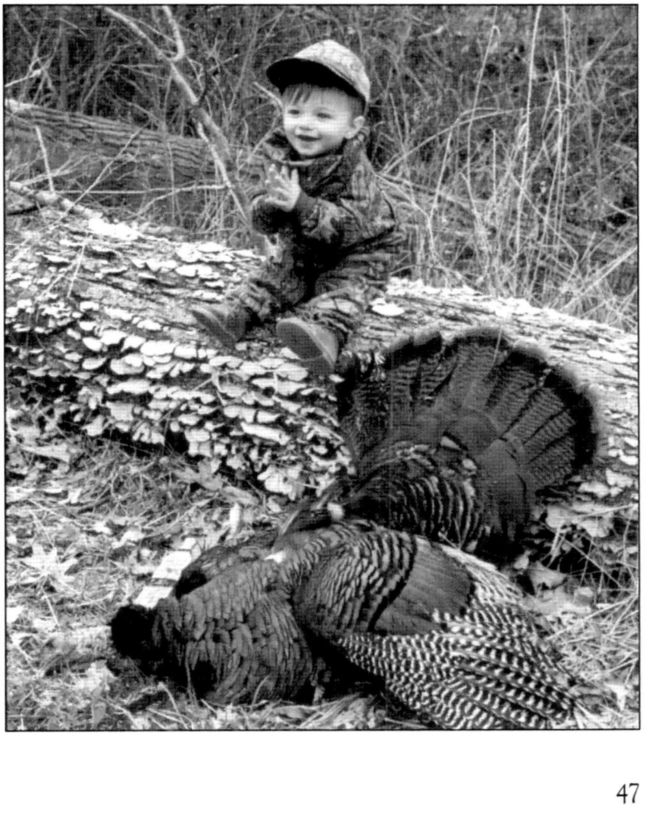

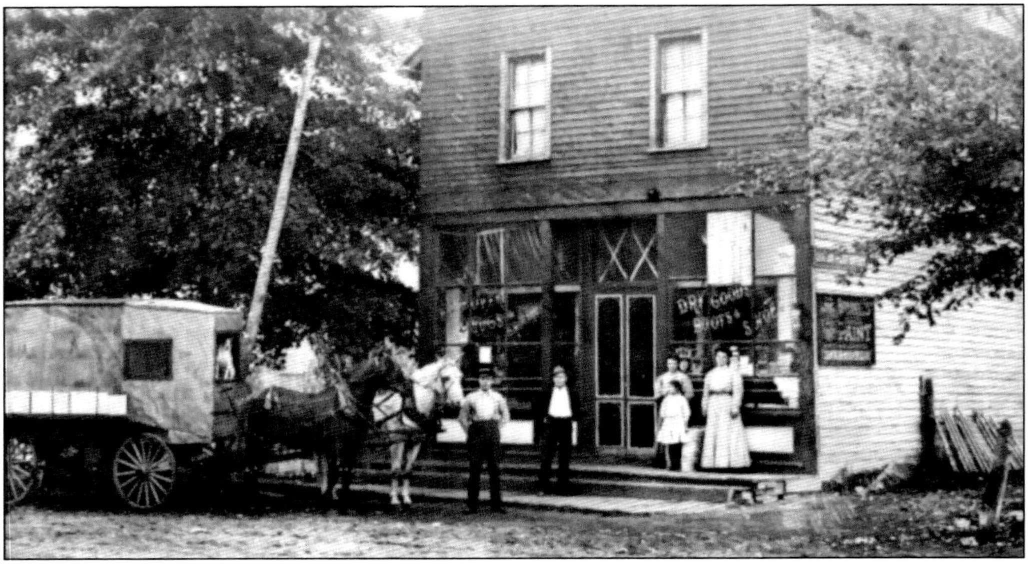

Leaton, now a cluster of residences, a softball diamond, and church at the corner of sections 19, 20, 29, and 30 in Denver Township, was named for Mount Pleasant attorney and prominent area landowner John C. Leaton. A stop on the Flint and Pere Marquette Railroad line from Coleman to Mount Pleasant, Leaton was established in 1880 with William Allenbaugh as postmaster of a post office in the store, above, until 1915. The 1940s Leaton baseball team, below, includes, from left to right, (first row) Kewn Cowden, Florek Zawacki, Victor Wizensky, Morse Graham, Floyd "Pat" Methner, and manager Frank Campbell; (second row) Buck Graham, Jack Morrison, Dan McConnell, Bob Davis, and Alfonzo Epple.

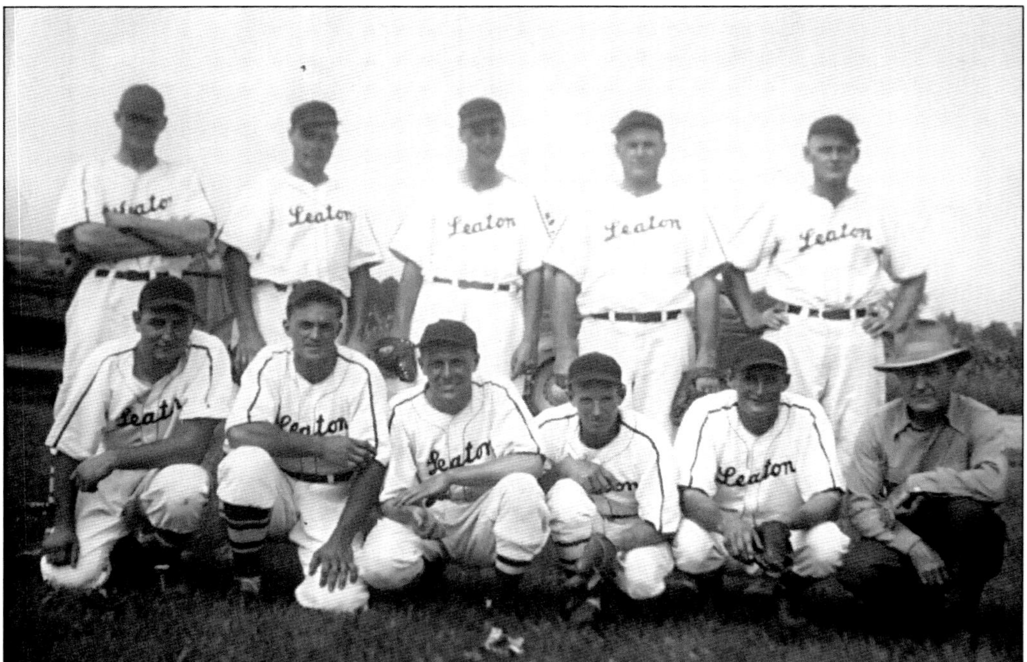

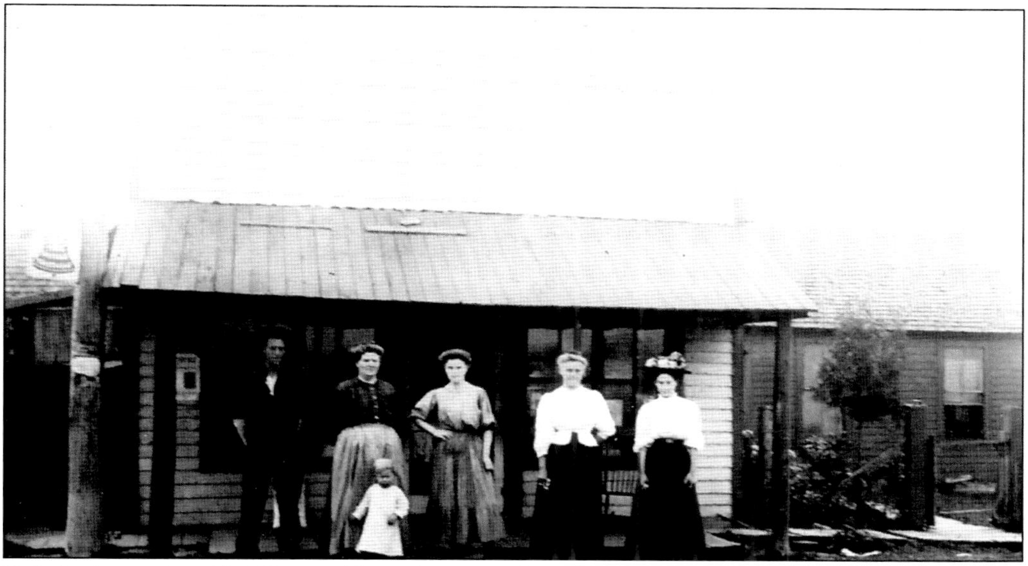

Delwin, in section 16 of Denver Township, was platted with only five blocks and 54 lots in 1888, having had a post office since 1880 with James Small as postmaster in Harrison's store on the south side of the town hall, above. Delwin, another busy lumbering center, was also a stop on the Flint and Pere Marquette Railroad's Coleman-to-Mount Pleasant spur with a substantial grain elevator, which is still operating on the site as modern Brown Milling Company and charcoal kilns. In 1906, it was lumbered out and the post office closed. In modern times, Delwin has shrunk to a cluster of residences, the gristmill operation, and the Denver Township Hall, below.

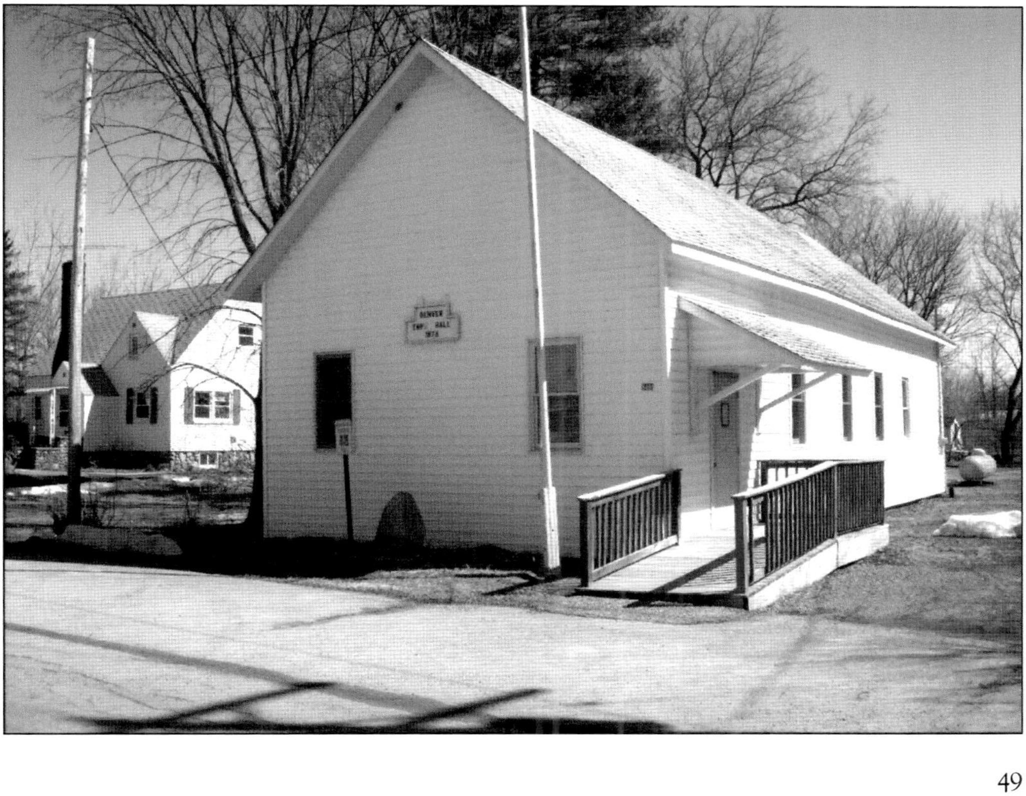

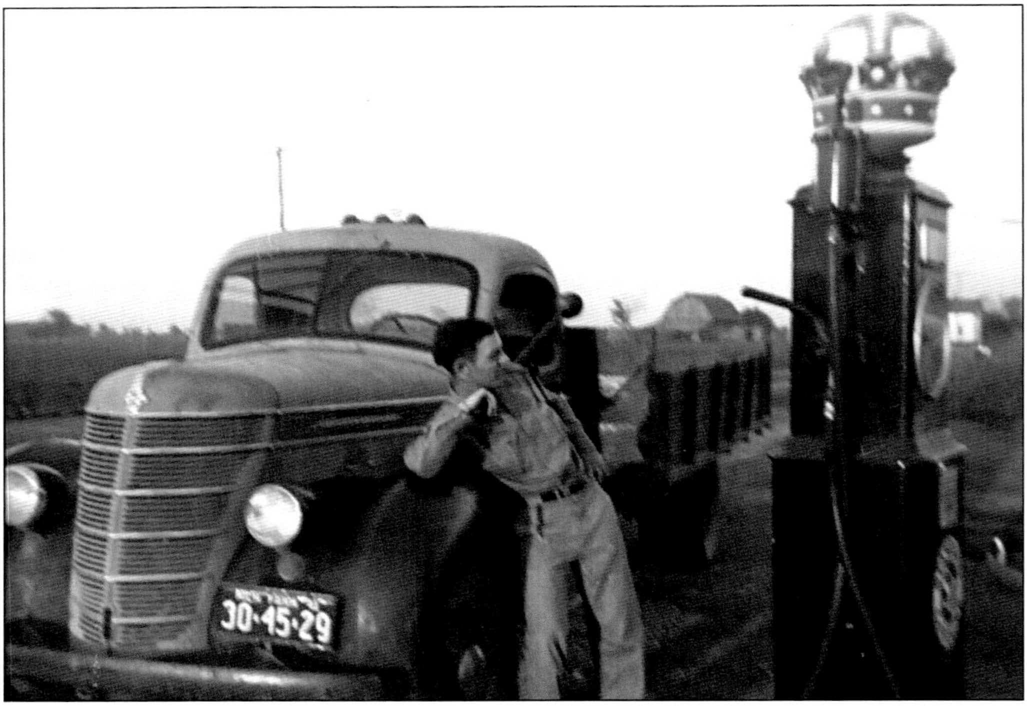

A 1940s customer fills up from the familiar crowned Standard gasoline pumps at Ackers Auto Service, above. Lowrence E. Acker and his bookkeeper wife Effie began his automobile repair business in a shed in his grandmother's backyard on the corner of East Coleman and Loomis Roads in 1936. The business soon moved to a 30-foot-square building across the street on Coleman Road and in 1948 expanded to automobile and small-engine sales and service, doubling in size. Lowrence and Effie retired in 1979, turning the now-defunct business over to son Richard L. Acker. Another Acker, Wally (below), resurrected a wooden manure spreader for a job on the Acker farm in 2004. (Courtesy of Carol Acker Sanford.)

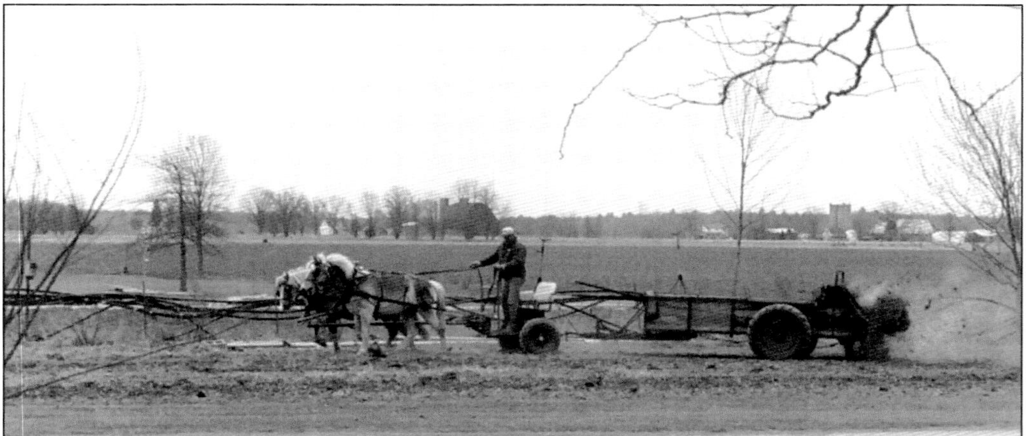

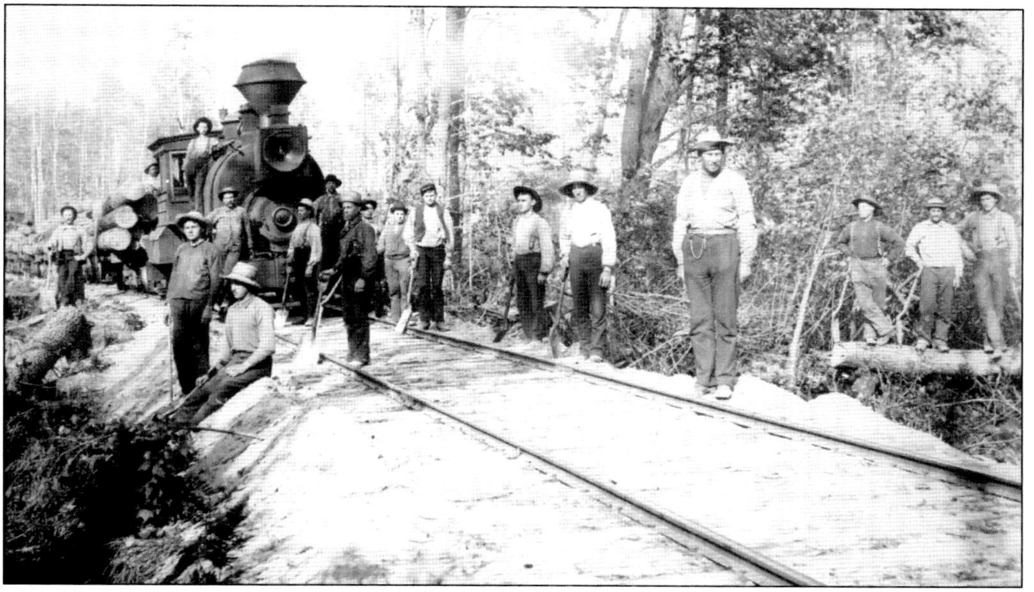

The Flint and Pere Marquette Railroad opened lumber trade lines from Mount Pleasant to Coleman (in Clare County) with the 1871 construction of a railroad line between those two communities. Besides offering year-round access to lumber markets, above, not dependent on weather like water routes, the new railroad spur opened previously isolated Isabella County villages like Longwood, Isabella Station, Jordan, Leaton, and Delwin to rail-passenger traffic, below, although sometimes passengers appeared to wonder "where's the town?" As was the custom of the time, railroad stops were placed about every two miles along the route, with some named stops never developed by settlement.

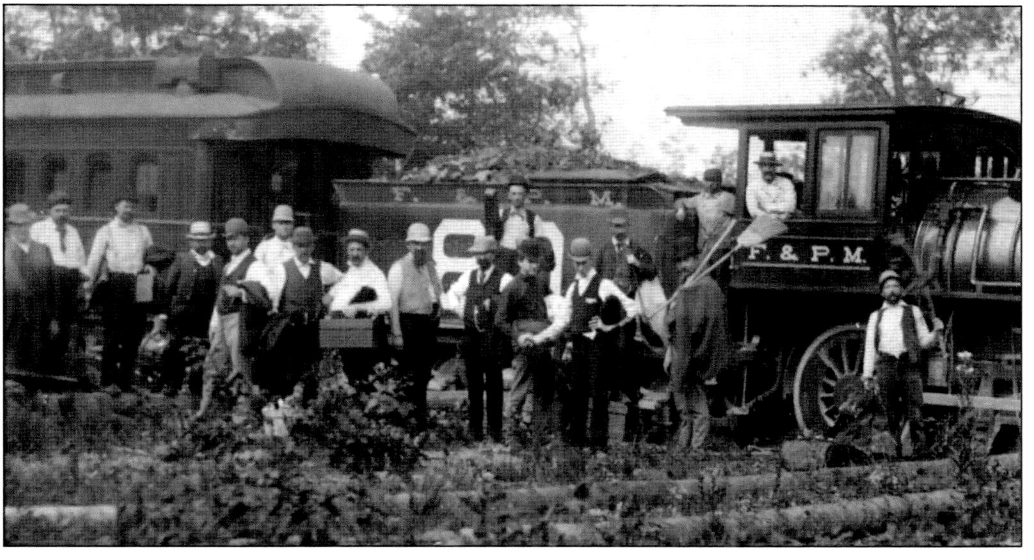

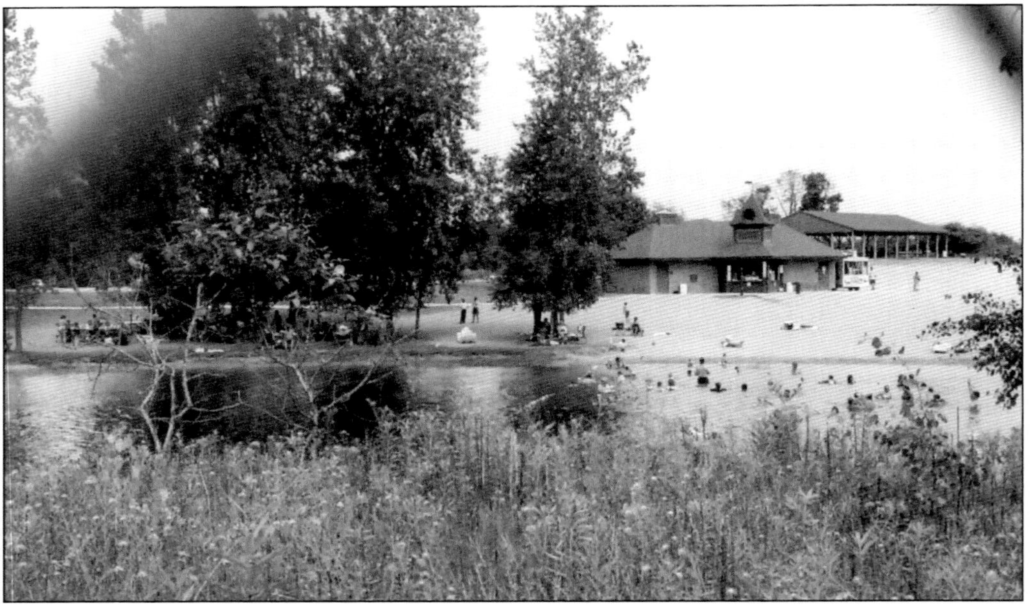

In 1969, gravel operator Paul Hubscher donated his pits, in sections 6 and 7 in Wise Township to Isabella County. In 1977, Ferdinand and Jacob Seibt gave land in the area to Isabella County in exchange for the use of land in another area. In 1983, 45 previously rustic campsites were converted into modern sites. Isabella County Herrick Park Recreation Area has grown since the early 1970s from two abandoned gravel pits to a first-class recreation facility. The north side, above, has a day-use area offering fishing, a playground, picnic pavilions, swimming, and a large sandy beach. The south side, below, offers 73 campsites, five rustic cabins, fishing, sand volleyball, and a small playground.

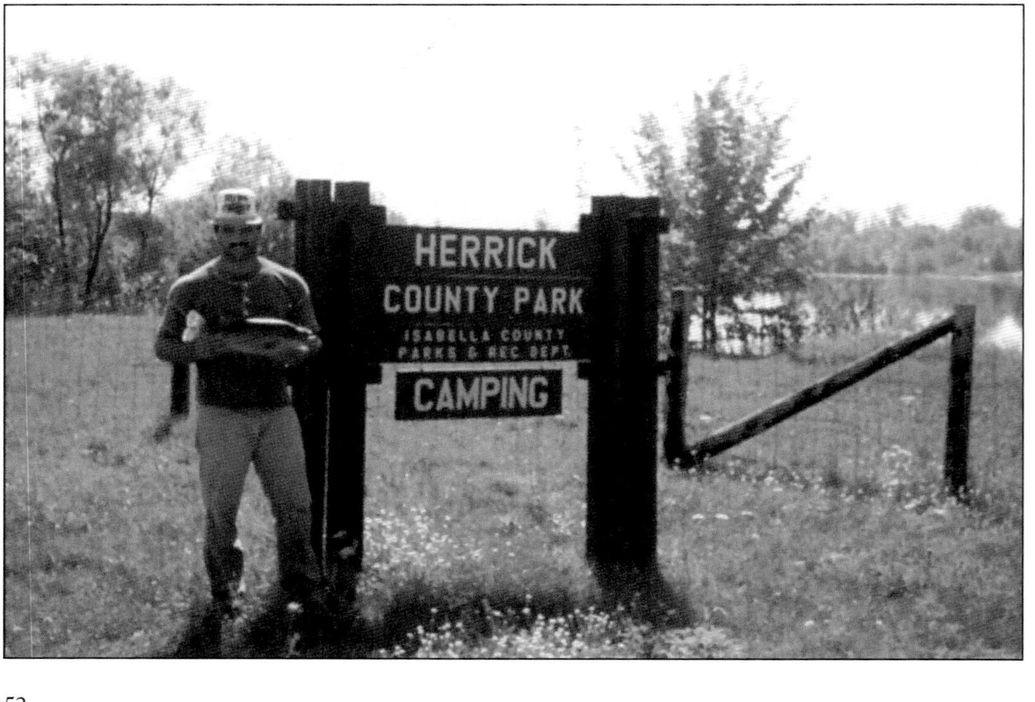

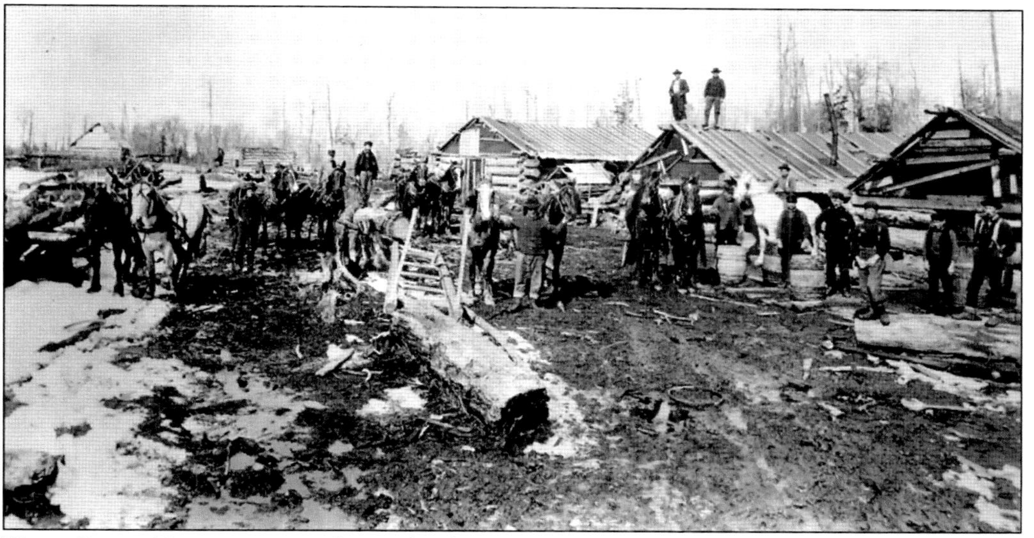

The village of Loomis sprang from a lumber camp straddling the line between sections 9 and 10 of Wise Township. The area began developing when Erastus Loomis, George W. Wise, and E. F. Gould built a sawmill and general store there in 1871, clearing land, above, and platting a village, then called Buchtel, to greet the arrival of the Pere Marquette Railroad line installed that same year. The post office opened as Buchtel in May 1871, but the name was changed to Wise in December of that year and remained so named until closing in 1915. In 1872, Wise Township was named after one of the village founders. Below from left to right, Cora Lyness, Emma Rockett, Thelma Lyness, Gladys Rockett, unidentified, and Harvey Rockett prepare for a Saturday jaunt to town in 1910.

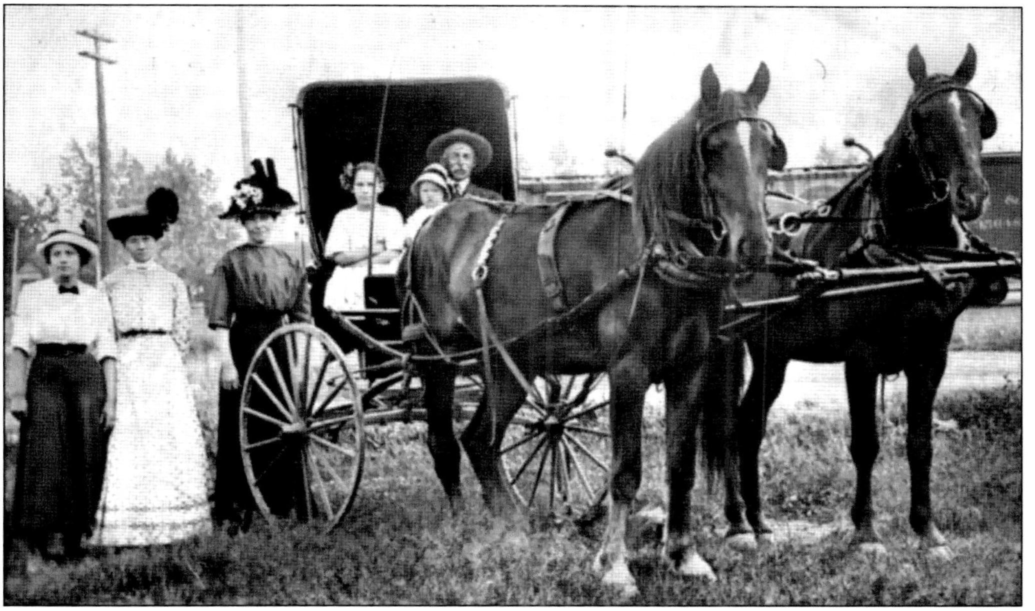

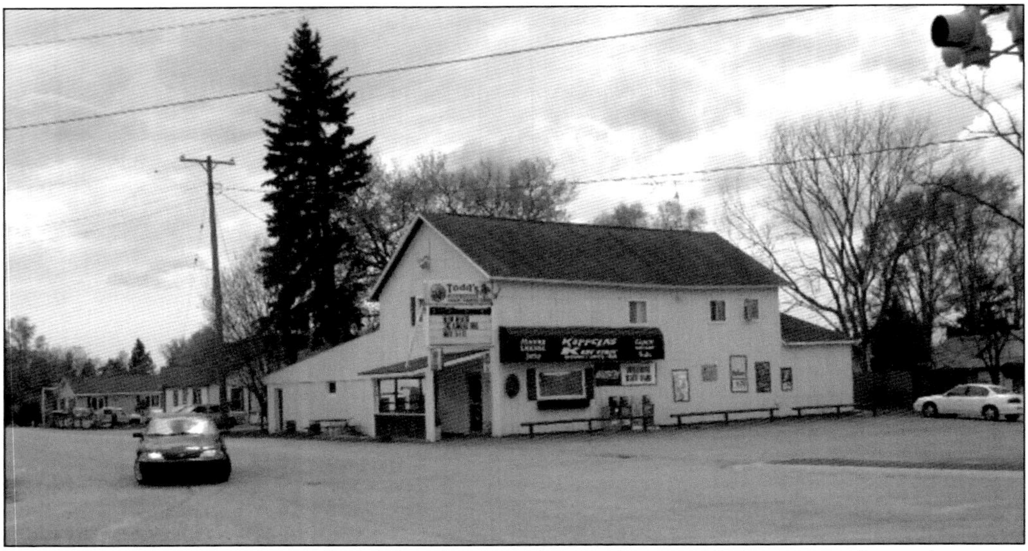

The 1871 arrival of the railroad heading southeasterly toward Saginaw, along the route approximately the same as followed by today's U.S. Highway 10, accelerated the growth of Loomis, above. By 1887, with Seth Bowdish as postmaster, the 400-person town of Loomis boasted an extract factory, two shingle mills, and a sawmill, along with a Methodist church and two hotels. Above, Todd's gasoline filling station and store (at the site of an original Loomis building, P. L. Tucker's store), some residences, a bar, and the Wise Township Hall are all that remain of the village. When Wise Township was organized in 1872, the first elections took place at the Loomis schoolhouse, below, and Isaiah Windover became the first township supervisor.

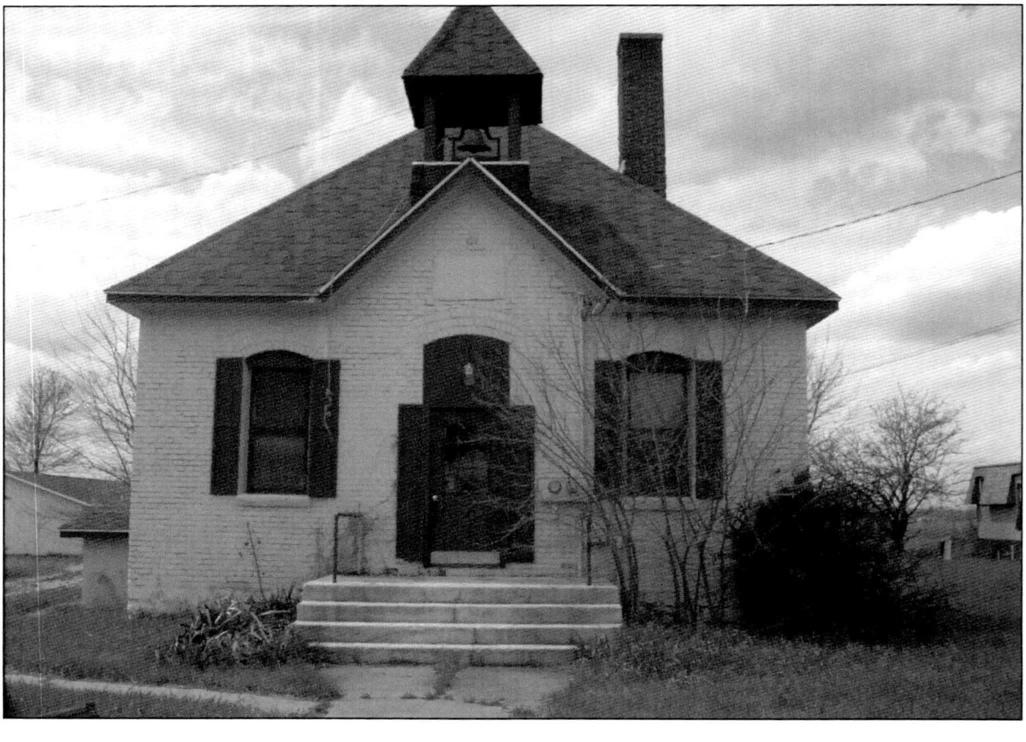

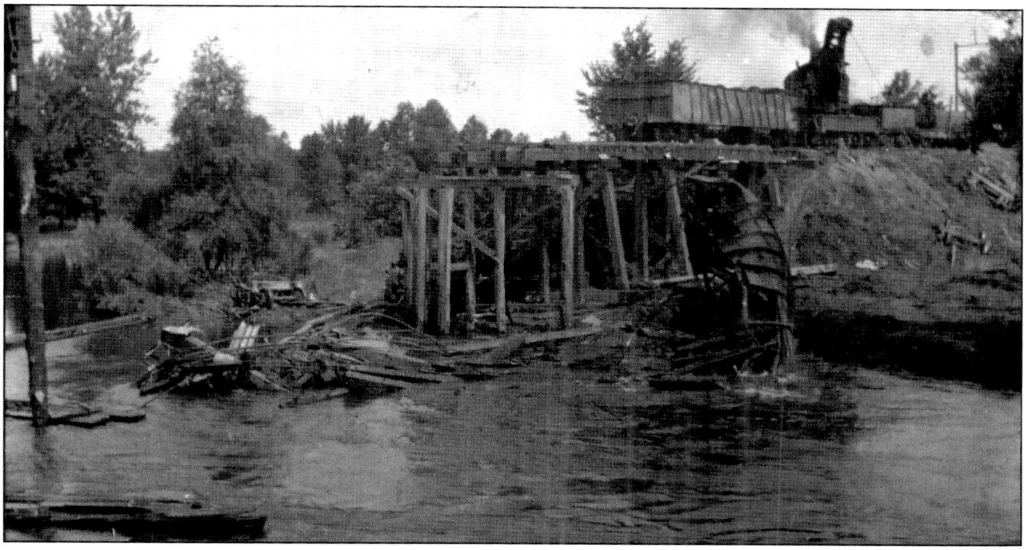

The original Pere Marquette Railroad spur between Mount Pleasant and Coleman encountered some difficulties, such as the 1878 collapse of the railroad bridge spanning the Chippewa River since 1871. The railroad line was replaced by a narrow-gauge line in 1879. At right, to help harvest northeast Isabella County sugar beets, reputed to be among the sweetest in the state, a homemade sugar beet harvester was developed and constructed by Floyd "Pat" Methner in the 1930s. The harvester operated with beets sent left to the truck and dirt and waste sent to the right.

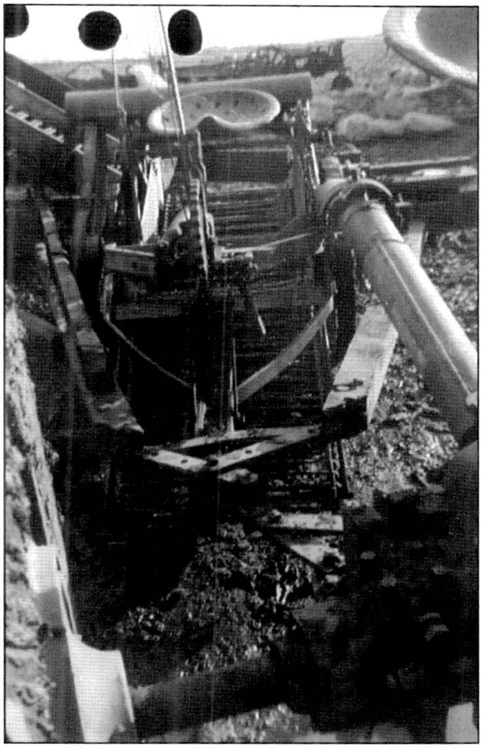

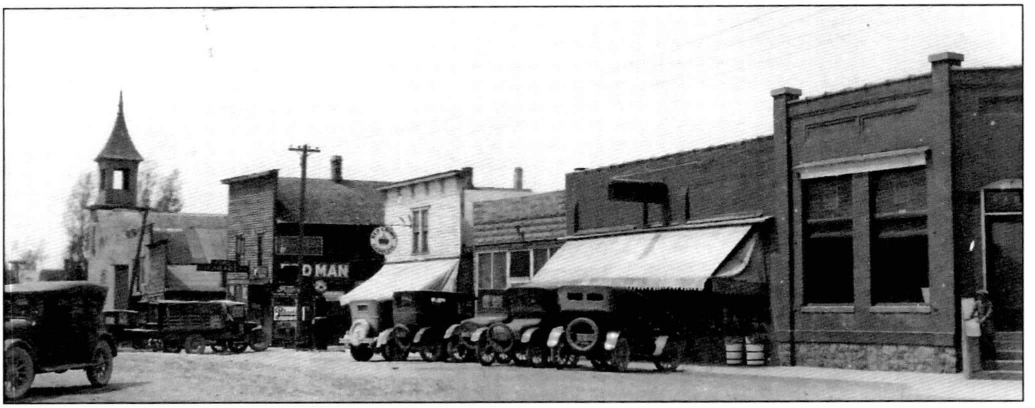

Travelers to Rosebush and Calkinsville from 1873 to 1889 or 1890 to 1903 went to the same place with both names. In 1868, James A. Bush platted a village around a store called Halfway in Isabella Township between Mount Pleasant and Clare. Bush gave land for a depot to the railroad if it was named after his wife, Rose Bush. Elias B. Calkins got a post office in his store in 1873, and it was called Calkinsville. So freight and passengers went to Rosebush and mail to Calkinsville until 1889, when the post office name was changed to Rosebush. All was fine until 1890, when the post office name changed back to Calkinsville and in 1903 back to Rosebush, which stuck that time. Above and below, downtown Rosebush is seen looking west from Mission Road in the 1920s and the present day, respectively.

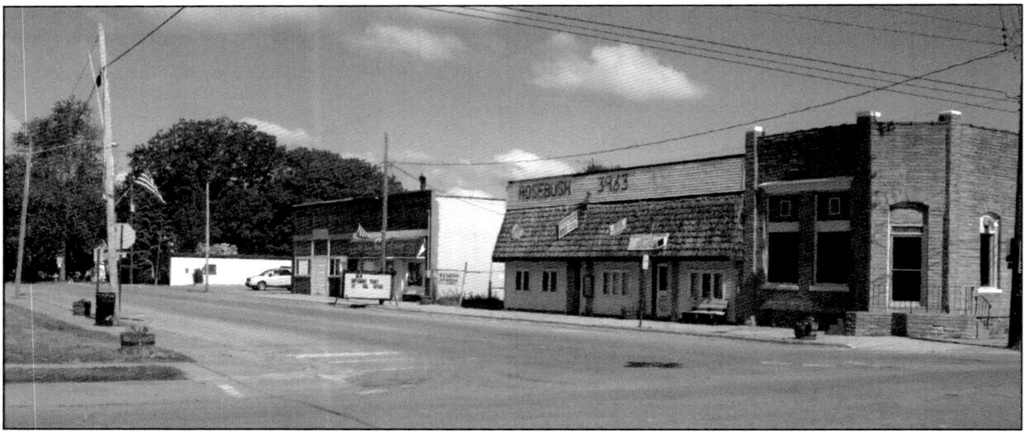

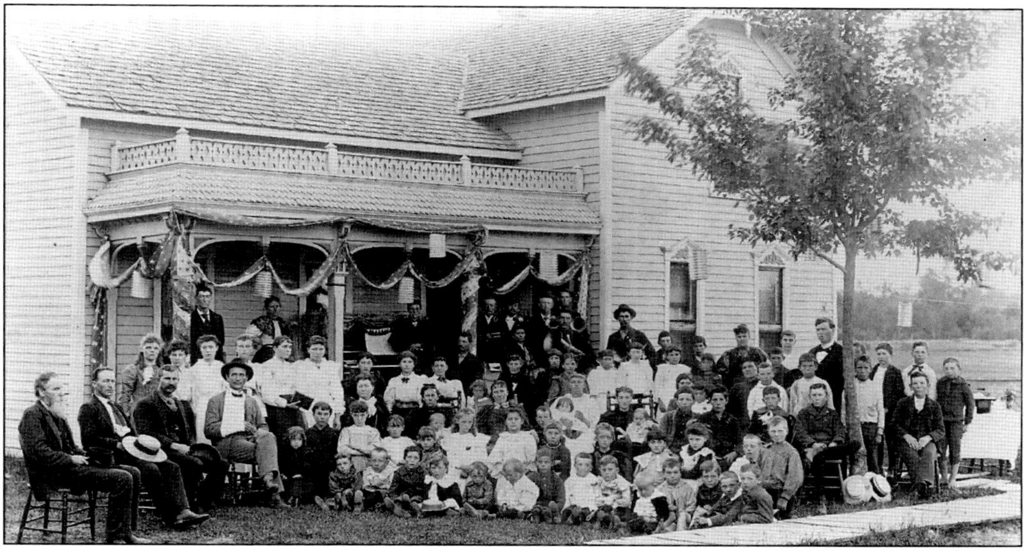

The annual Rosebush School social was held each year at the home of Dr. Bowman Corning Shaw, at left in the chair in the undated photograph above. Shaw was a medical doctor originally from Canada who spent time in the newspaper business, earned a medical degree, and practiced in Rosebush and Clare, then Rosebush again from 1900 until his 1917 death. Standing at the tree to the right is Samuel Cassidy, a longtime teacher at the Rosebush North School. On June 27, 1916, R. H. Muscott of Waters was awarded a United States patent for his "motor sleigh," the first snowmobile. The undated picture below, labeled simply "rural Rosebush," is not likely to be Muscott's first; it closely resembles the patent application drawings and must be among the earliest snowmobiles to do wheelies in Michigan winter fields.

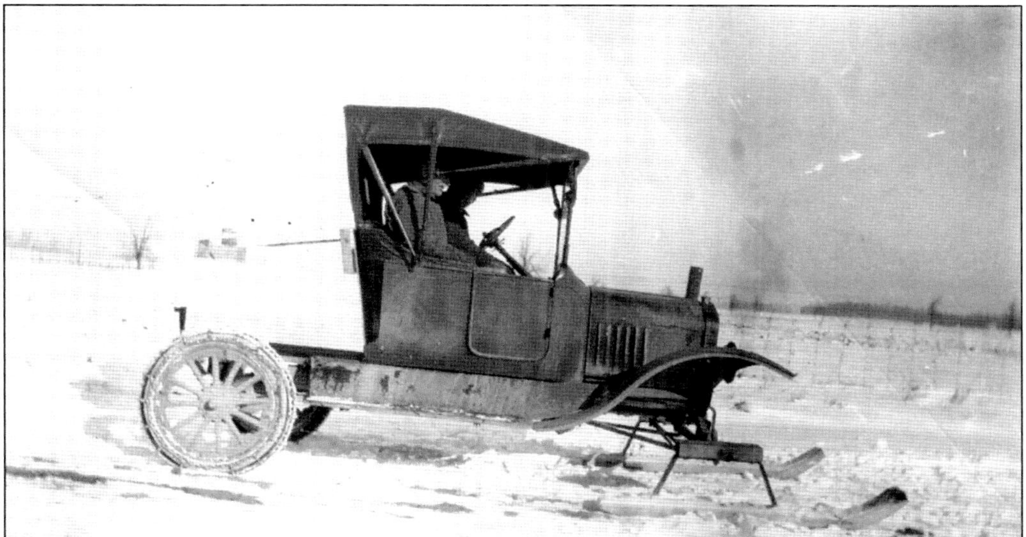

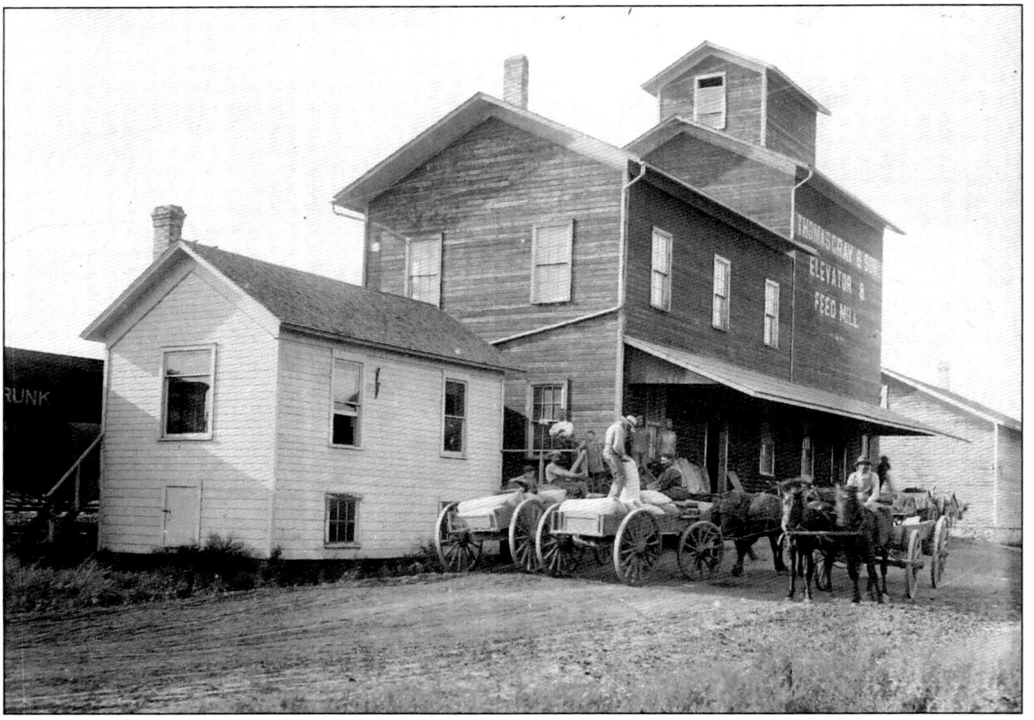

The Thomas Gray Elevator at Rosebush, above with Charlie Sefton lying in the closest wagon to the building, was bought in 1904 by Daniel Coyne, originally of Brampton County, Ontario, Canada, who came to Isabella Township in 1879 and farmed 80 acres in section 21 for 25 years. According to Kenneth Simmer of Midland, whose father worked at the elevator for 40 years, Lou Moon acquired the business from Coyne. The building pictured burned to the ground in 1940 and was rebuilt in the same location. A dapper group of mail carriers, below, prepares to fan out on their rural route from a central post office in Calkinsville or Rosebush, depending on when the photographer captured them at their tasks.

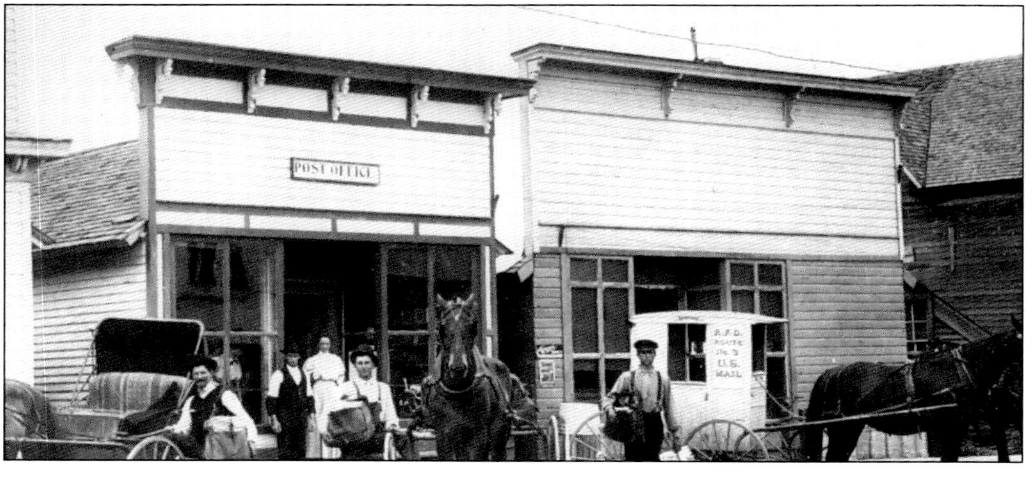

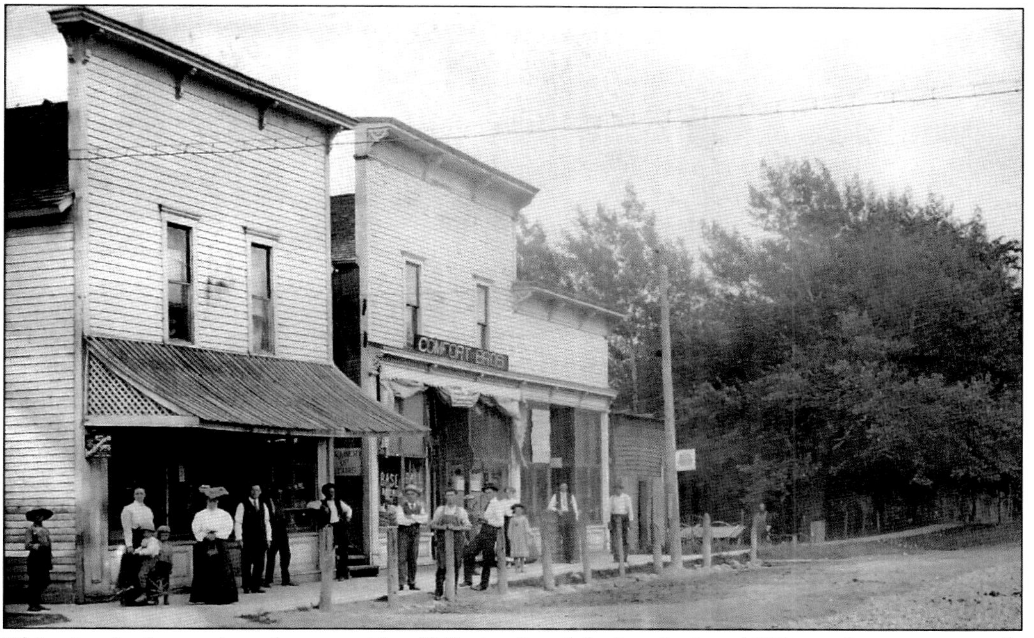

This view looks north at the west side of Mission Road during the late 1800s, at the area presently housing the offices of the Rosebush village and, since 2007, the Faith M. Johnston Memorial Library in a new building at far right corner. The little boy in front of the lady second from the left is on one of the large front-wheeled tricycles that typify the era.

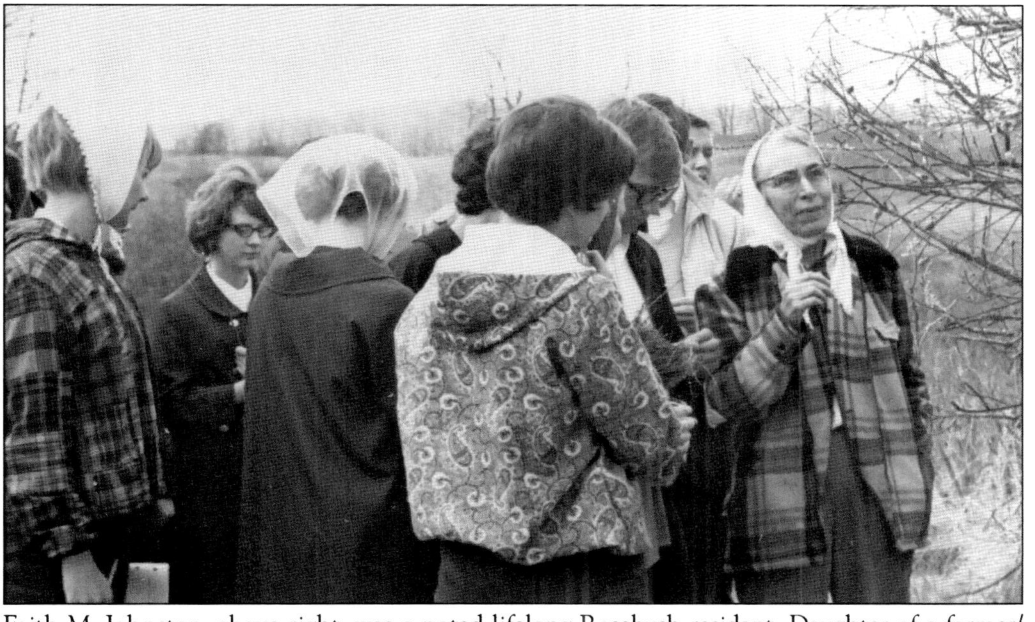

Faith M. Johnston, above right, was a noted lifelong Rosebush resident. Daughter of a farmer/minister, Johnston was a biology professor at Central Michigan University for 46 years in addition to authoring books about mid-Michigan life and a regular column for the Mount Pleasant *Daily Times-News*. Upon her 1998 death at 95, the Rosebush Library, housed in her father's former church, was renamed the Faith M. Johnston Memorial Library.

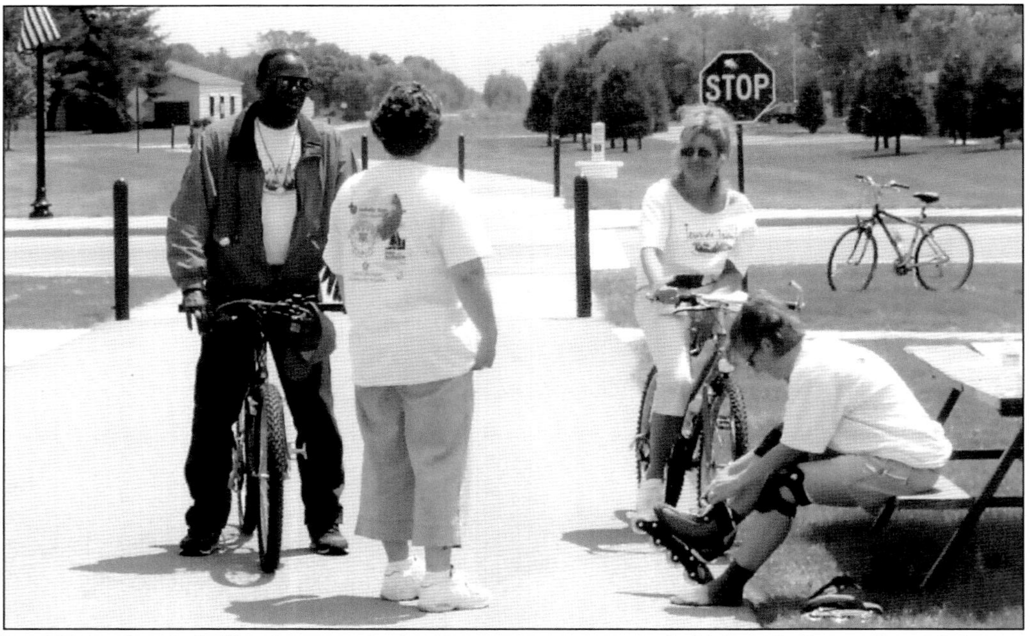

In 1998, the Isabella County Parks Department received $960,283 from the Michigan Department of Transportation to improve the rail trail segment acquired from Midland County in 1997 for $10. The following year, Isabella County received $482,762 for trail improvements from the Michigan Natural Resources Trust Fund (rooted in oil and gas revenues from state-owned mineral properties). The Isabella County Pere Marquette Rail Trail segment extends 8.3 miles through Wise and Vernon Townships, above. The 14-foot-wide linear park connects with Midland County's 18 miles of trail, providing Rollerblading, biking, walking, and jogging venues. The Isabella County Lawrence A. McDonald Wildlife Sanctuary, below, in Wise Township just off the Pere Marquette Rail Trail, is an 11-acre wetland area given to the county by De Etta McDonald, Margarita Hughes, and Dorothy Collins in 1984.

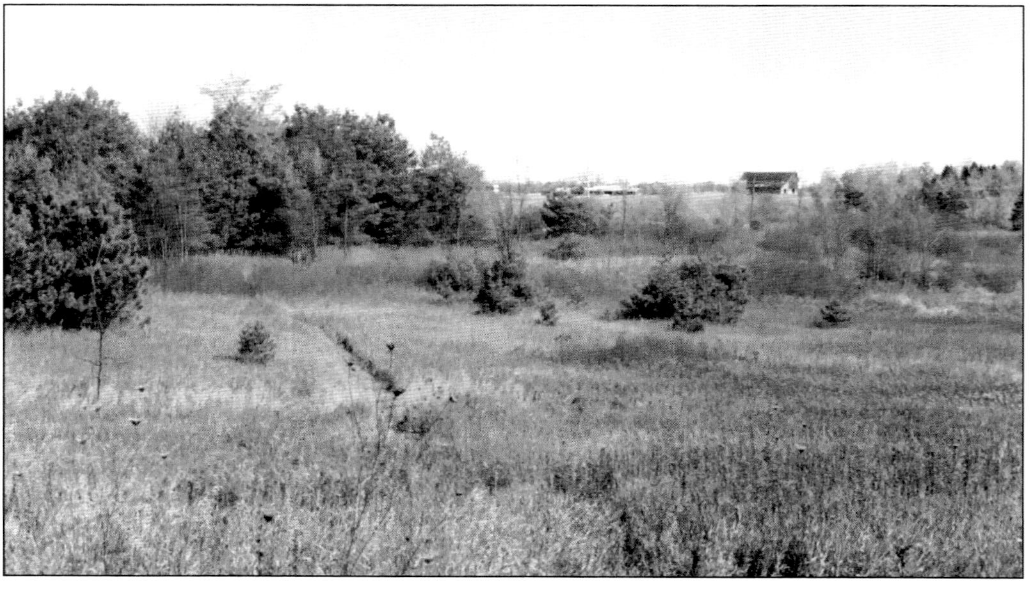

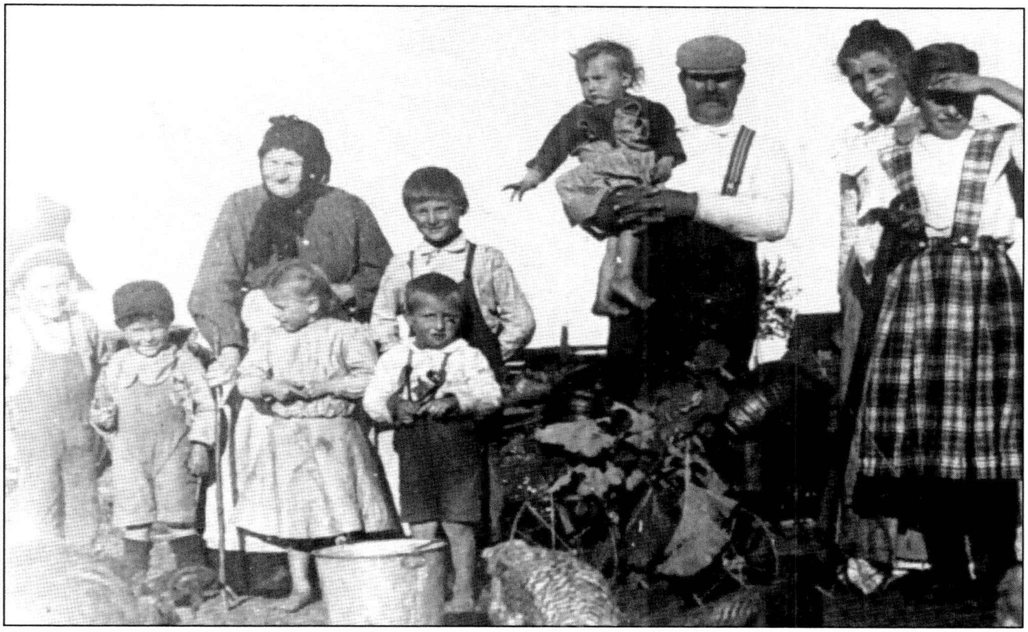

Three generations of Wise Township residents are seen above, from left to right: Jason; Elmer; Emma; Henry Methner; great-grandmother Mary Klashak; Floyd "Pat" Methner; Fern in the arms of the Methner brood's father, Fredrick Methner; his wife, Pauline Methner; and Suzie Methner. Below, Fredrick prodigiously added to the fourth generation pictured in the top picture. Fredrick's 12 sons had a baseball team that played the Detroit Tigers and won two games out of three in the 1920s. Shown in 1922, the Methner ball team consisted of, from left to right, (first row) August, Joseph, Edward, Floyd, Elmer, and William; (second row) Jason, Henry, Fritz, and Otto; (third row) John, Frederick (father), and Frank Methner.

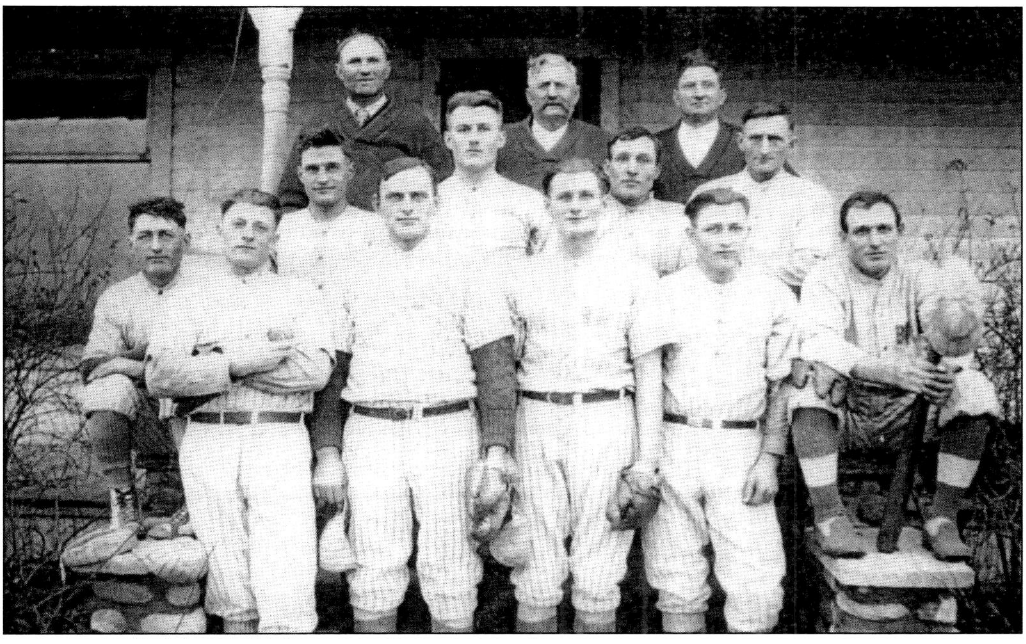

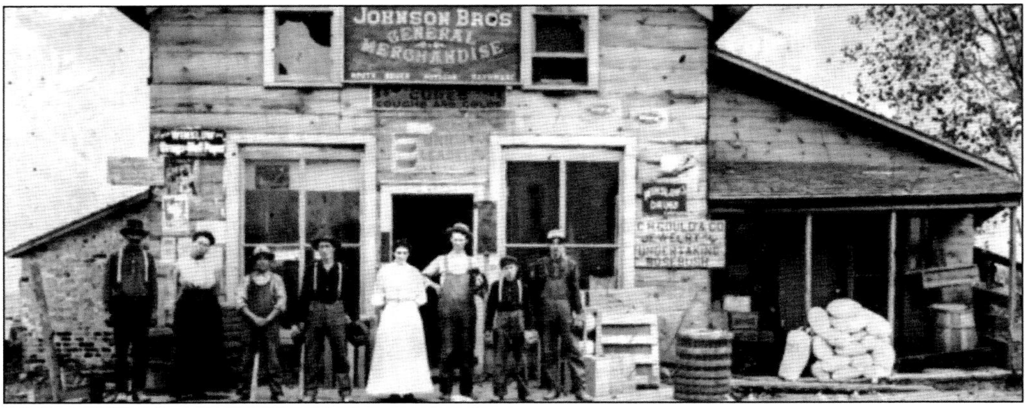

Wise was in section 2 of Denver Township and was first known as Freeney's Mills after John H. Freeney, the first to settle there. In 1884, the store at Wise was granted a post office with Freeney as postmaster. The post office closed in February 1892, reopened in 1903, and was renamed Wise, until closing in 1906. In front of the newly opened Johnson Brothers store, above, in 1908 are, from left to right, Harry Ohler, Beulah Ohler, John Ohler, Wes Lattimer, Daisy Rockett, Cecil Johnson, Charles Strauch, and Ray Strauch. Below, an 1895 hunting party from Mount Pleasant prepares to brave the forests of northeastern Isabella County; from left to right are Chester R. Gorham, unidentified, Dr. G. F. Richardson, Charles McKenney, and P. C. Taylor

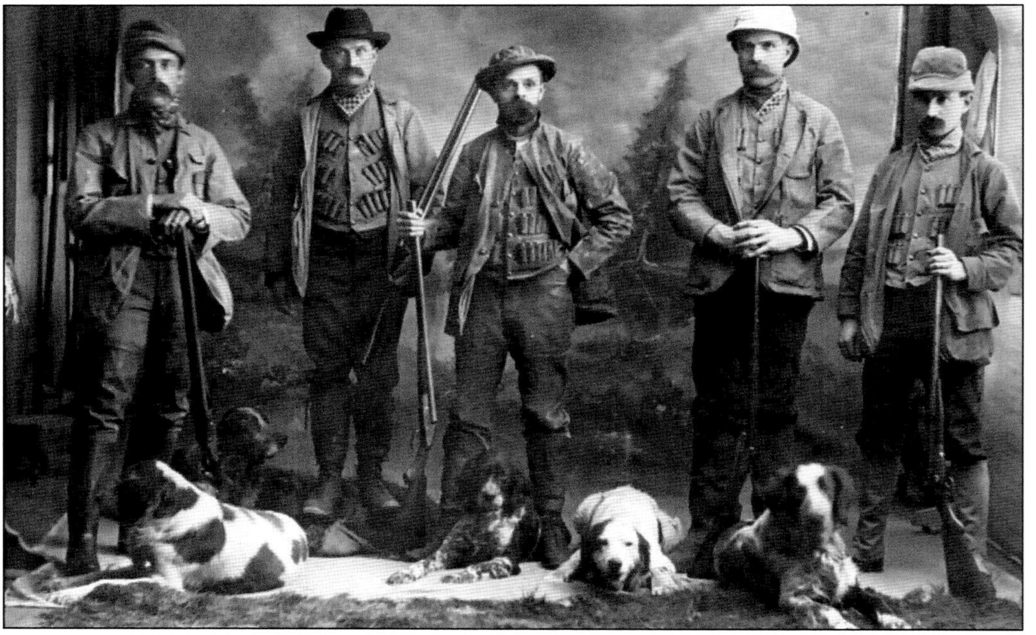

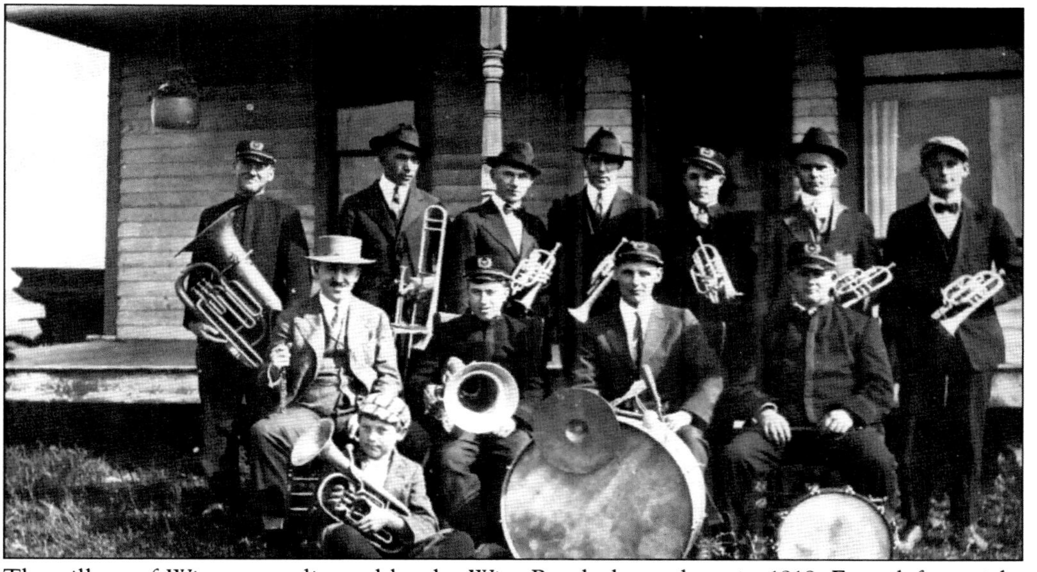

The village of Wise was enlivened by the Wise Band, shown here in 1918. From left to right they are (first row) Elmer Gross; (second row) A. Hanna, Art Brookman, Ray Strauch, and C. Burton; (third row) Rollin Gross, Pete Pelcher, Glen Mitchell, Charles Strauch, Jake Carrick, Tim Oiler, and Floyd "Pat" Methner. The village of Wise, more than a mile from the Coleman/Mount Pleasant spur of the Flint and Pere Marquette railway and victim of changing times as the Freeney lumber mill closed, declined as a population center. The Wise Presbyterian Church, below, was the last standing remnant of the village of Wise and was torn down in 1978.

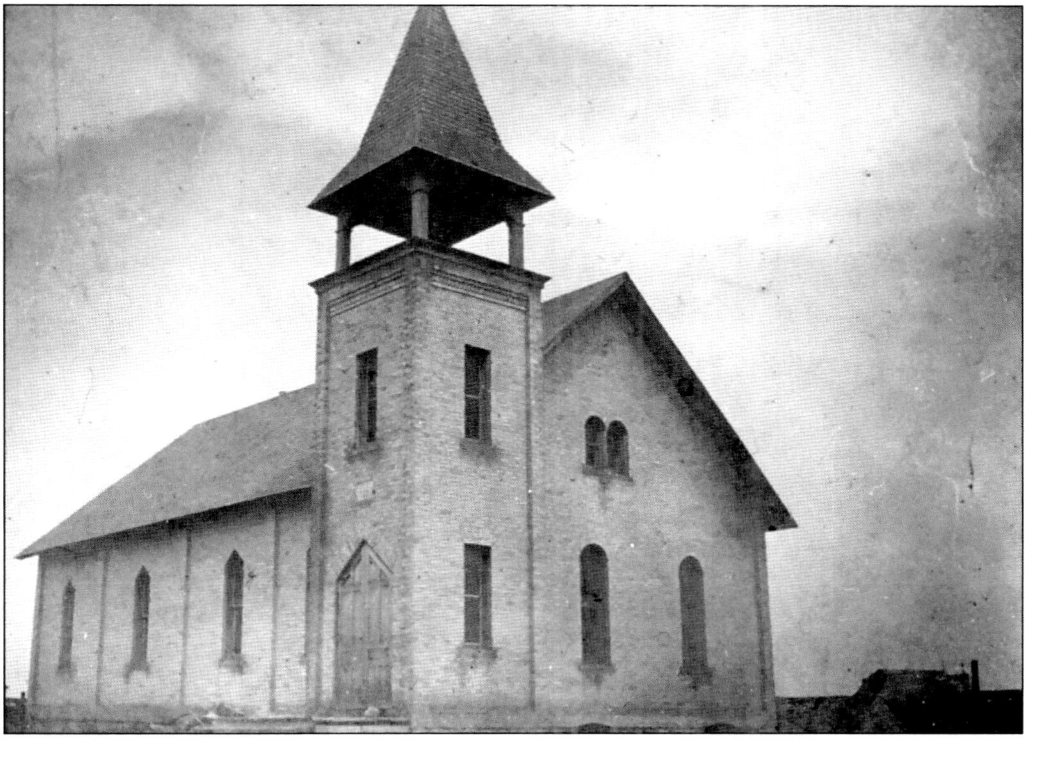

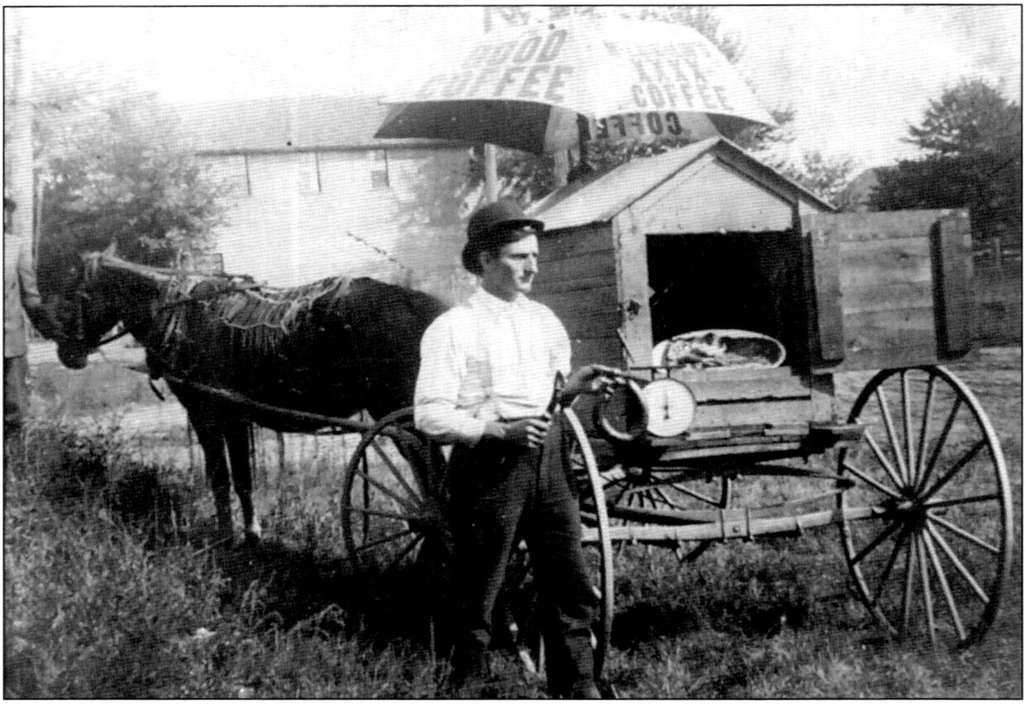

Located in the extreme northeast corner of Isabella County, distance caused Wise residents to associate themselves more with Clare and Coleman (closer in Clare County) than Isabella County communities. Thus the Methners butchered and processed meat on their Wise Township farm, but their retail meat market was in Coleman. The trip to and from Coleman was not wasted, however, since the Methner "meat wagon" maintained a retail route in the surrounding area, manned above by Otto Methner. Looking forlorn in a blasting snowstorm, below, the Methner family crew hauls ice from a nearby lake to the Methner enterprise in this undated picture.

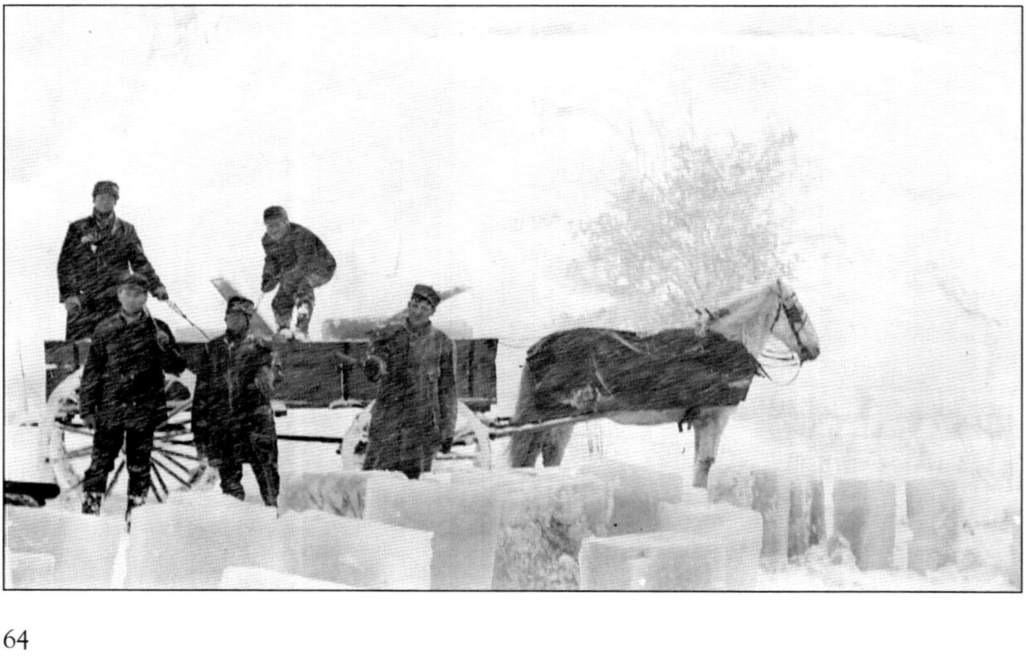

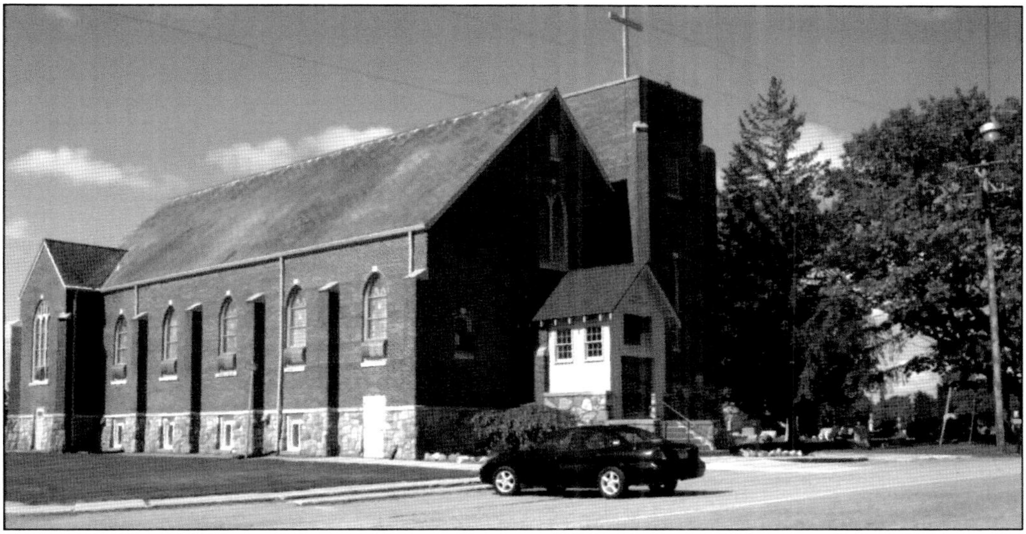

Vernon Township was organized in 1866. In October 1874, the Catholic Mission of Vernon began when the Reverend Richard Sweeney of East Saginaw said mass for Roman Catholics in the area. Mass was said in area homes until a church, school, and rectory, all named for the bishop of Grand Rapids' patron saint, St. Henry, were built at the southwest corner of section 35. St. Henry's became an independent parish in 1905, and the original wooden church burned to the ground in 1922, with the cornerstone of the present brick church, next to the cemetery, above, laid in 1923 but not completed until 1941. Improved transportation caused parish and school consolidations, reducing the church to visiting priest mission status in recent years. The school, below, closed in 2001 but is still used as a parish community center.

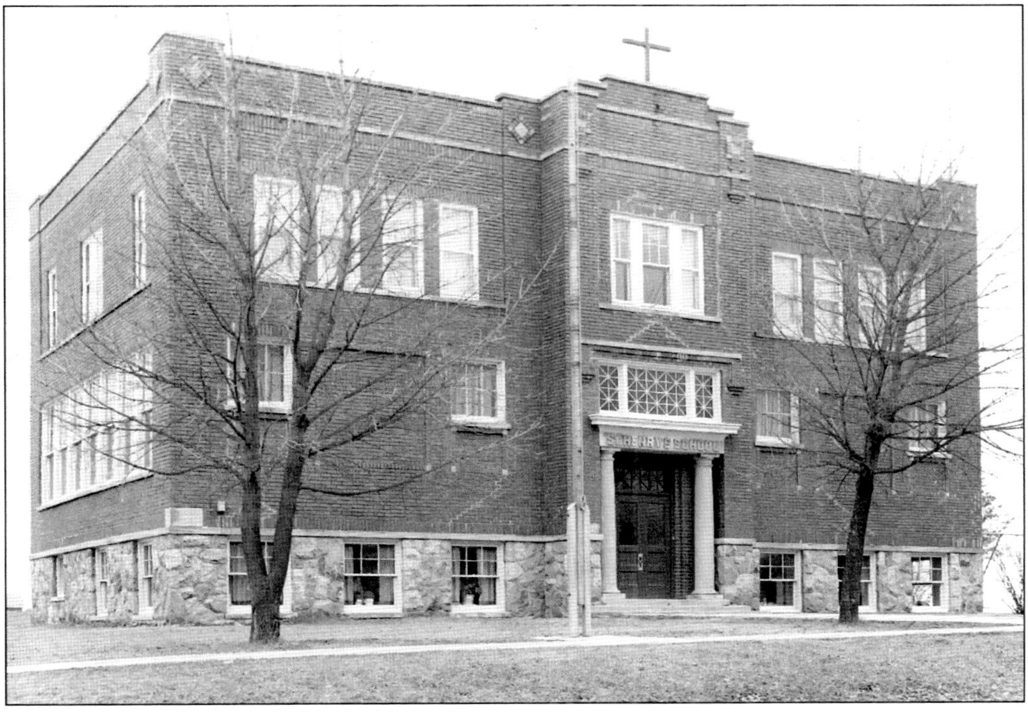

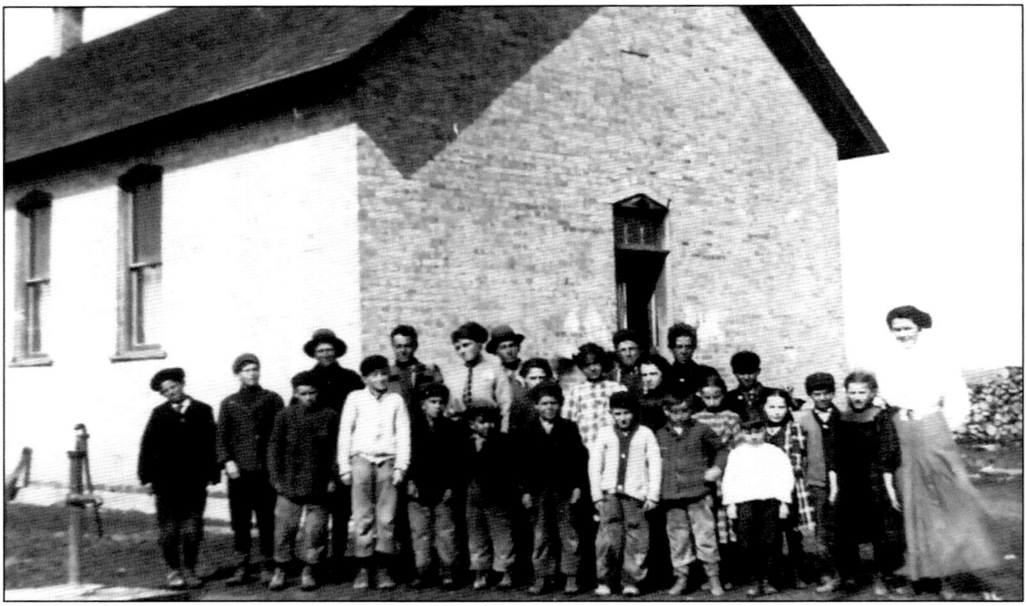

In 1908, under the direction of teacher Alma Preston, above far right, the student body of Andersonville School in Wise Township included, from left to right, (first row) Jason Methner, Homer White, Wellington Pelcher, Homer Pelcher, Dutch Zinser, Ike Methner, Amos Worden, unidentified, Ethel White, Clifford Raymond, and Emma Methner; (second row) Ralph Smith, Elmer Bowen, Sam Bowen, Earl Acker, Lena Zinser, Elva Bowen, Ruth Raymond, Sarah Miller, Erwin Zinser, Kathryn Zinser, Lillie Weadle, Earl Wilt, and Glenn Wilt. Andersonville School was also known as Wise School District No. 5. Below, the school's faculty and student body in this undated photograph includes, from left to right, (first row) Mary Smith, Frances Ernest, Rose Ann Raymond, Helen Raymond, Hazel Seaton, Rosie Hinkle, Minnie Bowen, Charlotte Smith, Thelma Acker, Ethel White, Mildred Bowen, Nellie Seaton, Ronald McNerny, Henry McNerny, Charlotte Raymond on teacher Frank Sheahan's knee, Homer White by the flag pole, unidentified, Manley Smith, Anna Ernest, and Hazel Owens; (second row) Otto Wilt, Rennie Smith, Vern Owens, Amos Woden, Cliff Raymond, Dutch Zinser, Alonzo Bowen, unidentified, unidentified, Kathryn Zinser, Ruth Raymond, Lester Beers, Hurley Wilt, Anna Fish, and Nina Seaton.

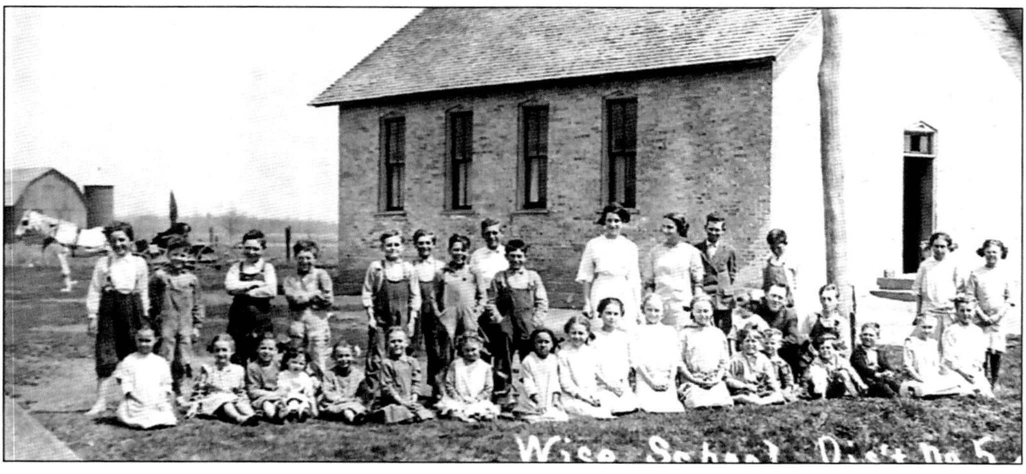

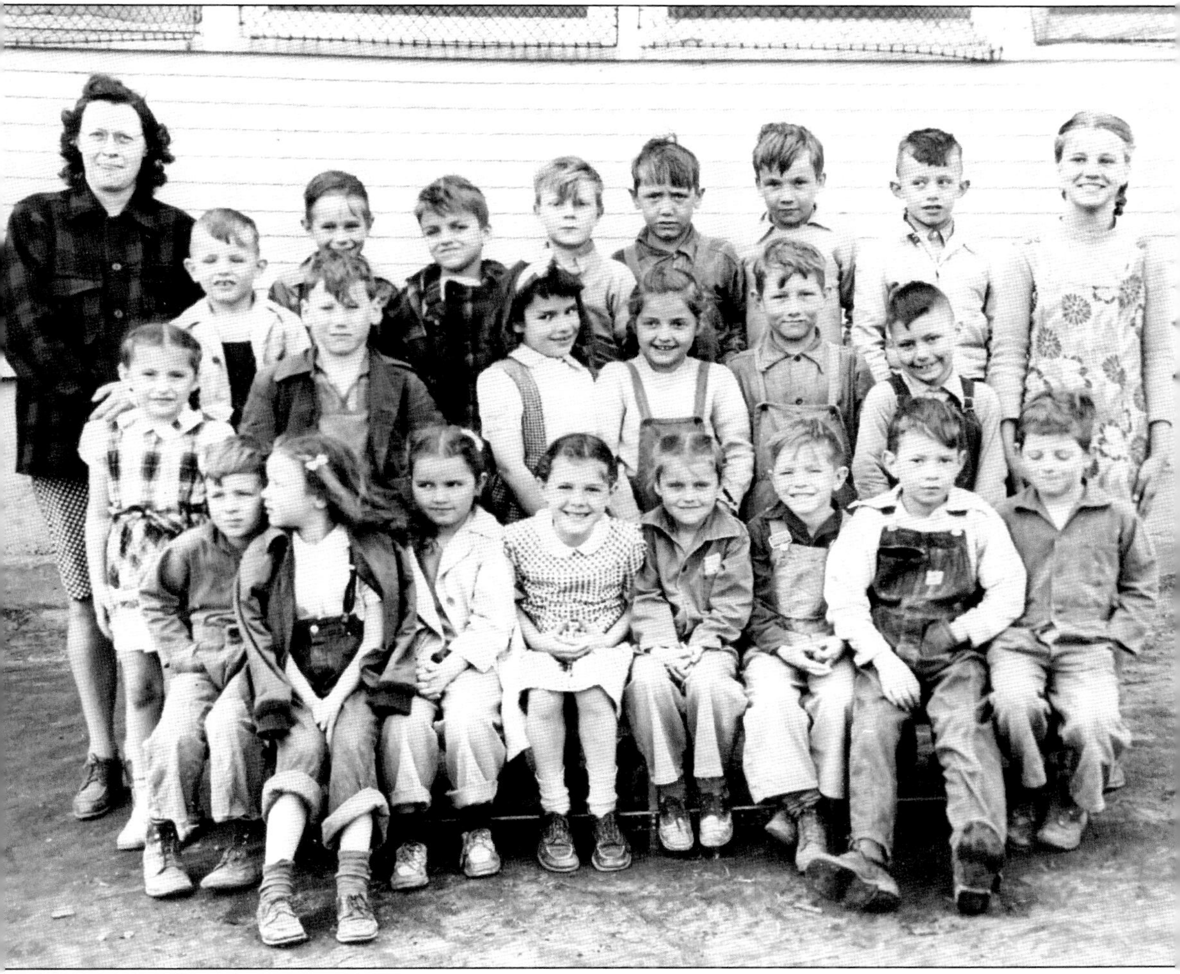

The pictorial saga of the Andersonville school ends with a 1948 look at the teacher and student body after the brick school in the previous two pages burned near the end of the 1930s and was replaced by a wooden building. From left to right are (first row) Jack Smith, Sandra Russell, Carol Acker, Judy Glasky, Sharon Doan, Ronald Drake, Richard Zinser, and Wyman Smith; (second row) Sandra Methner, Gene Weadel, Sandra Davenport Smith, Christine Porter, ? Grant, and Sonny Doan; (third row) teacher Ellen Zinser, Donald Zinser, Elmer Mogg, Richard Davenport Smith, Kenneth Slocum, Gail Grant, Daniel McNerny, William Zinser, and Martha Hefner.

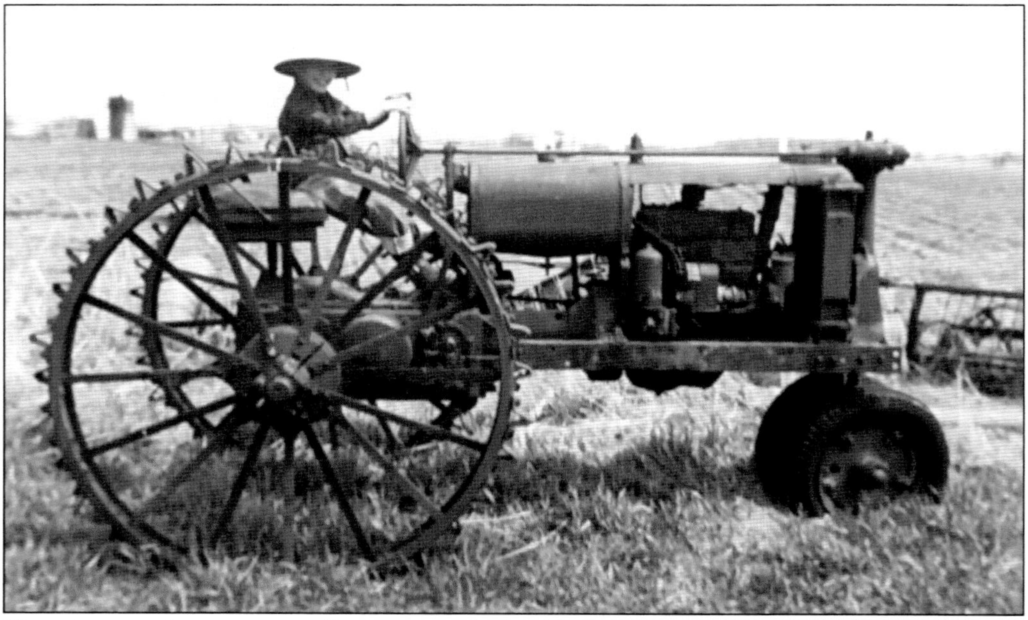

This photographic scenario tells the story of a farm lad, two tractors, a man, and his dog. Above on the Wise Township farm of Floyd and Lelia Methner, 10-year-old Dean Methner proudly pilots the family's F-12 tractor in the 1930s. Dean's brother Floyd went off to World War II, and when he returned in the mid-1940s it was with Butch the Wonder Dog, who promptly made himself a part of the working farm scene by becoming a tractor driver. History does not record whether Butch could plow a straight furrow, but it is known that he was willing to work for table scraps.

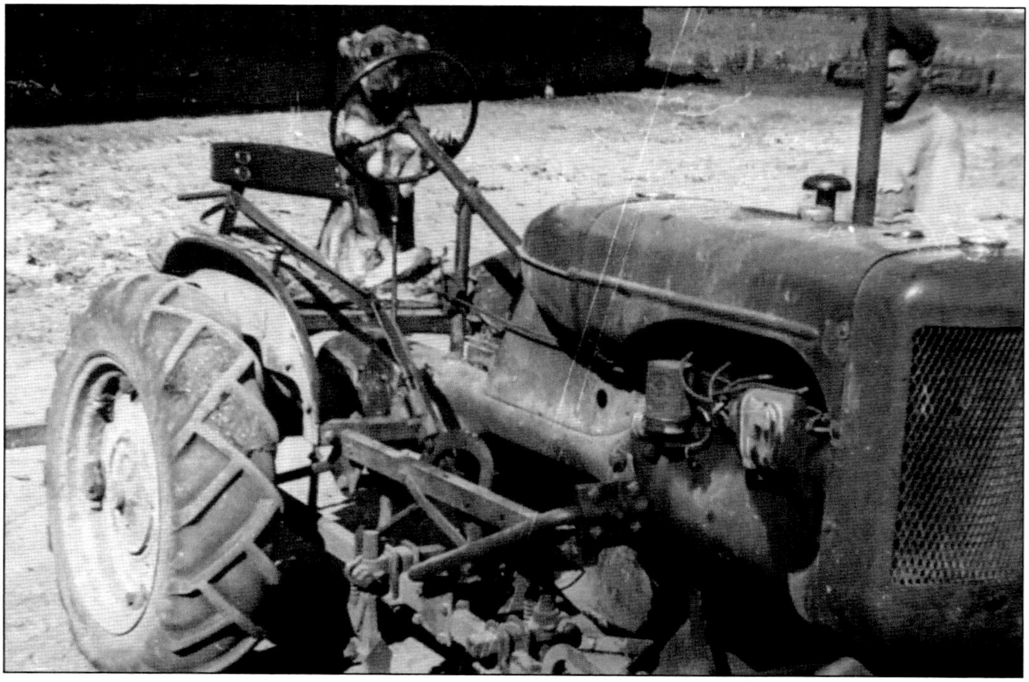

Three

Southeastern Isabella County

The southeastern quadrant of Isabella County is now traversed south to north by U.S. Highway 127 and east to west by Michigan State Highway 20. At the start, natural water highways led to lumber camp growth, translating to settlements, to make this the most populous of Isabella County quadrants.

Chippewa Township was established in 1856 in Midland County and became part of Isabella County in 1859. This township and Union Township are home to the main body of the Saginaw Chippewa Indian Reservation, established by the Treaty of 1855, Saginaw Chippewa tribal headquarters, and the Soaring Eagle Resort and Casino, one of the largest casinos east of the Mississippi River and Isabella County's biggest employer.

Chippewa Township settlements, none existent at present, were Alembic, where storekeeper Norman Payne was postmaster 1874–1905; Denver, a railroad station from 1875 to 1900 that never had a post office; and Floyd, which was in the extreme southeast of the township, with a post office from 1861 until 1895.

Coe Township is named for Albert G. Coe, Michigan lieutenant governor when Michigan Act No. 151 established the township in 1855. To attend township supervisor meetings, first Coe Township supervisor William B. Bowen journeyed 18 miles along the Pine River through swamp, marsh, and forest to the Midland County seat until Isabella County was established in 1859.

Settlements in Coe Township, all gone except Shepherd (see pages 95–98), were Burdick, a railway stop appearing on maps until 1900; Coe, with a post office from 1891 to 1904; Cohoon (Cahoon), the shortest-lived post office in Isabella County, with Morris B. Cohoon the only postmaster from November 21, 1891, until January 9, 1892; and Wiota, one of the first Isabella County settlements to receive a post office, from 1857 to 1871.

Lincoln Township, named for recently assassinated Pres. Abraham Lincoln, was established in 1863. Defunct Lincoln Township settlements were Crawford, four miles west of Shepherd, which had a post office from 1863 to 1904; Jerseyville, southwest of Shepherd, which had a post office from 1892 to 1906; Strickland, with a post office from 1870 to 1904; and Summerton, on the Gratiot/Isabella County line, was granted a Gratiot County post office in 1870 until 1876, which was restored in 1882, and in 1902 was transferred to Isabella County and operated until its 1905 closing.

Union Township, settled in 1854 by John Hursh and family, is the most heavily populated of the county. Established on March 9, 1861, when the board of supervisors showed patriotism for the Union during the Civil War, Union Township is home to the county seat and Central Michigan University (see page 80) and is the hub of railroad, milling, lumbering, oil exploration and production (see pages 86 and 87), and other commercial activities in Mount Pleasant (see pages 71–93). It is the largest community in Isabella County.

Union Township settlements, all gone or absorbed by Mount Pleasant, included Blunt, also known as Blunt Court House, northeast of Mount Pleasant, which had a post office from 1863 to 1865 when it was transferred to Isabella; Boyden, which was never a settlement, but postmaster Lucy Boyden operated a post office from the Boyden family farmhouse from 1892 to 1906; Brodie (see page 88), a whistle-stop on the Ann Arbor Railroad just southwest of Mount Pleasant with no settlement and no post office; Gough, near the Union/Deerfield Township line, which had a rural post office operating from January 24 until June 28, 1882; Indian Mills (see page 71), later to be Isabella City and Isabella Center, which was the first Chippewa Indian settlement of any kind in Isabella County following the Treaty of 1855; Isabella City (known variously as Albany, Longwood, and New Albany and now colloquially as Dogtown), platted in 1861, given a post office in the same year until 1866, and restored as Longwood in 1871 until closing in 1878; and Martha, a stop two and a half railroad miles above Mount Pleasant on the Ann Arbor Railroad that appeared on maps from 1892 until 1905.

Mount Pleasant was made county seat in 1860, platted in 1863, recorded in 1864, and incorporated as a village in 1875 and as a city in 1889. South Mount Pleasant appears on some maps in the early 1900s and was absorbed by present-day Mount Pleasant. Taylors was a tiny settlement and flag stop three miles south of Mount Pleasant until about 1900. Transport was shown on railroad timetables four-tenths of a mile north of Mount Pleasant in the 1880s but engulfed by the larger place by 1900.

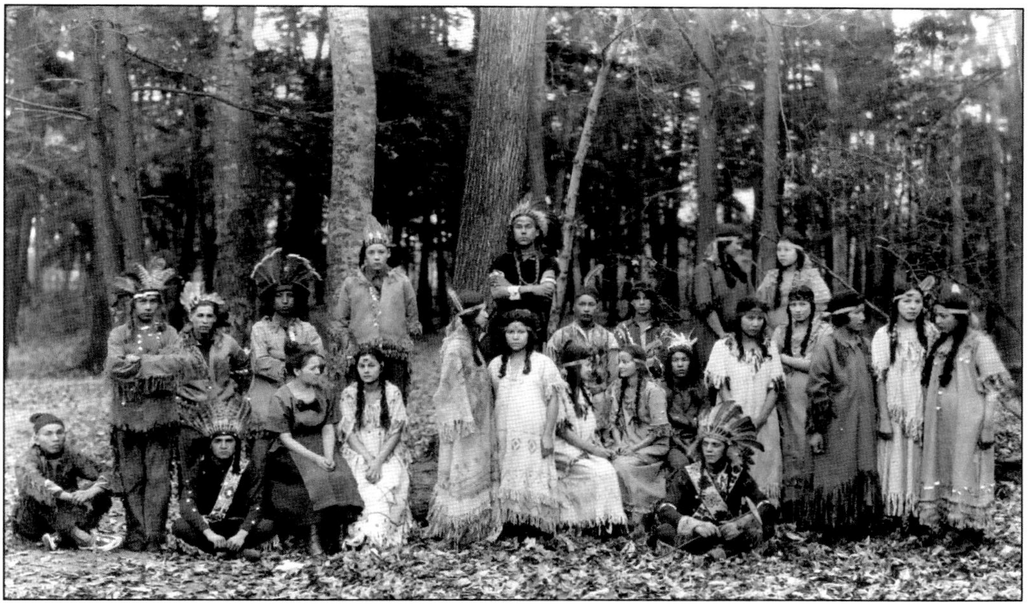

Carved from contiguous named lands in an 1831 legislative act, Isabella County was formally organized in 1859. An 1855 treaty granted lands in six of the county's townships to individuals in the Chippewa tribe, previously scattered, and established some reservation land in trust. With nothing here to sustain them, "Indian mills" to grind corn were built, and American Indians began gathering here, as did merchants. Indian Mills became Isabella City, then Isabella Center.

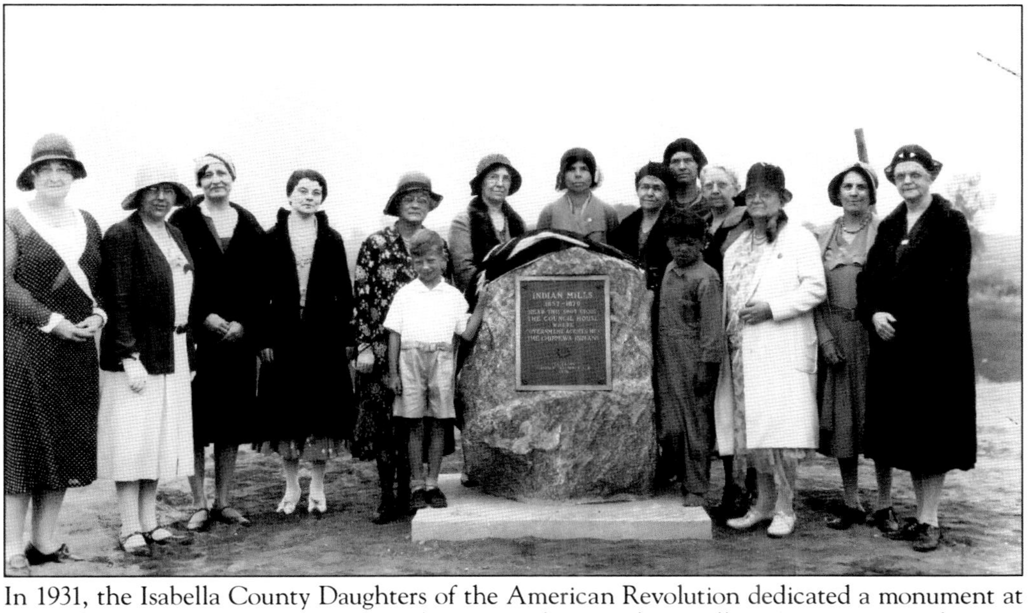

In 1931, the Isabella County Daughters of the American Revolution dedicated a monument at the Chippewa River north of Mount Pleasant reading, "Indian Mills 1857–1870. Near this spot stood the Council House where government agents met the Chippewa Indians." Second from the left is chapter regent Jessie Grambau, whose son Raymond and Mount Pleasant Indian Industrial School student David Green flank the monument. Longwood was south side of the Chippewa River.

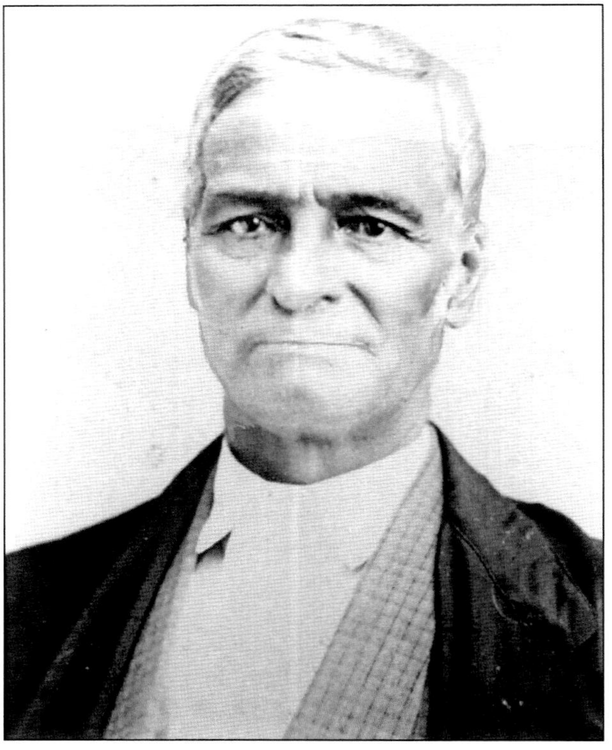

John and Elizabeth Hursh and their six children settled on land north of the Salt River in 1855 on a homestead that was the Mount Pleasant area farm later subdivided to become the site of Central Normal School. Elizabeth gave birth to a daughter, named Isabella for the new Hursh home territory. It was two years before the Hursh family had any neighbors.

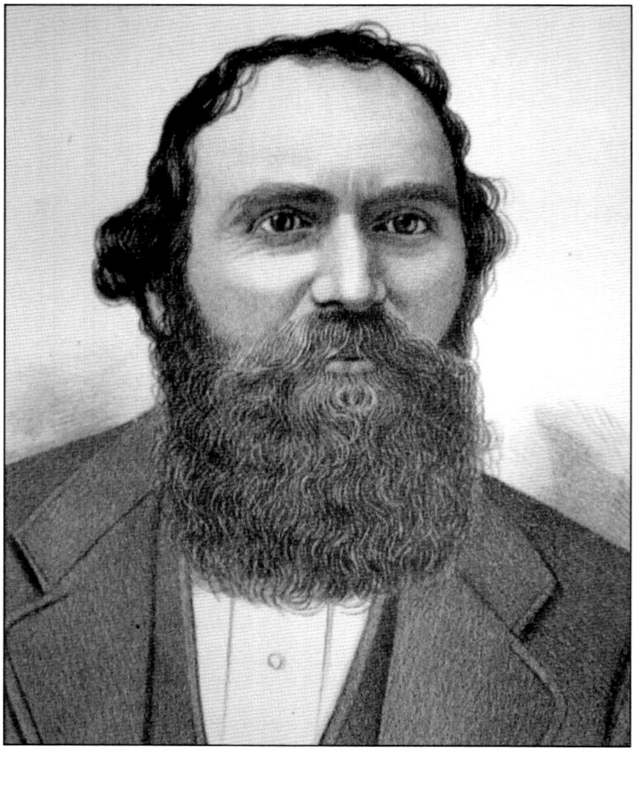

John T. Landon came to Chippewa Township, Isabella County, at age 22 from his native Canada in September 1862. He worked a year for $15 a month and board for he and his wife. In 1863, he went into debt to buy 40 acres, and in 1873, now a prominent landowner, lumberman, and farmer, he built a brick family residence in section 27, the county's first brick structure.

The first European visitors in over 200 years came to the middle Michigan pine and hardwood forests in the 1830s to harvest the forests to satisfy the nation's growing hunger for lumber. New York lumberman and Michigan's first lumber millionaire, 27-year-old David Ward, at right, donated a five-acre lot for a courthouse in 1860, on the condition that the Isabella County seat move to Mount Pleasant from Isabella Center.

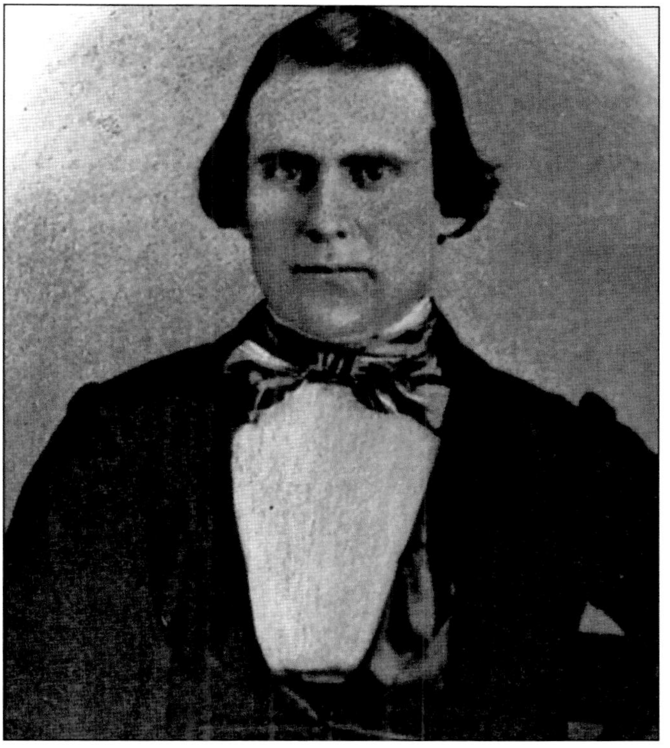

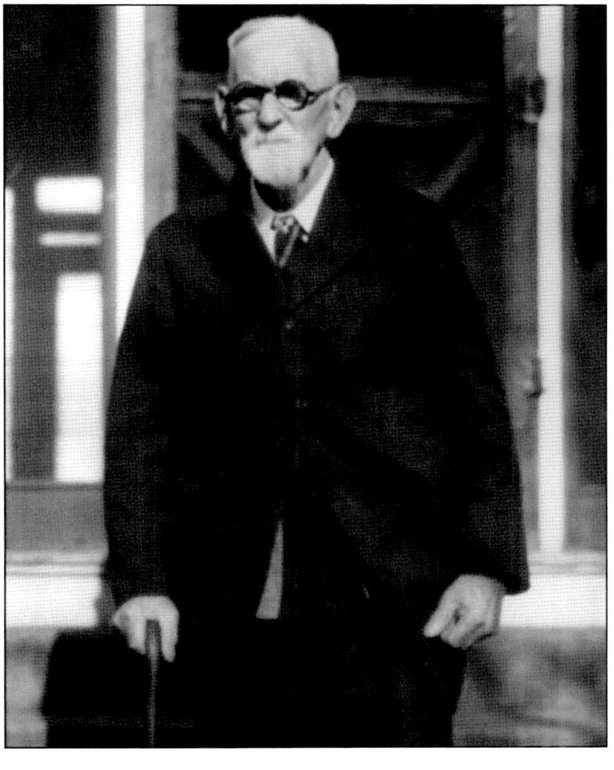

Attorney/surveyor Isaac A. Fancher, shown near his 1934 death at 100, came from New York on July 4, 1863, to survey and plat Mount Pleasant. Fancher established a farm southeast of Mount Pleasant and stayed to become a farmer, practicing attorney, merchant, congressman, and historian. A Mount Pleasant avenue and an elementary school are named for him.

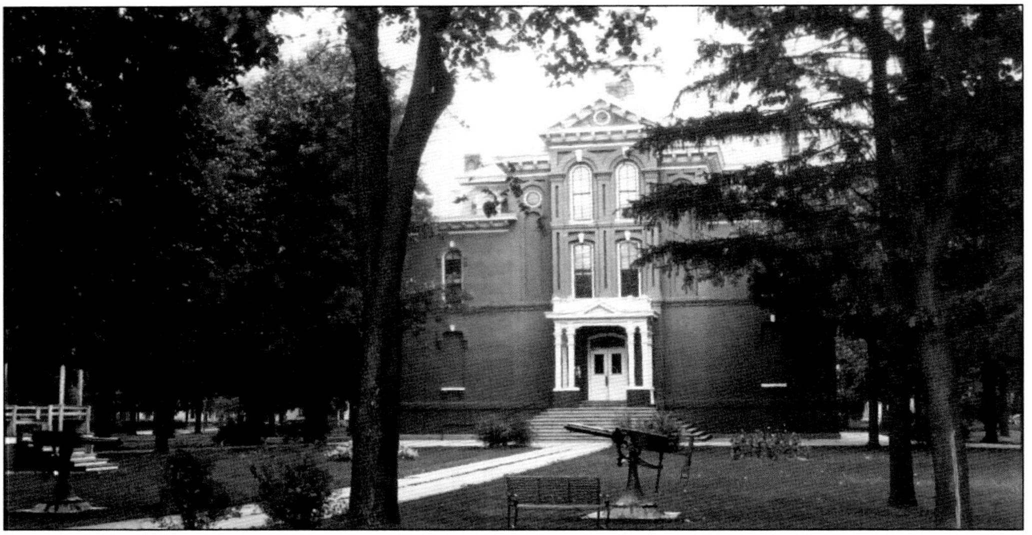

Following the establishment of Isabella County in 1859 and the 1860 designation of Mount Pleasant as the county seat, the second log Isabella County courthouse was built in the 200 block of North Main Street, facing Court Street. Built at a cost of $140, this courthouse served the citizens of Isabella County until 1878. The courthouse was joined in 1870 by a county jail at the same location. Both were replaced by Victorian structures, the courthouse in 1878, above facing Main Street, and the county jail in 1880, below facing Court Street. Both were demolished by 1972 to make room for new structures.

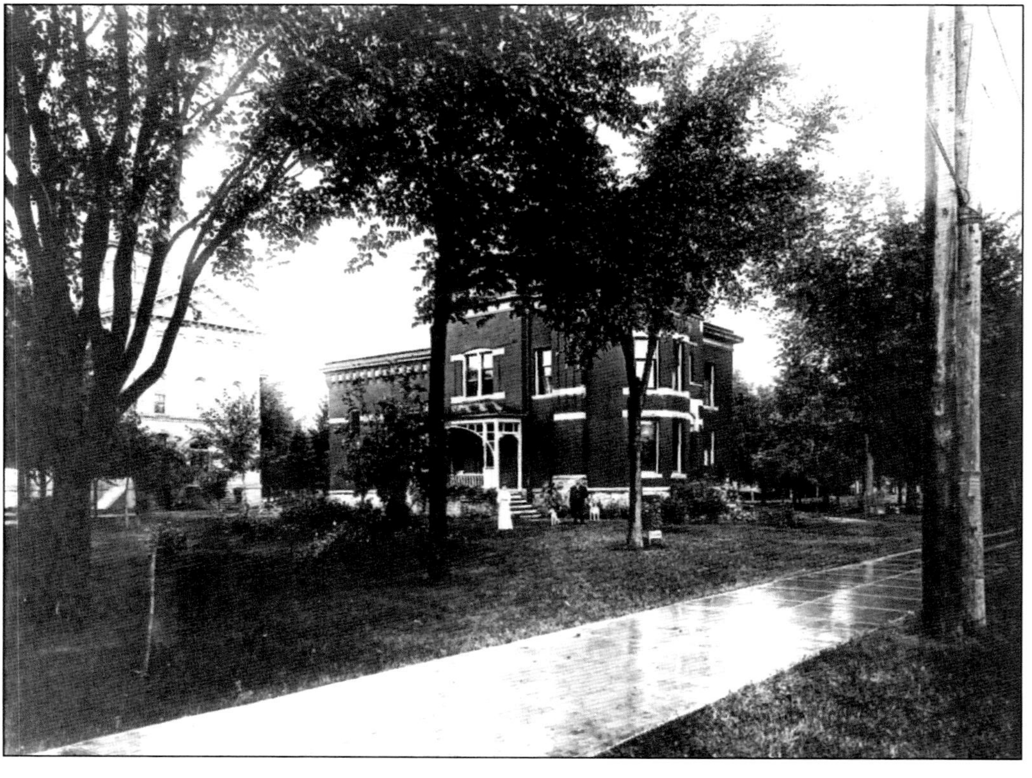

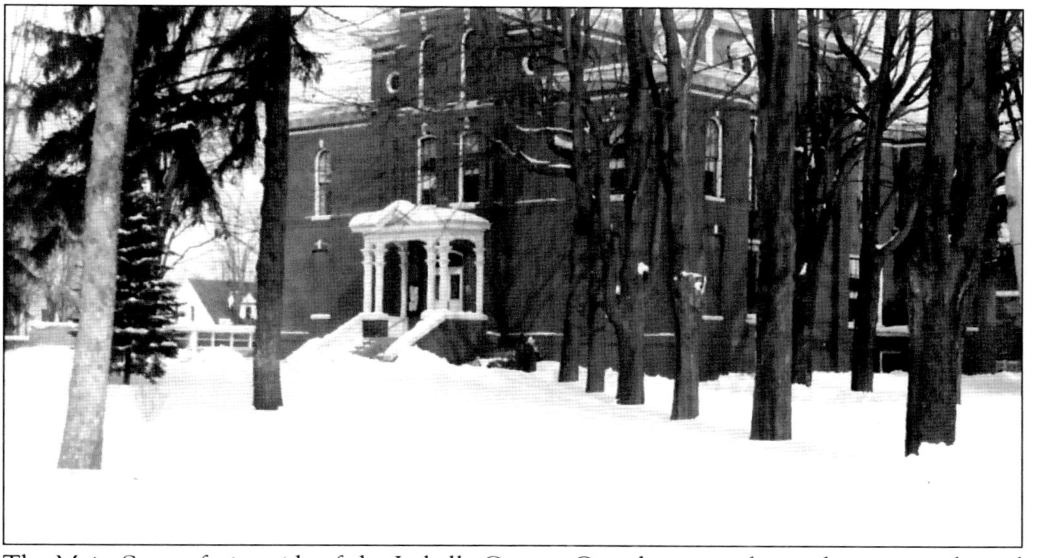

The Main Street–facing side of the Isabella County Courthouse, with its white pine–adorned grounds, lent a parklike feel to downtown Mount Pleasant. In February 1922, a sleet storm glazed the area, causing tree damage on the Isabella County Courthouse and Jail grounds. The next day, Isabella County's worst recorded rainstorm struck, enabling canoeists to paddle their way up parts of Main Street in record floodwaters.

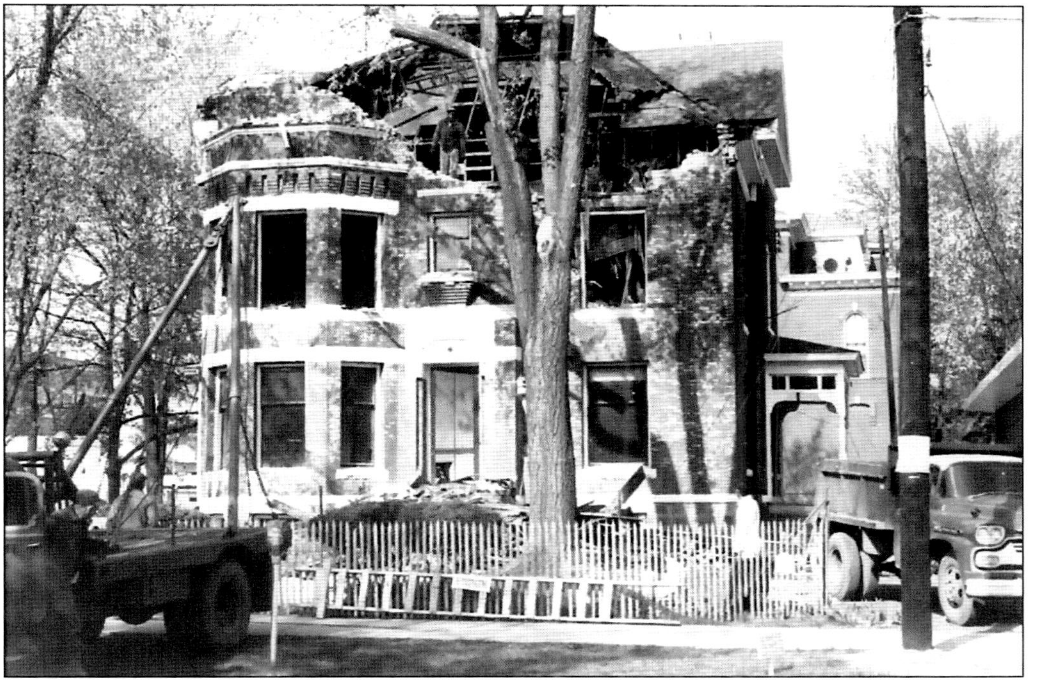

The Victorian-styled Isabella County Jail was the first of the architecturally stunning county buildings at Mount Pleasant's North Main Street complex to fall to the wrecking ball in 1962, while the courthouse in the background seems to sadly contemplate a similar fate, which followed less than a decade later.

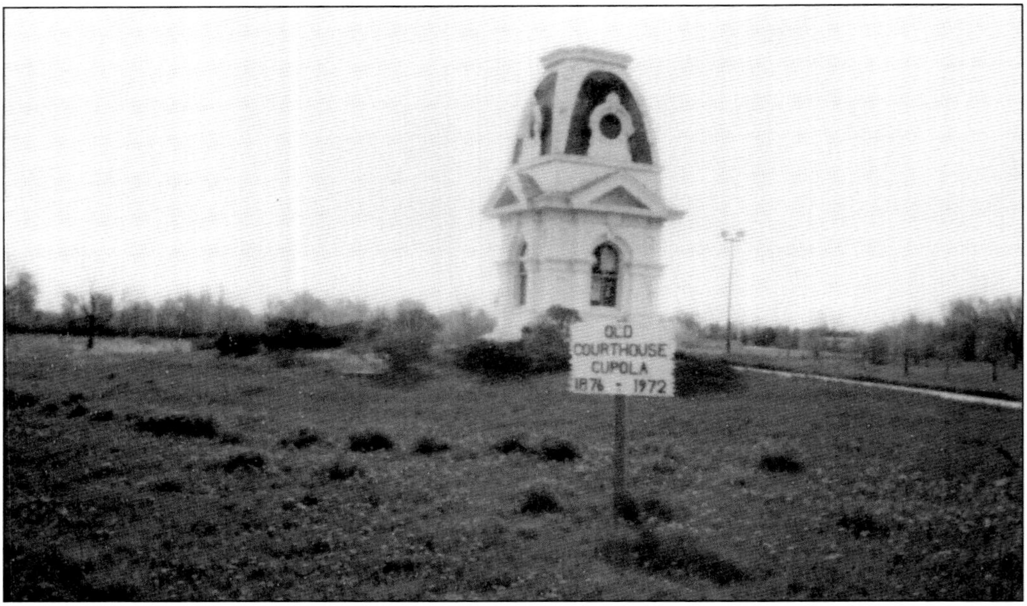

An ornate gingerbread cupola graced the top of the Isabella County Courthouse from its initial 1877 construction until demolition in 1971. The cupola stayed on the old courthouse grounds until finding a temporary home at the new Isabella County Fairgrounds in Isabella Township north of Mount Pleasant, above, when the Isabella County Youth and Farm Fair venue moved from Island Park in 1978. Through the efforts of private citizens, the cupola was returned to the Isabella County government complex grounds in 2007, below, refurbished in preparation for the 2009 Isabella County sesquicentennial and is shown below along with the county courthouse built in 2000, far left, alongside the administration building built in 1972.

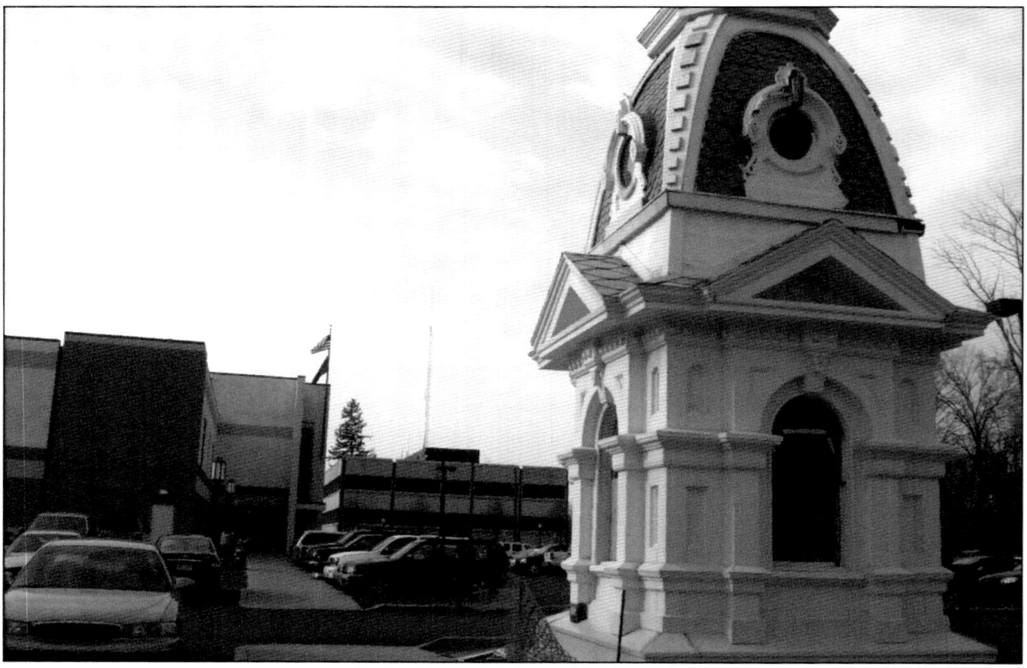

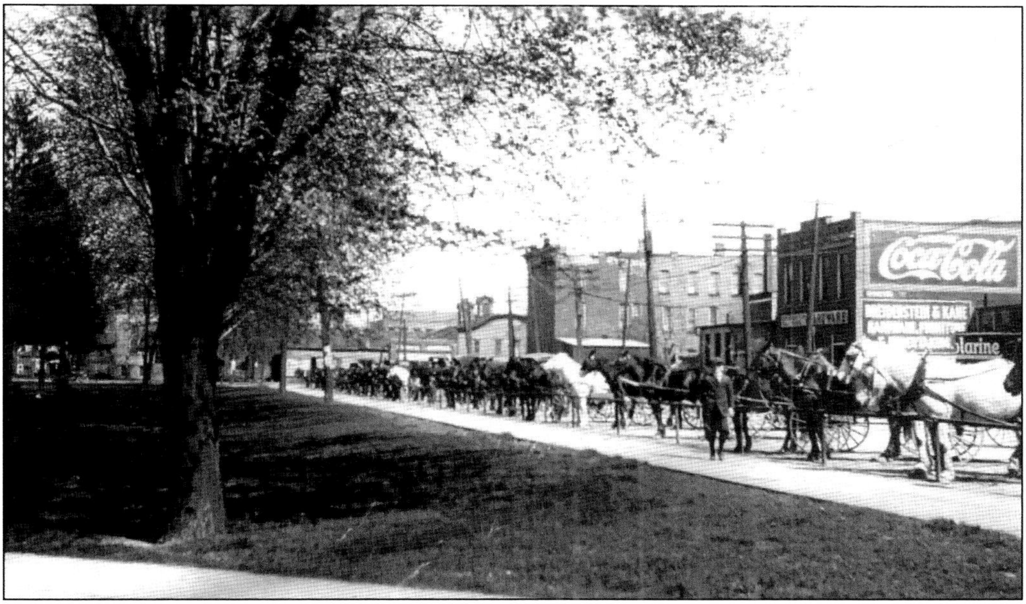

State Street, between Main and Court Streets south of the Isabella County Courthouse immediately behind downtown Mount Pleasant businesses facing Broadway Street, became known as "Jockey Alley." It was where those conducting county business parked horses, carriages, and sometimes their drivers, above. Later automobiles replaced the carriages, and the municipal parking lot continues to modern times to be known colloquially as Jockey Alley. The trees, left, were replaced by the western extension of Mosher Street from Fancher Avenue to Main Street, below, where a Michigan Department of History historical marker was installed on the Isabella County Administration Building grounds in the 1990s, commemorating the 1860 designation of the city as the county seat.

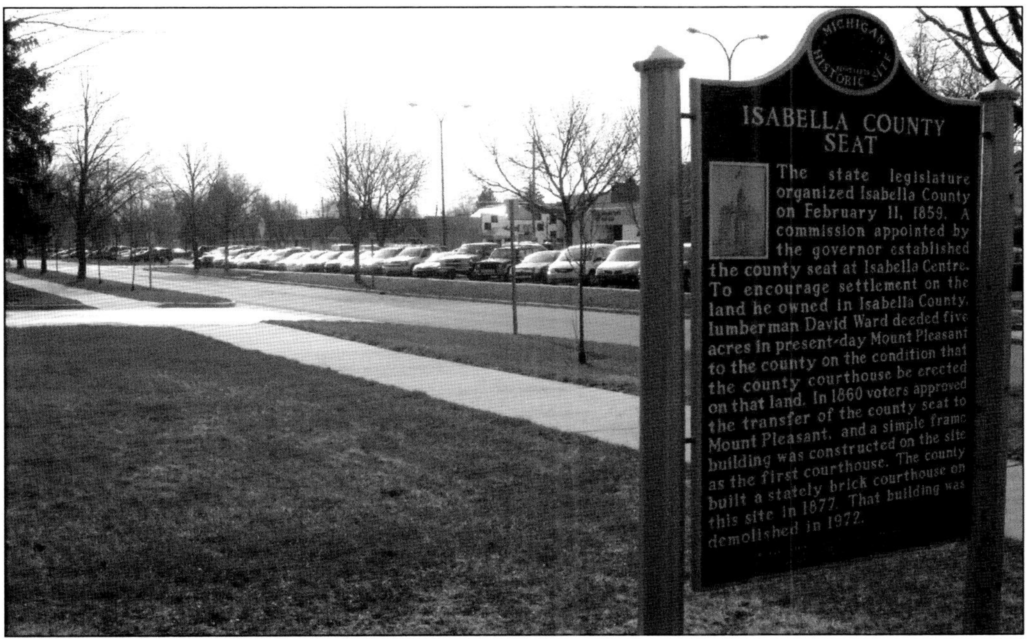

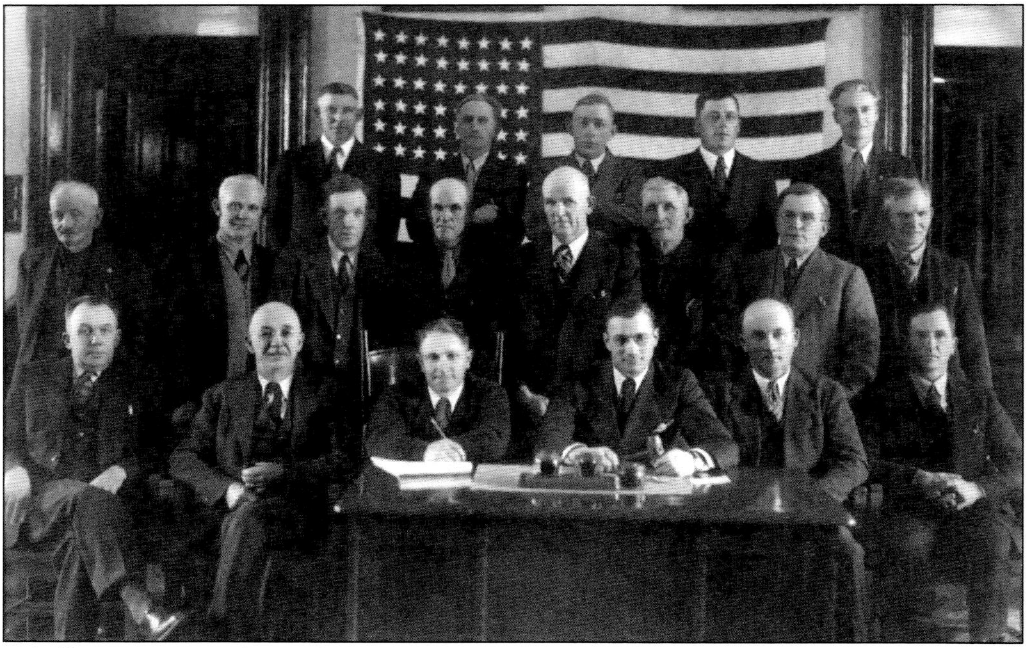

Isabella County township and county officials pose on April 1, 1941, above, including, from left to right, (first row) Earl Willie, Ed Winslow, Maynard Gilmore, Frank Gruss, Fred Sponseller, and Fred Hutchinson; (second row) Heistand Perry, Russell Collins, Jimmie Walsh, Bert Bunting, Art Foster, Tom Prout, Bob Kane, and Alva Cumming; (third row) Dwight Curtiss, Clyde Forbes, Joe Bollman, Ernest Schmidt, and Elmer Childs. An 1880s Mount Pleasant Woman's Club, below, from left to right includes (first row) unidentified, Blanche Maybee, Effie Sheline, Mrs. Carey Taylor, Bernice Battle, and Mabel Doughty; (second row) Lois Wilson, Nan Northway, unidentified, Edith Dusenbury, Maude Keeler, Hattie Dodds, Virgilene Collins, and Hannah Vowles; (third row) Ethel Taylor, Elizabeth Chatterton, Minnie Brown, Mrs. Cockran, Hester McNutt, unidentified, Mrs. Newberry, Sara Gorham, Arminta Kelly, Mrs. Bennett, Maggie Sanford, and Lizzie Foster. In the fashion of the time, some married women's first names were not published.

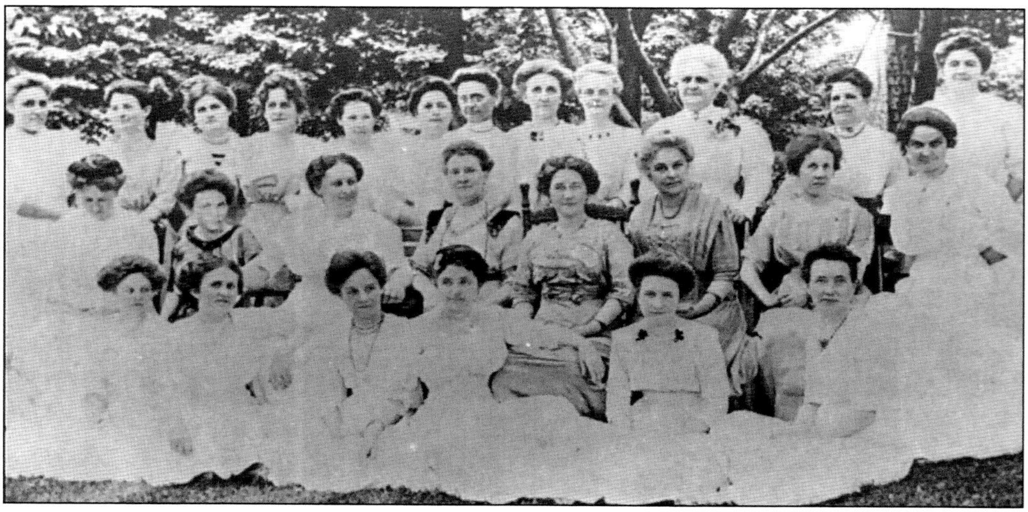

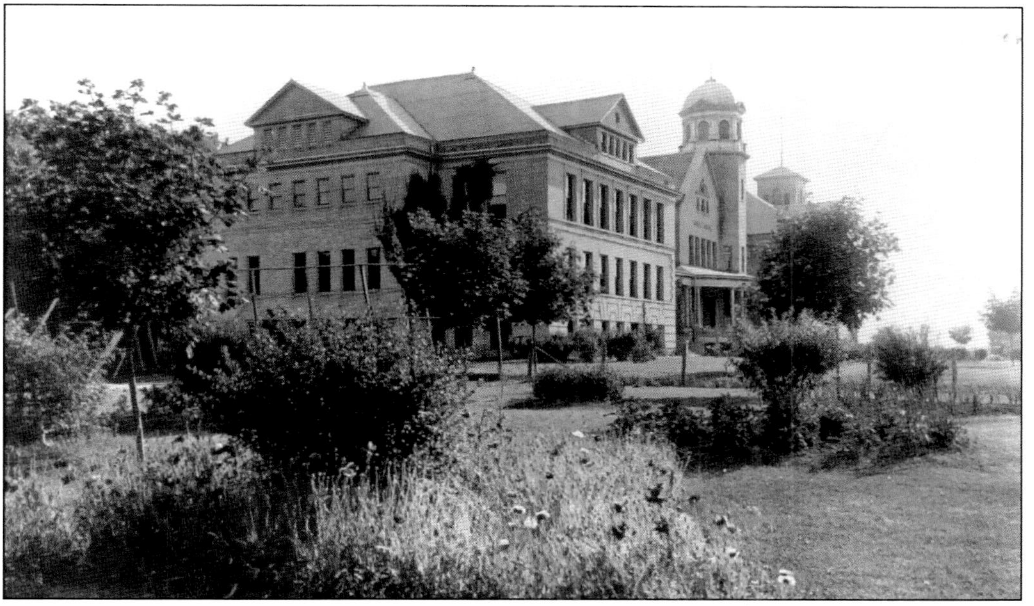

In 1892, the Mount Pleasant Development Company sold 224 lots for $10 each, leaving a 10-acre plot in the southern part of town for the Central Michigan Normal and Business Institute, which became a state teachers training school in 1895 and is now Central Michigan University, the fourth-largest university in the state with a 27,000-student enrollment, 19,000 at the 258-acre home campus. The first building was the normal administration building, above, which burned to the ground in 1925 and was replaced by Warriner Hall on the same site. At commencement ceremonies on July 2, 1896, the graduating class from Central's first full academic year as a state school were four Mount Pleasant and two Evart students, from left to right above, Paula Foster, Maud Hepburn (Evart), James Kennedy, Jessie Martin (Evart), Mary McCue, and Clara Saunders.

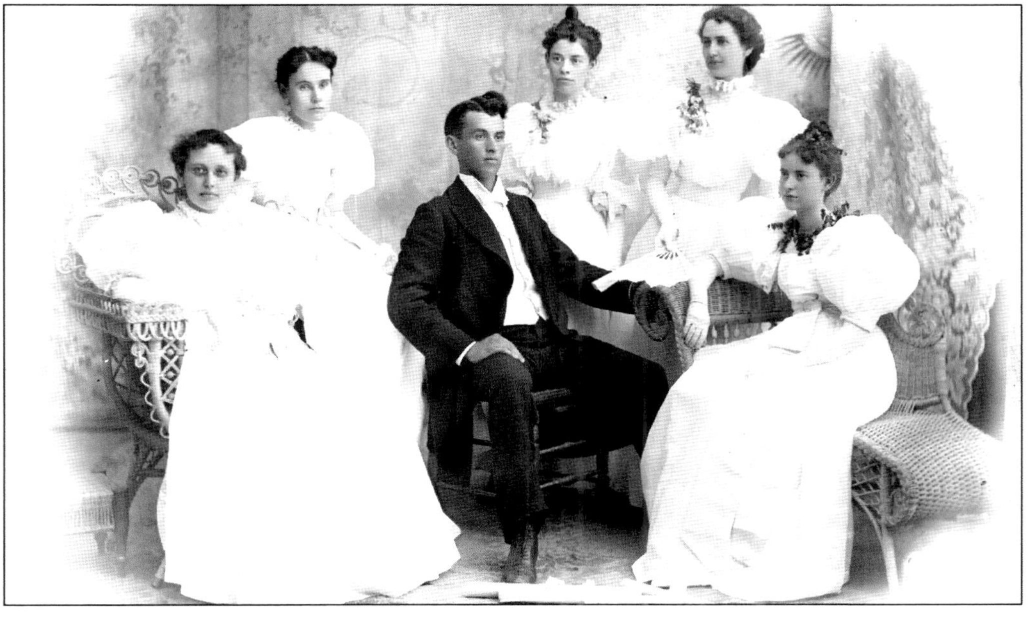

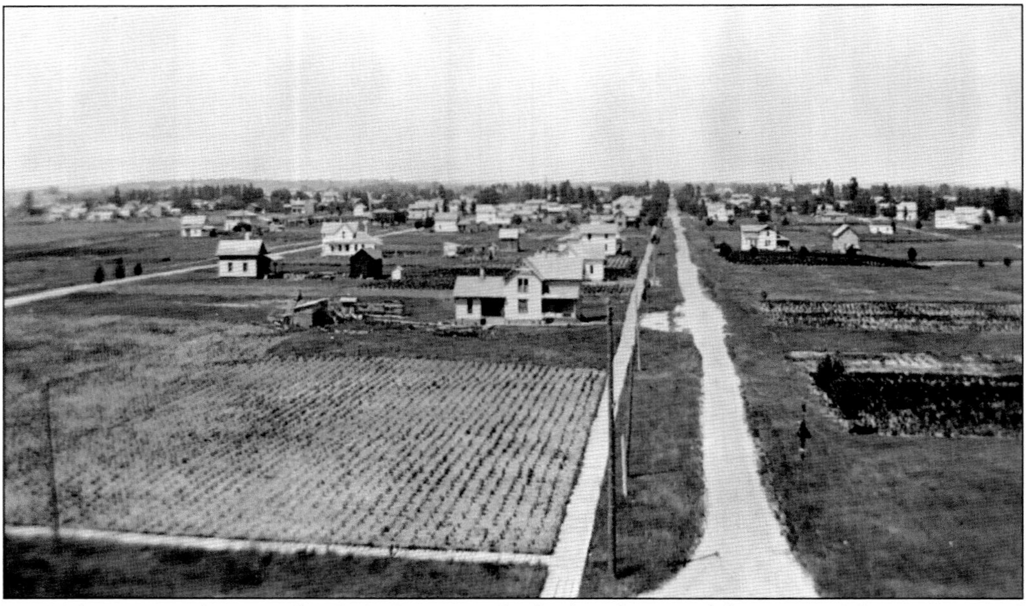

In 1896, amateur photographer J. C. Freeman climbed to the top of the tower of the new Central Michigan Normal School's main building, where Warriner Hall is now located, to snap a view of Church Street, above, looking north toward downtown Mount Pleasant. Church Street was renamed Normal Avenue, and with the changes to the school's status, it was renamed College Street in the 1920s and University Avenue in 1959.

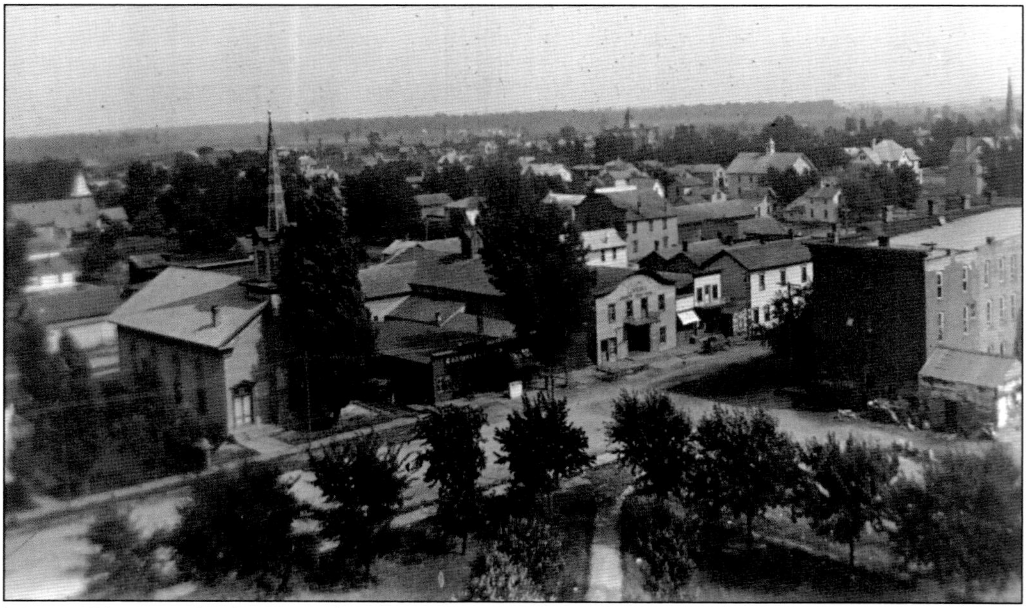

Mount Pleasant, looking southeast in the early 1900s from the cupola of the new county courthouse at the corner of Court and State Streets, is seen here. At the left is the steeple of the Presbyterian church and the McDonald Livery and Sale Stable (round-roofed building). In the center just below the horizon is the cupola of the Union School, and at the far right is Sacred Heart Academy and the steeple of the Sacred Heart Catholic Church.

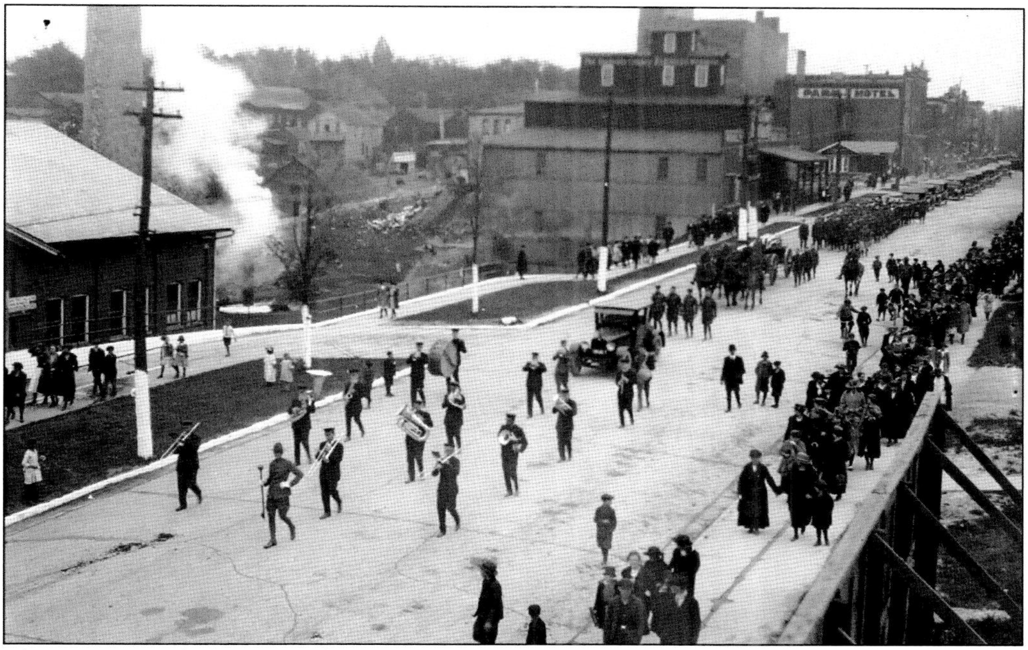

The crown jewel of Mount Pleasant's West Broadway industrial strip, the Borden Condensed Milk Company creamery, left above, was built in 1907 and processed the output of more than 2,000 cows in a 10-mile radius. Borden closed the plant in 1960, and for a time, it was used by Bader Milling Company as a fertilizer warehouse before abandonment in the 1980s. A revitalization project of the building was undertaken in 2006 with plans calling for the Mount Pleasant city government offices and others locating on the site. Note the Isabella County Courthouse cupola at the right above and as the centerpiece of the 1930s downtown Mount Pleasant aerial view below, with Harris Milling Company in the lower-left corner.

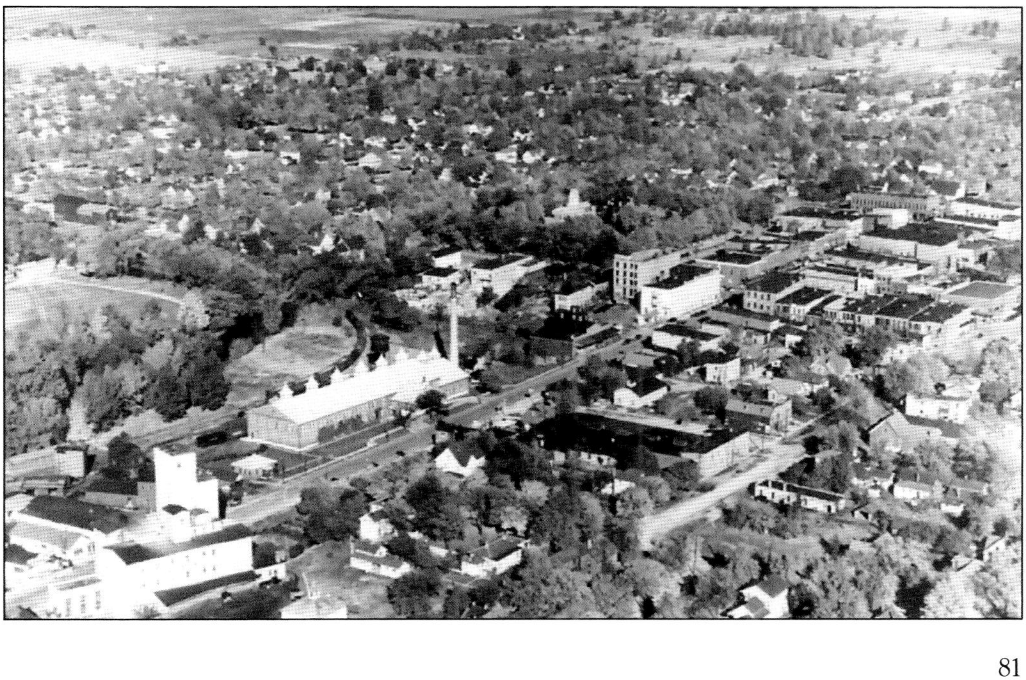

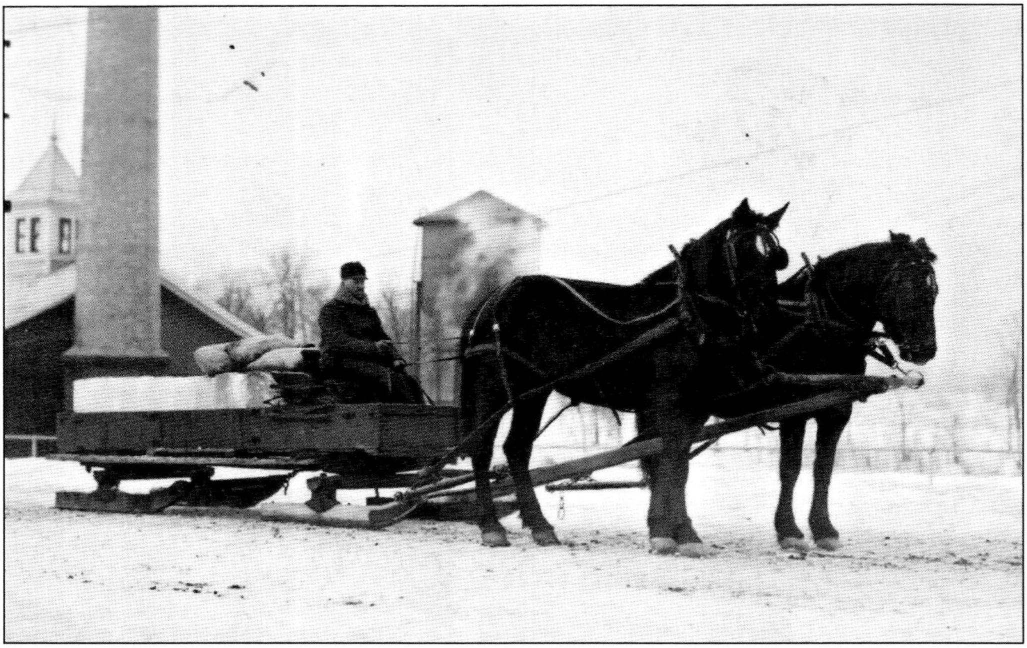

The Borden Condensed Milk Company building was a favorite background when folks wanted to lend authority to photographs of themselves. Above, Chippewa Township farmer and 10-year township treasurer Albert Gilmore pauses in front of the condensery smokestack with a load of ice cut from the Mount Pleasant Millpond on the way to his East Deerfield Road home. Albert's son Maynard Gilmore was the Isabella County clerk from 1948 to 1972.

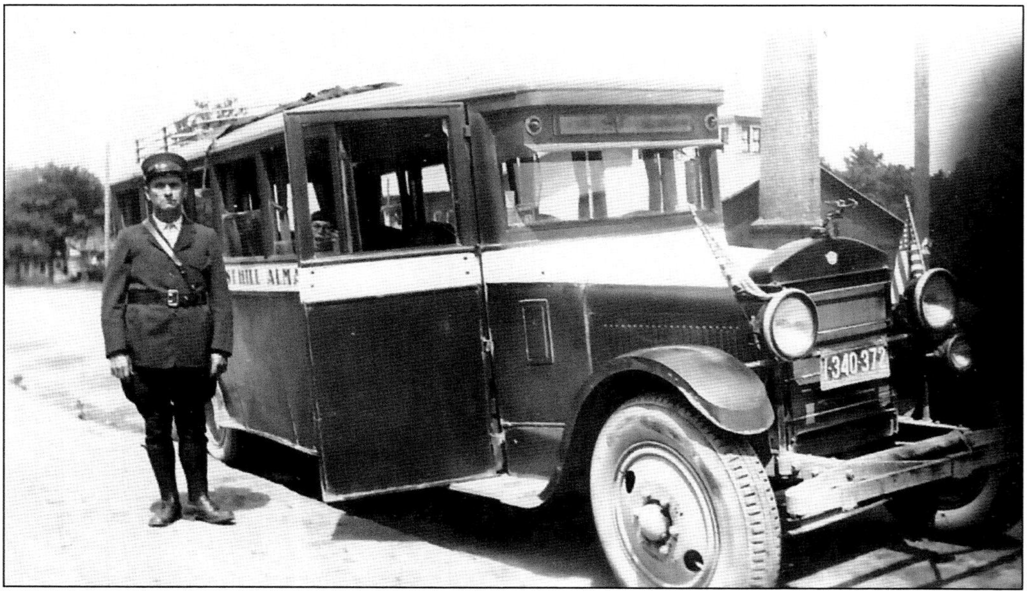

Likewise, Clarence Hart, a 40-year veteran of the taxicab and bus business, used the Borden building as backdrop for a promotional photograph of his new cab, with wife Elanor inside, in 1923 as they posed in front of his bus, cab, and automobile dealership in the 200 block of West Broadway. (Courtesy of Pat Wilmot.)

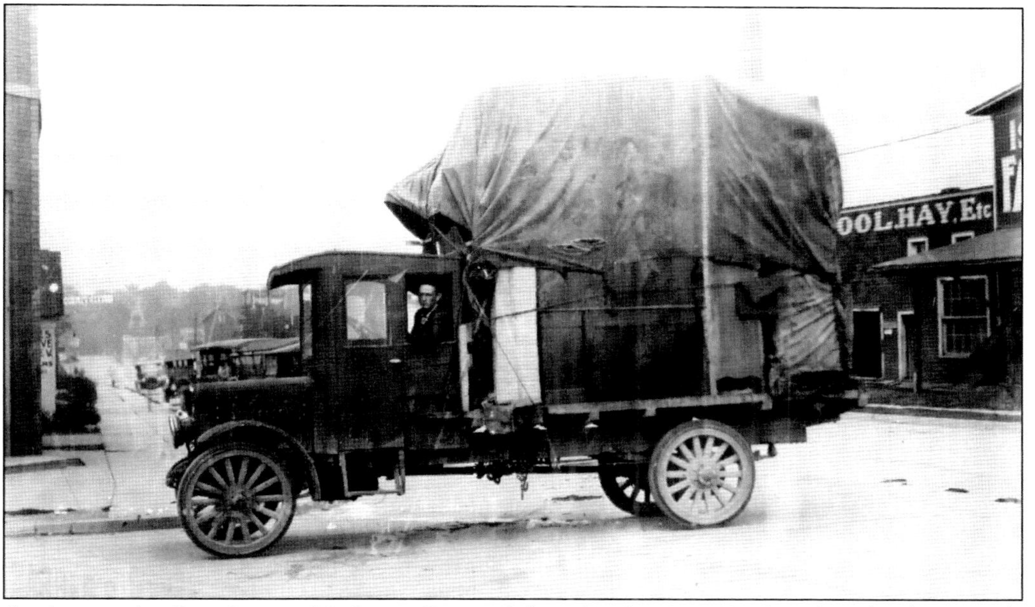

At the popular Broadway at Michigan Street, Sidney Sowle, the 1900 founder of today's Sowle and Son Moving and Storage, above, shows off his brand-new 1919 moving van, the first built by Mount Pleasant's Transport Truck Company, a local manufacturer that produced more than 1,000 trucks from its West Pickard Street location before closing in 1925. William Francis "Young Sid" Sowle later took over the business and, upon retirement, passed management to his son Bill Sowle. Below, a 1919 locally manufactured transport truck was Mount Pleasant's first motorized fire truck. It is being paraded down Normal (now University) Avenue by Fire Chief Roy D. Hafer and his toddler son Roy in 1920. (Above, courtesy of Bill Sowle.)

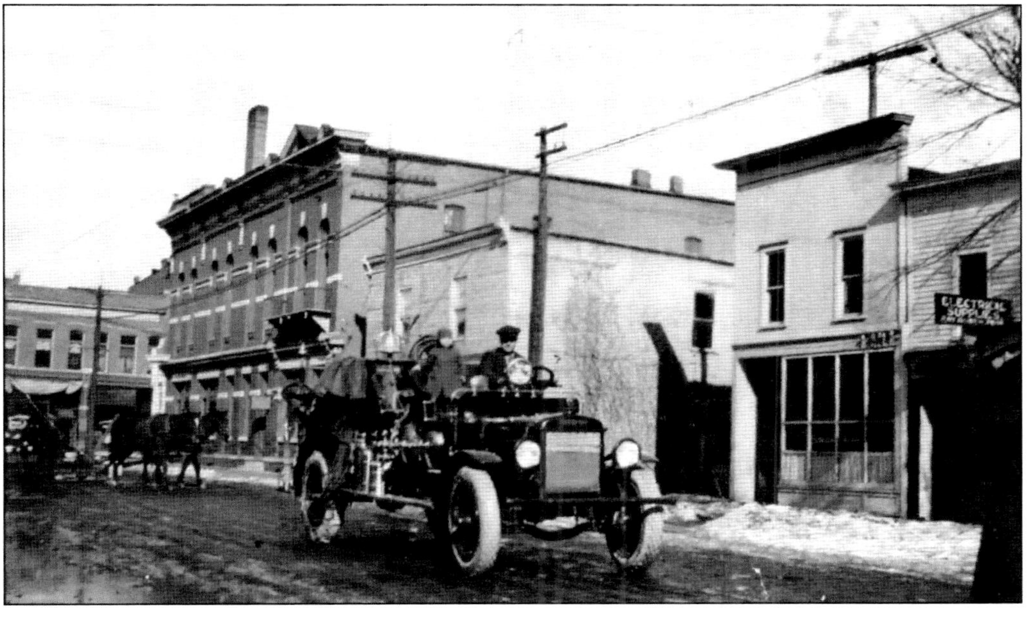

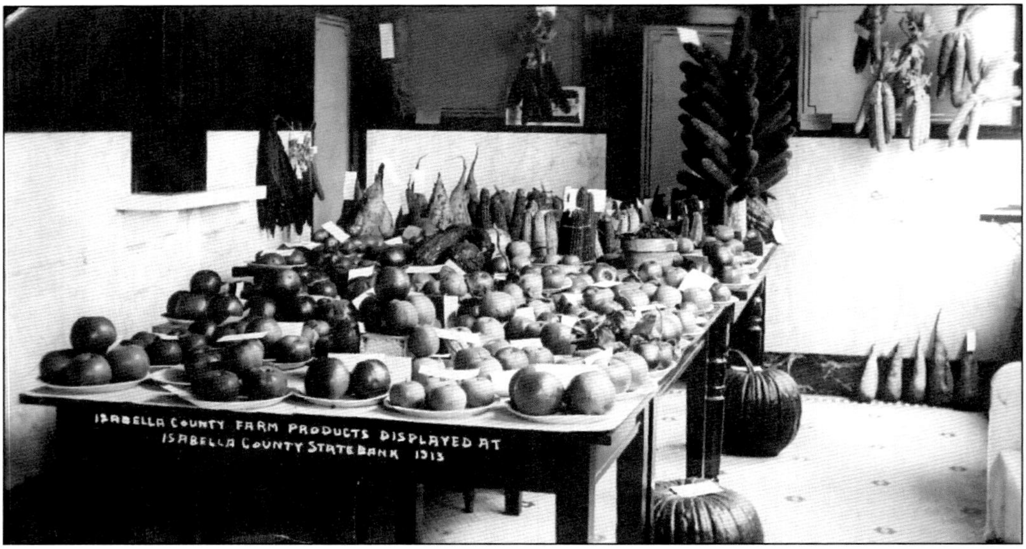

In the postcard view above, the 11-year-old Isabella County State Bank, now Isabella Bank, displayed Isabella County farm products in agricultural pride during fair week in 1913. Besides the apples, corn, cherries, pumpkins, squash, tomatoes, turnips, and wheat on display, the county soil proved ideal for raising chicory, a coffee substitute now a homeopathic medicine cultivated and processed in the 1890s to the 1930s, and sugar beets processed from 1919 until 1947, both at separate plant facilities on Pickard Street on the north side of Mount Pleasant. Additionally the city was a center for gristmills, lumber, and basket and brick manufacturing. Below, a 1939 queue of sugar beet–laden railcars line up at the Mount Pleasant sugar beet processing plant on West Pickard Street. (Above, courtesy of the Richard Brandell collection.)

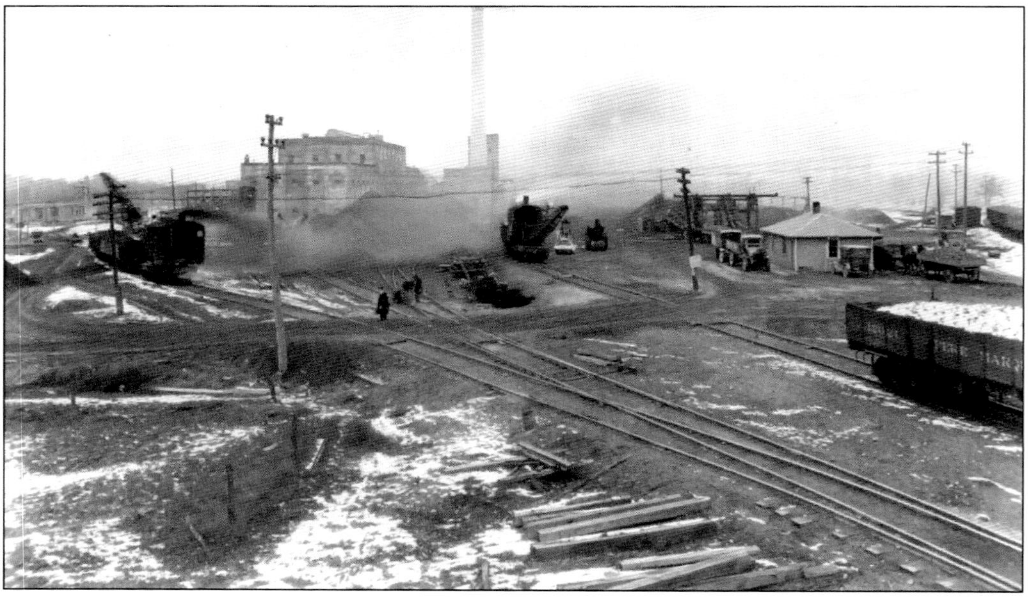

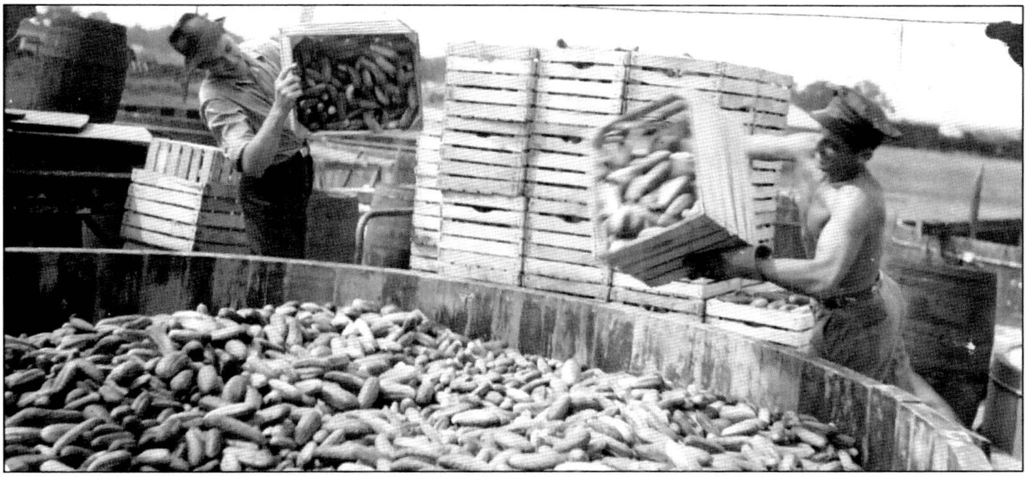

An August 20, 1942, front-page article in the *Isabella County Times-News* newspaper, read, "The receiving of the crop at the C. C. Lang salting station on North Kinney Street is going along at a rapid rate with a crop nearly double last year's expected." Among many in Isabella County, Lang company's station and H. J. Heinz's station were located at the northern end of Mount Pleasant.

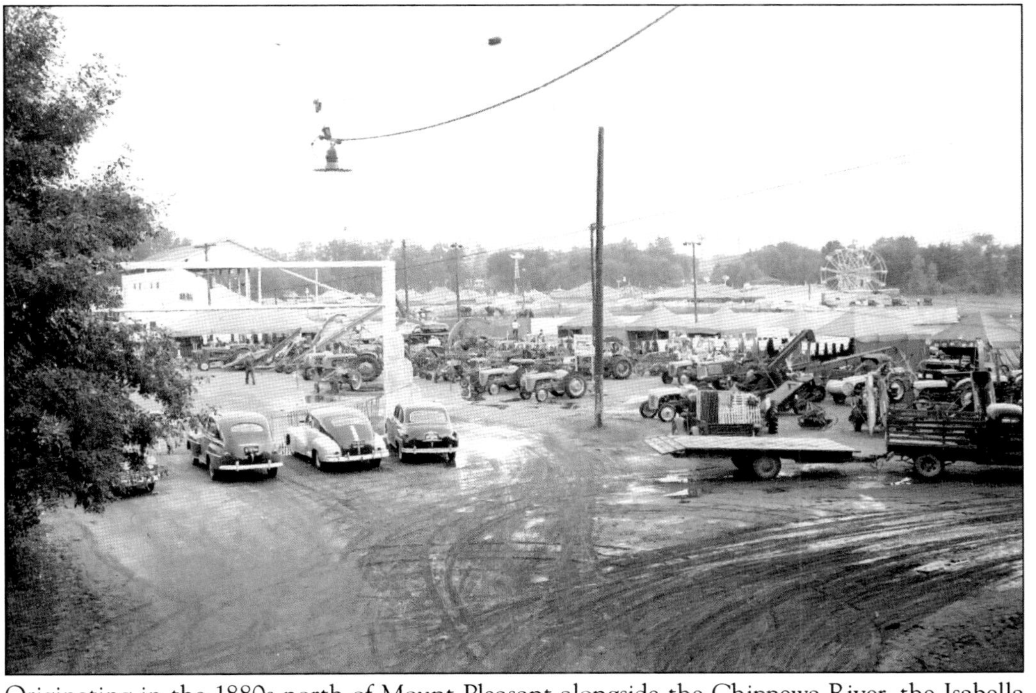

Originating in the 1880s north of Mount Pleasant alongside the Chippewa River, the Isabella County Fair sold part of its grounds to Dow Chemical Company in 1899 and made an agreement for the event to take place annually at Mount Pleasant's Island Park, above. The Isabella County Youth and Farm Fair outgrew Island Park, acquired grounds on Mission Road, and the fair located north of town again in 1978.

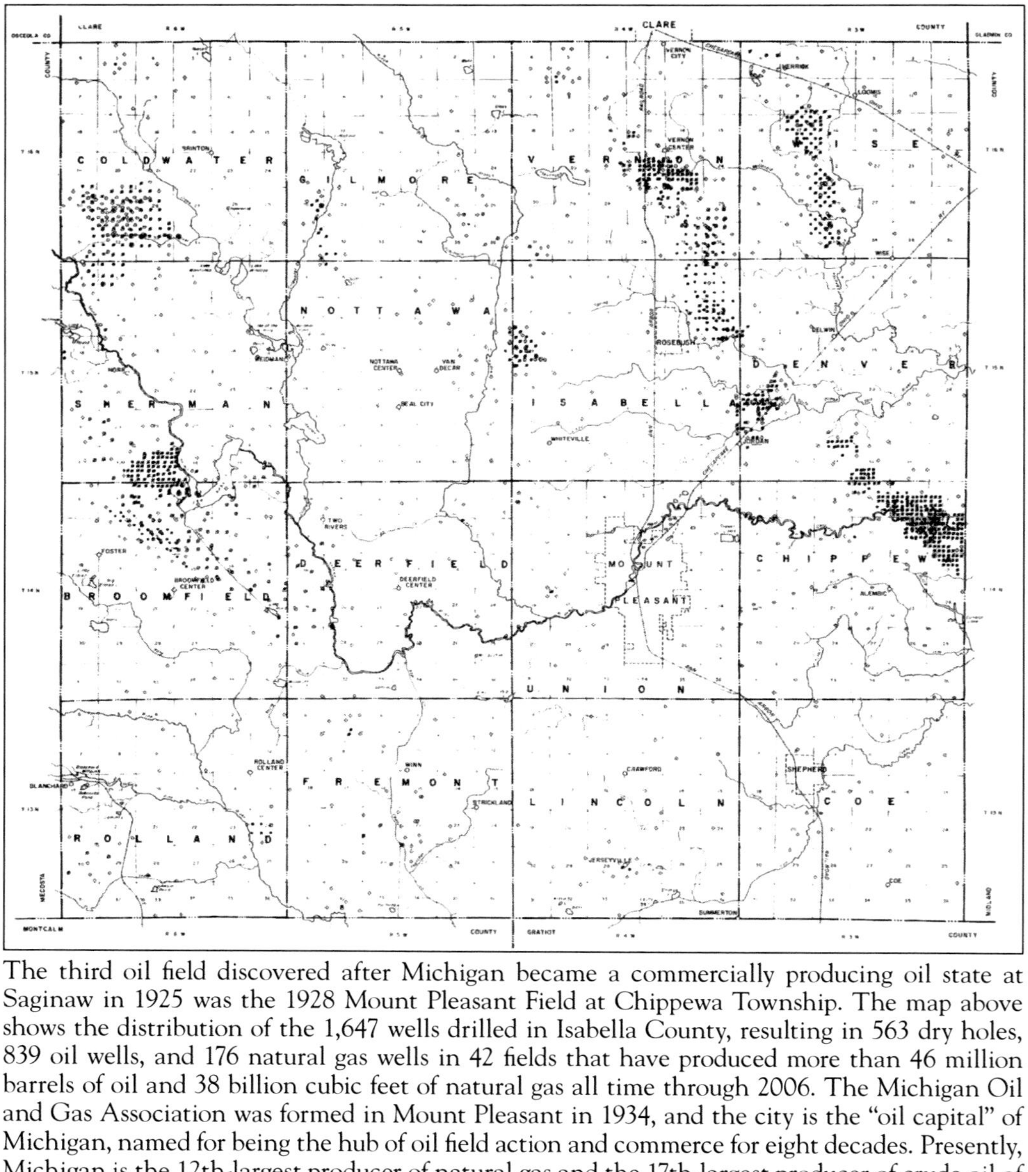

The third oil field discovered after Michigan became a commercially producing oil state at Saginaw in 1925 was the 1928 Mount Pleasant Field at Chippewa Township. The map above shows the distribution of the 1,647 wells drilled in Isabella County, resulting in 563 dry holes, 839 oil wells, and 176 natural gas wells in 42 fields that have produced more than 46 million barrels of oil and 38 billion cubic feet of natural gas all time through 2006. The Michigan Oil and Gas Association was formed in Mount Pleasant in 1934, and the city is the "oil capital" of Michigan, named for being the hub of oil field action and commerce for eight decades. Presently, Michigan is the 12th-largest producer of natural gas and the 17th-largest producer of crude oil of the 34 states producing oil and gas.

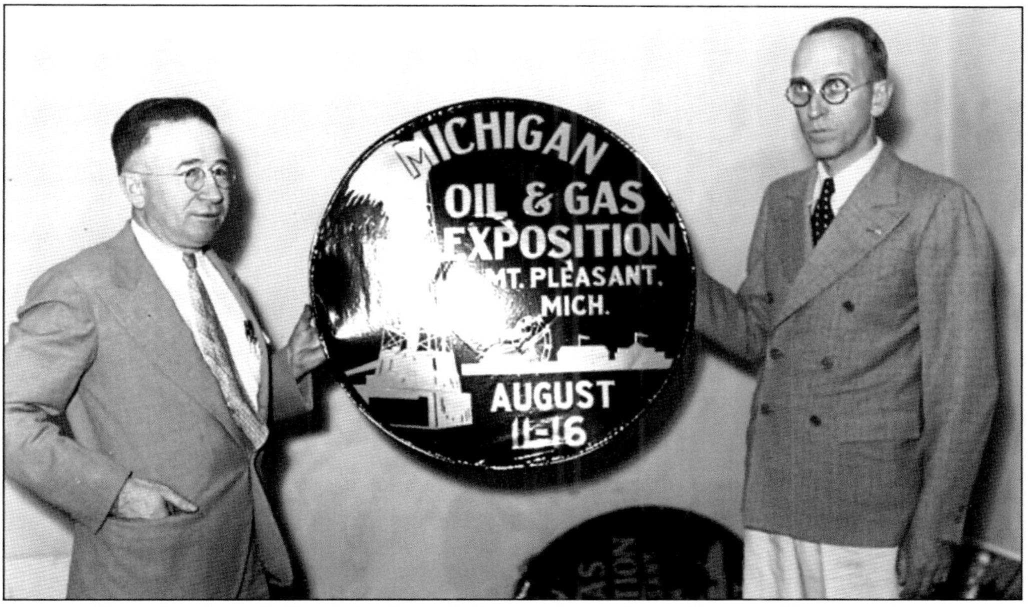

Central State Teachers College's Dr. Joseph Carey of the Mount Pleasant Planning Commission and chamber of commerce president, left, and N. G. "Harry" Gover hold a sign for the 1935 Michigan Oil and Gas Exposition, which drew more than 25,000 people to town. A parade was led by a mock hearse containing an effigy of "Ole Man Depression," symbolizing industry activity having shielded the area from the financial devastation of the Great Depression.

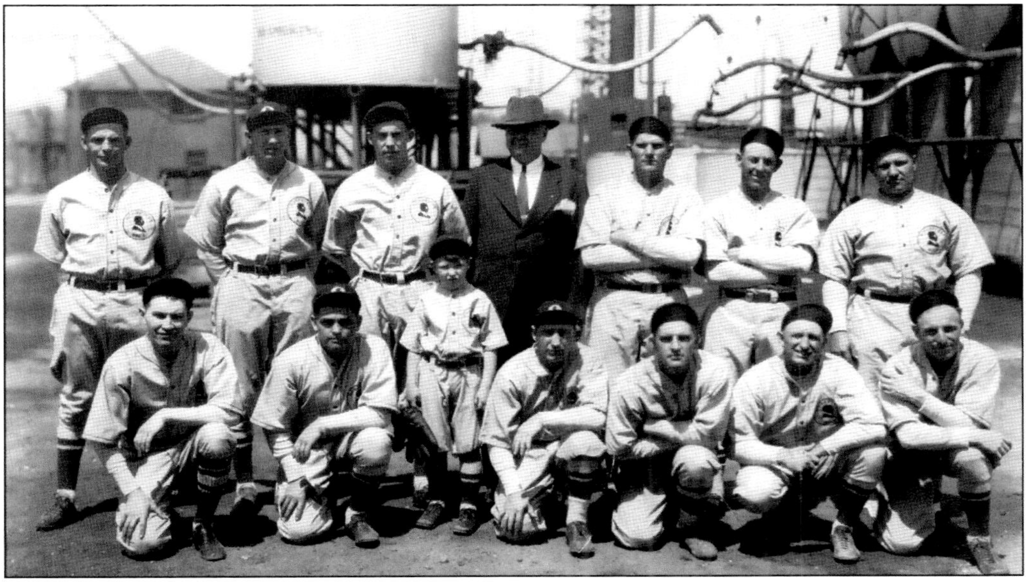

Oil was important to both economic and sports life in Mount Pleasant. The 1934 Roosevelt baseball team went to the final tournament of the Michigan amateur baseball league; from left to right they are (first row) L. Randall, D. Mathews, R. D. Cowden (standing, mascot), H. Cowden, R. Stauffer, R. Cowden, and L. McCullum; (second row) O. Mathews, C. Hamilton, M. Georgia, refinery president C. L. McGuire, D. Lehman, W. Thompson, and D. Gabystak. (Courtesy of Joe Prout.)

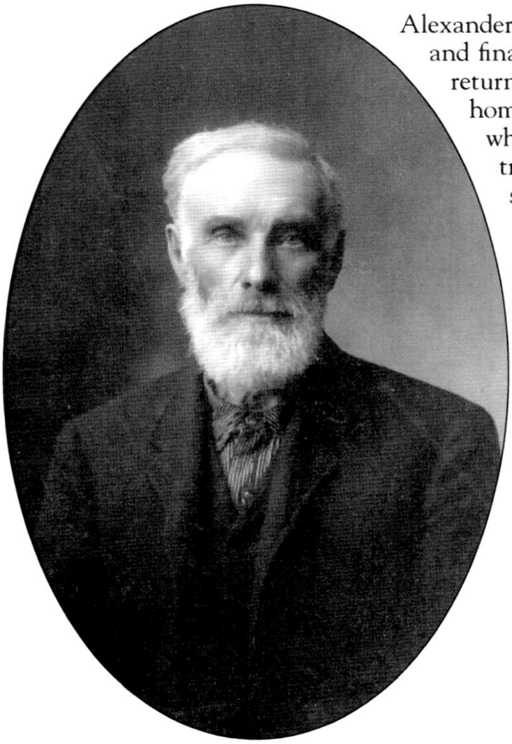

Alexander Brodie was born in 1834 and came to Michigan and finally Isabella County in 1859 on a prospect trip, returning the following year to settle on a 160-acre homestead just southeast of Mount Pleasant, where Wal-Mart is located today. Isabella County treasurer for four years, he was Union Township supervisor for a time and on the school board for his district. He died in 1913.

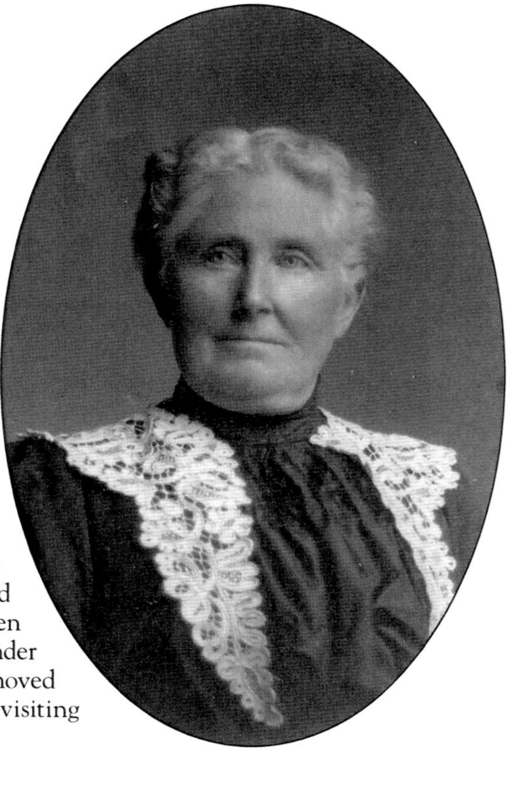

Janet "Jennie" McLeod Brodie came to Isabella County at 18 with her family in 1840. An accomplished photographer, she had a gallery opposite the courthouse square. She captured the first-known camera image of the wooden courthouse in the 1860s. She married Alexander Brodie in 1866 and raised four children, then moved to Florida while Alexander stayed in Michigan, visiting her often. She died in 1922.

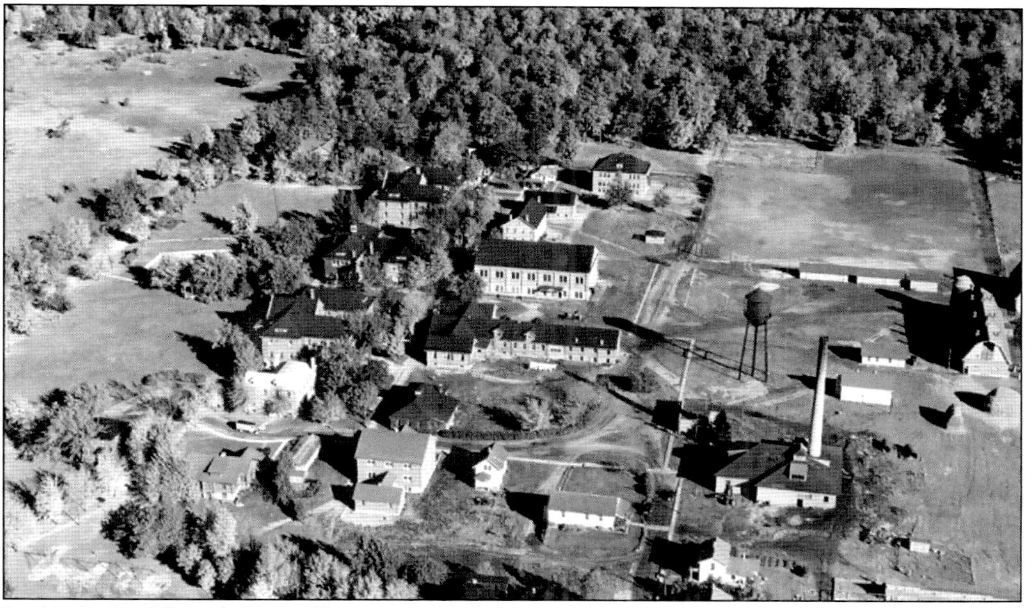

In 1893, the United States Department of the Interior opened the Mount Pleasant Indian Industrial School on 320 acres in the northwest corner of town. The nine-year boarding school and self-supporting farm, designed to acclimate primarily Chippewa Indian children to the "white man's ways," grew from 1 to 11 buildings, above, and from 59 to 300 students per year before closing in 1934. Reports of the experience vary from discontent to gratitude for a steady environment with regular meals. In 1938, more than 600 Chippewa alumni of the school held a powwow there to celebrate their years at the school. The grounds, below in 1972, were deeded to the State of Michigan and were converted to Mount Pleasant Home and Training School for the mentally challenged in 1934, known now, after many name changes, simply as the Mount Pleasant Center.

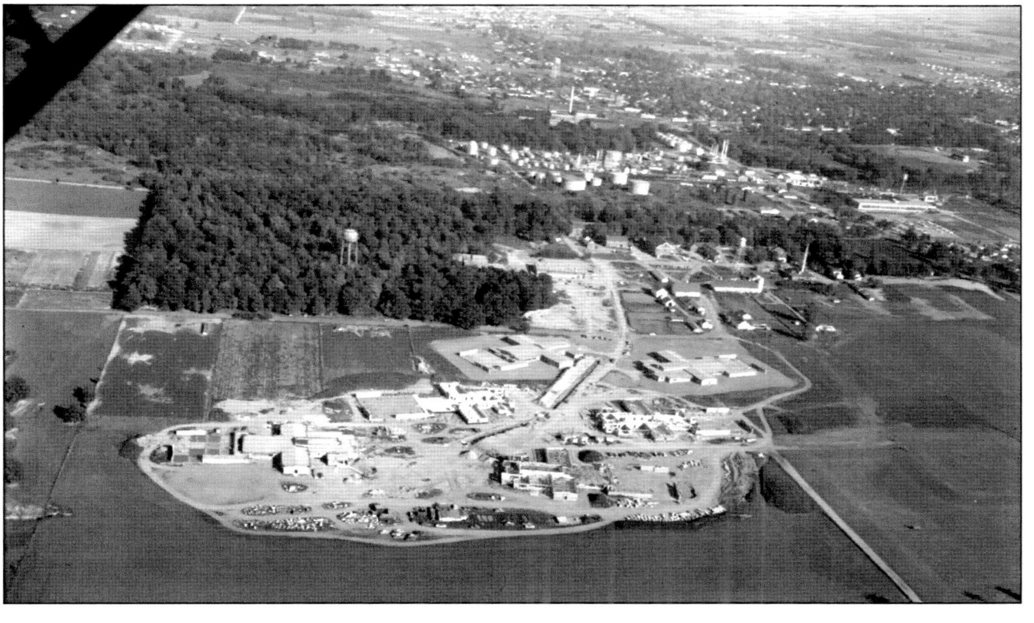

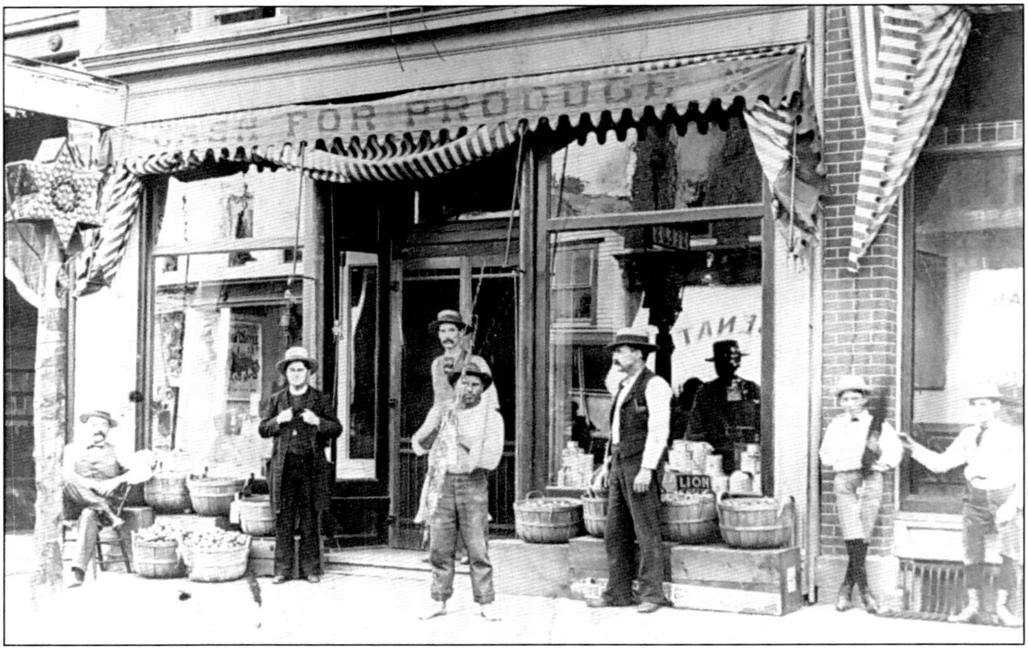

Canadian Frank A. Sweeney, in the doorway of his store at 114 South Main Street in Mount Pleasant (the site of today's Book Garden bookstore), came to Isabella County on foot looking to secure land and timber, bought a horse in Salt River (now Shepherd), and came the rest of the way to Mount Pleasant in 1873. In 1881, he opened the mercantile store on Main Street. In the 1920s, his son Frank J. Sweeney expanded to deal in seeds and beans and opened the Sweeney Seed Company store and grain elevator at 110 South Washington Street, where it remains. In the photograph below, the elder Sweeneys celebrated 50 years of marriage in 1925 with an ice-cream social at their 304 South Washington Street home with family and friends. (Courtesy of Mary Ellen Brandell.)

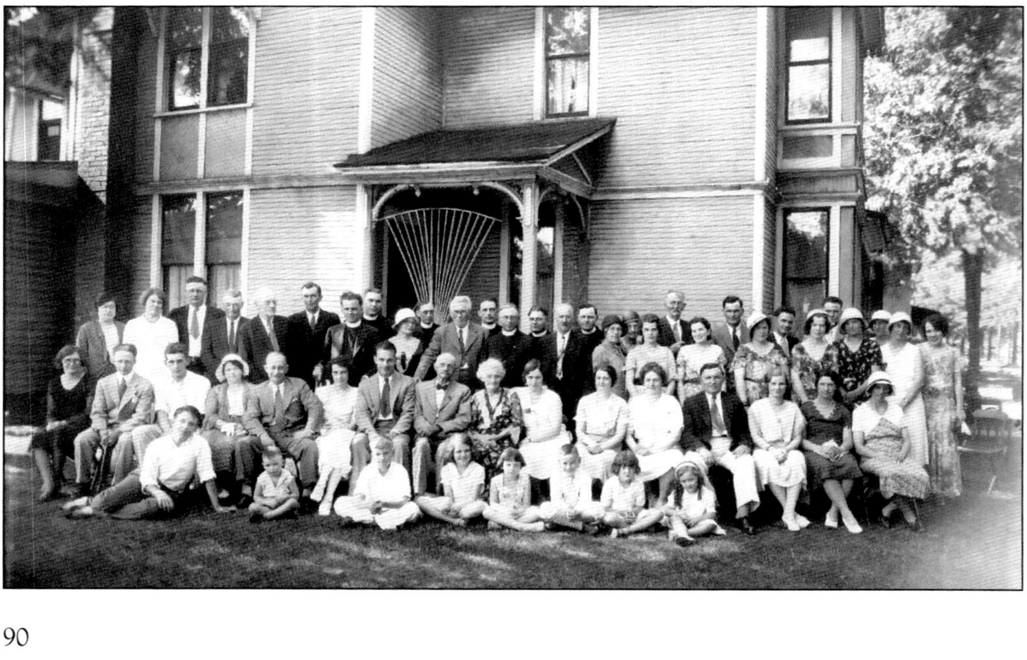

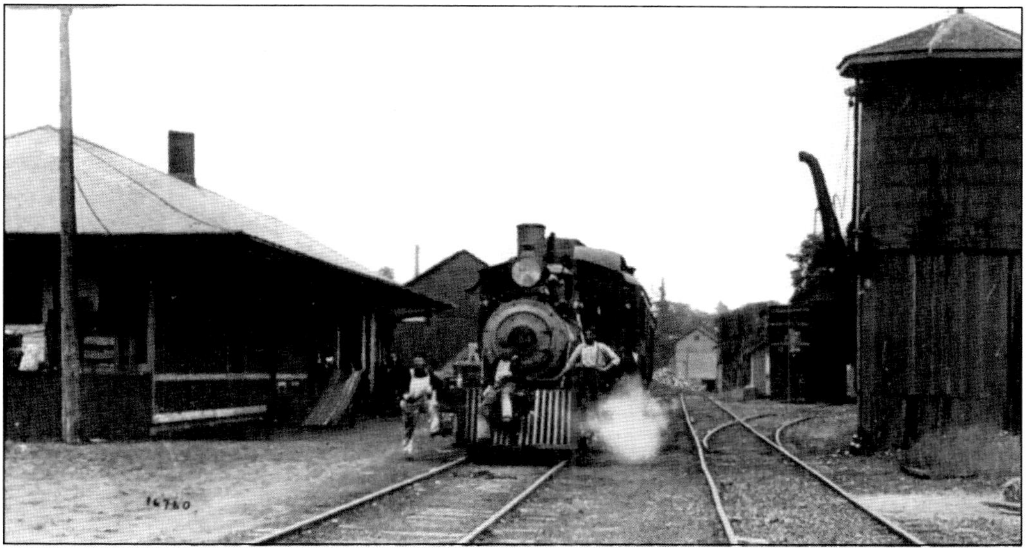

The first railroad in Isabella County was the 1871 line run by the Flint and Pere Marquette Railroad from Coleman, which ran south below the Isabella County side of the county line to reenter Clare County at Farwell. In 1879, a narrow-gauge railway was built to Coleman from Mount Pleasant, with the depot above located on North Main Street, which is now a parking lot just south of the post office.

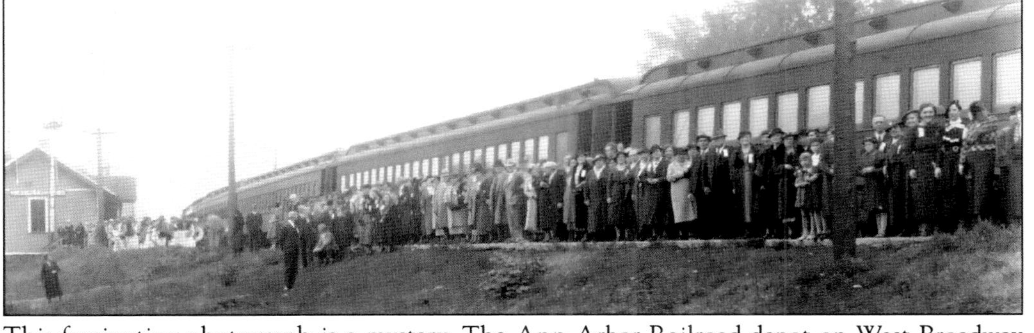

This fascinating photograph is a mystery. The Ann Arbor Railroad depot on West Broadway in Mount Pleasant was opened with the line's arrival from Owosso in 1885 and served as the line extended north to Cadillac. The depot was the scene of a massive unidentified assemblage sometime between the 1920s and 1940s, which hours of research have failed to identify. The building is now a brewpub steakhouse.

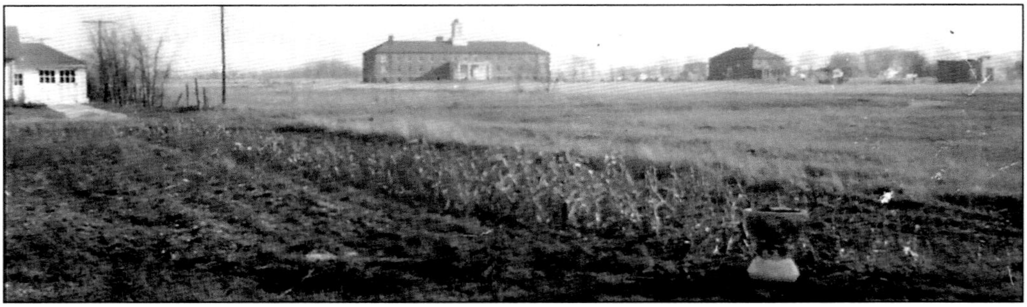

Small private hospitals, notably the Bronstetter Hospital on Court Street and the Northway Clinic at Main Street and Broadway, operated in Mount Pleasant before the community hospital opened in 1934 on the grounds of the recently closed American Indian industrial school (see page 89). Nine years later, the Central Michigan Community Hospital opened in a remote area east of town at Maple and Brown Streets. The remoteness of the now heavily populated area would be hard to grasp without the 1943 picture looking southeast from Anna Street at about Wisconsin Street, above. In a short time, below, residential sprawl began in the now densely populated area. (Above, courtesy of Monica Barrett.)

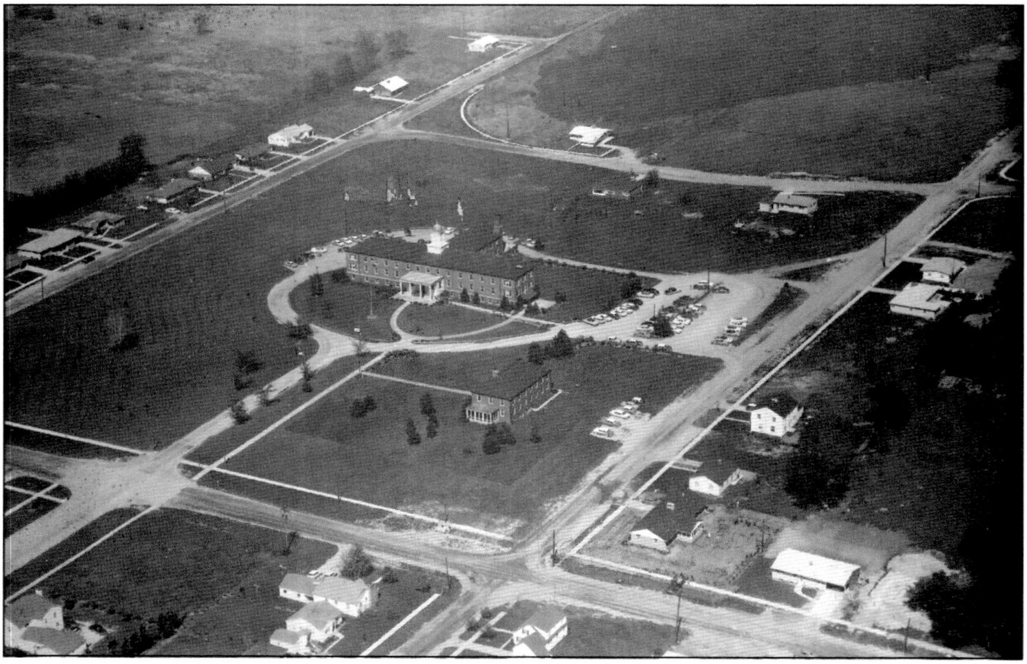

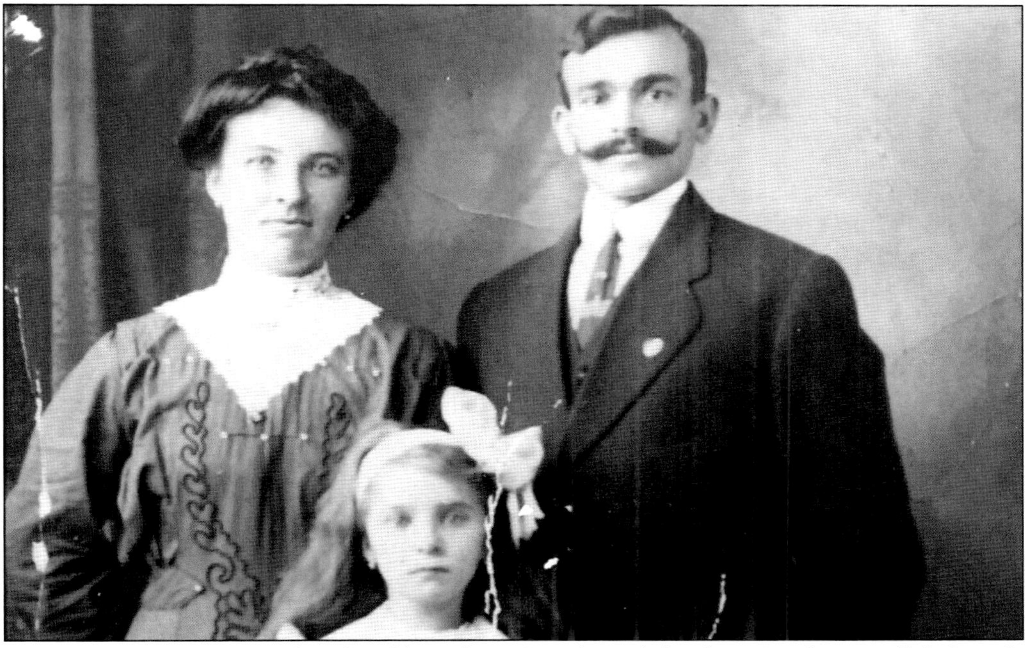

Illustrating the county's cultural meld, Barbara, Joseph, and daughter Cecilia "Lucille" Gostola pose for a 1912 portrait in Budapest, Hungary, before immigrating to Isabella County. Lucille married Carey Robinson, son of Irish/English/Dutch Isabella County couple Arvilla and W. B. Robinson. Carey and Lucille's daughter Colleen married Robert Campbell, great-grandson of Patrick Donovan, founder of the Donovan House (Park Hotel) in downtown Mount Pleasant. (Courtesy of Colleen Campbell.)

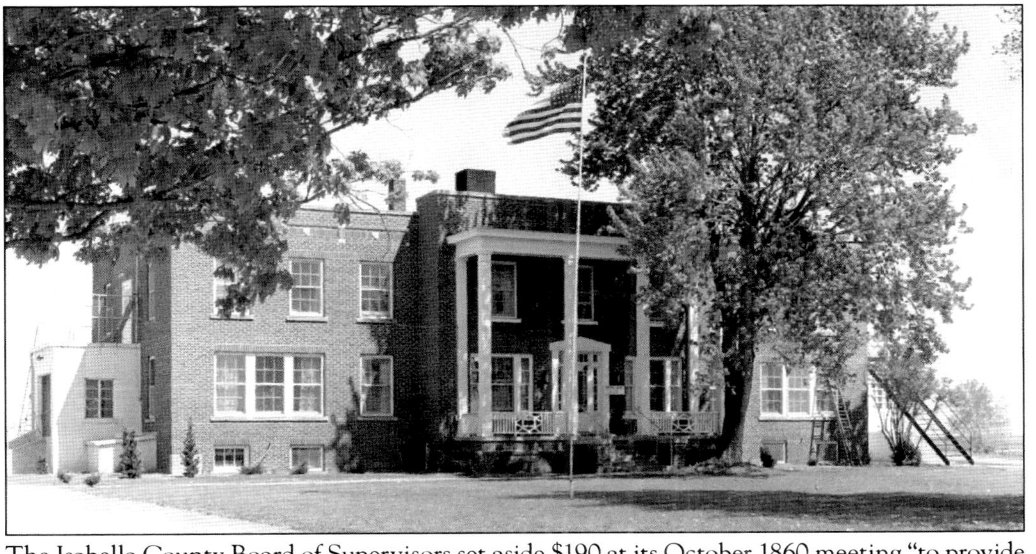

The Isabella County Board of Supervisors set aside $190 at its October 1860 meeting "to provide for the poor." In 1865, a 160-acre farm was purchased in Chippewa Township as a county poor farm. From 1929, it was renamed the Isabella County Infirmary and Farm, later again renamed Broomfield Convalescent Hospital, until 1953, when it was sold to private interests, to operate in the 1970s as headquarters for the Gould Rexall drugstore chain.

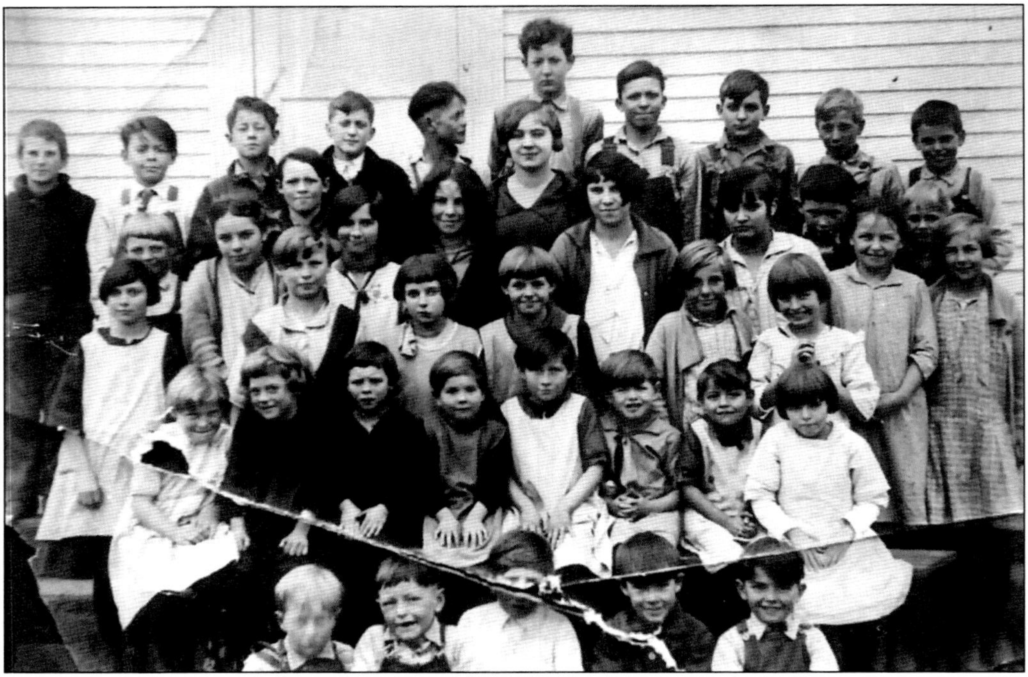

Above, Lincoln Township, section 6, Lincoln Center School in 1927 includes, from left to right, (first row) Hugh Beebe, Wayne Dowling, Elmer Kyser, Loren Loomis, and Jack Caszett; (second row) Sophia Klumpp, June Beebe, Dorothy Kyser, Coral Loomis, Dorothy Recker, Evelyn Caszett, Lillian Recker, and Genevieve Wallace; (third row) Margarite Hartford, Marjorie Klumpp, Elizabeth Kyser, Dorothy Cole, Helen Arnold, and Marie Wallace; (fourth row) Alfred Klumpp, Evelyn Kyser, Ada Humphrey, Mildred Dowling, Hazel Parks, Margarite MacDonald, Claude Dowling, May Dowling, Lewis McDonald, and Ilene Arnold; (fifth row) Harold Parks, Murry Van Liew, Paul Caszett, Wayne Cole, Donald Diehl, Arlo McDonald, an unidentified teacher, Dewayne Kyser, Glen Cole, unidentified, Darwin Beebe, and Raymond Wallace. Below, brothers Ray Sponseller (right), Fred Sponseller (sitting), Arthur Sponseller (with the team), and a logging crew are at work in Lincoln Township. (Below, courtesy of George and Sherrie Sponseller.)

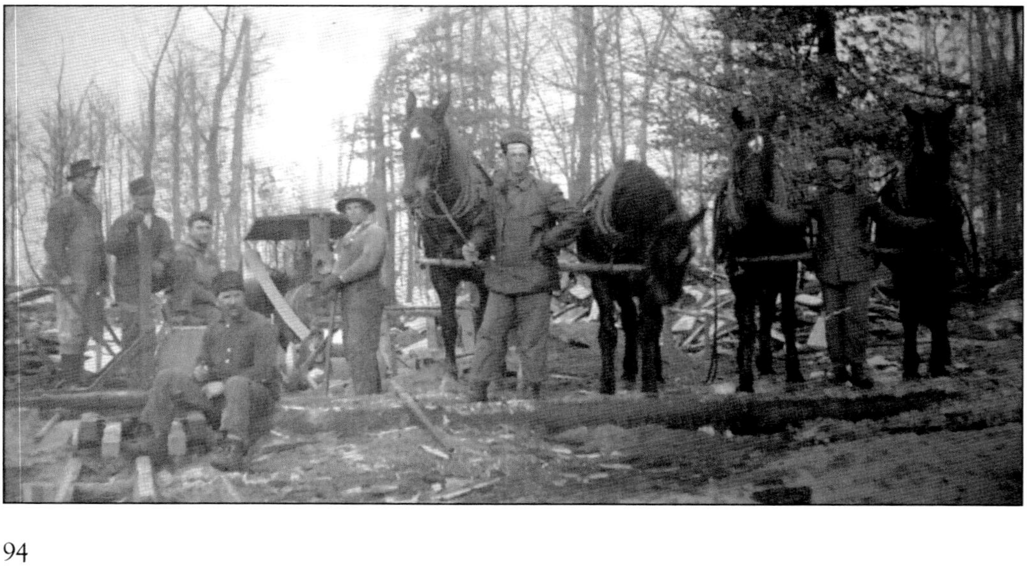

Shepherd's Electric Light and Power Plant, at right, was built in 1908 during the era when towns generated their own power. The coal/gas engine–powered 35-kilowatt dynamo operated from 1909 to 1912, and outside power was distributed through the facility from 1913 to 1925, until Consumers Power Company bought the distribution system. Part of the building was used as a village council hall until 1957. The water tower was razed in the late 1960s, and the site, facing Wright Avenue, is now a city park. Still standing, the brick power plant building has served as a museum and home to the Shepherd Historical Society since 1982. Below, a former Chippewa District 2 school is preserved as the Shepherd Historical Society Little Red Schoolhouse Museum.

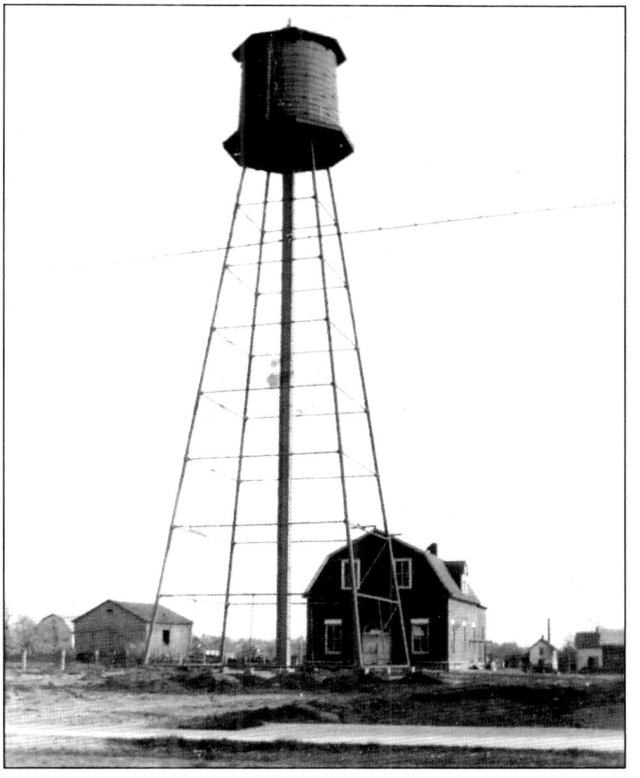

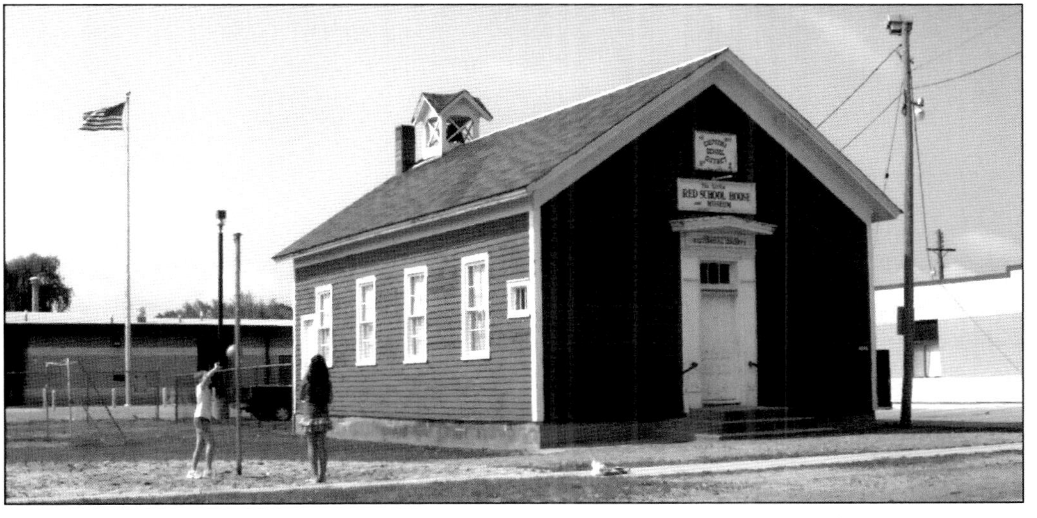

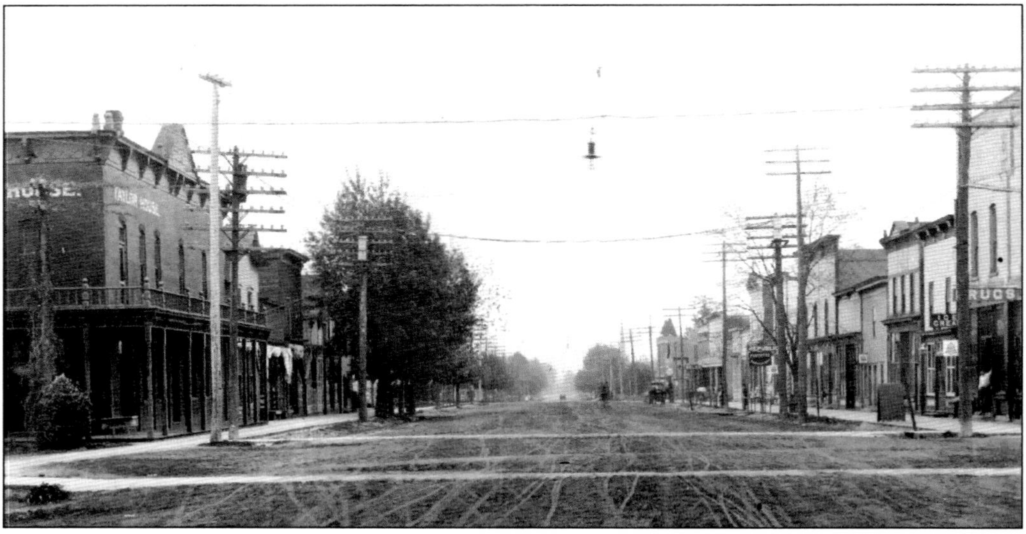

Above, Shepherd's main thoroughfare, looking west along the newly widened Wright Avenue from Second Street in the 1920s, shows that the presence of electricity is apparent by elaborate power lines. Fire destroyed a great deal of Salt River that year, and Salt River was included in Shepherd, below, looking west along the north side of Wright Avenue. Downtown Shepherd also suffered three more conflagrations, along the north side of Wright Avenue in 1888, along the south side of the same avenue in 1927, and Jack Arndt's Garage on the northwest corner of Wright Avenue and Third Street in 1947. Below, note the famous Taylor House, later called the Calkins House, a block from the train station at the northeast corner of Wright Avenue and Second Street.

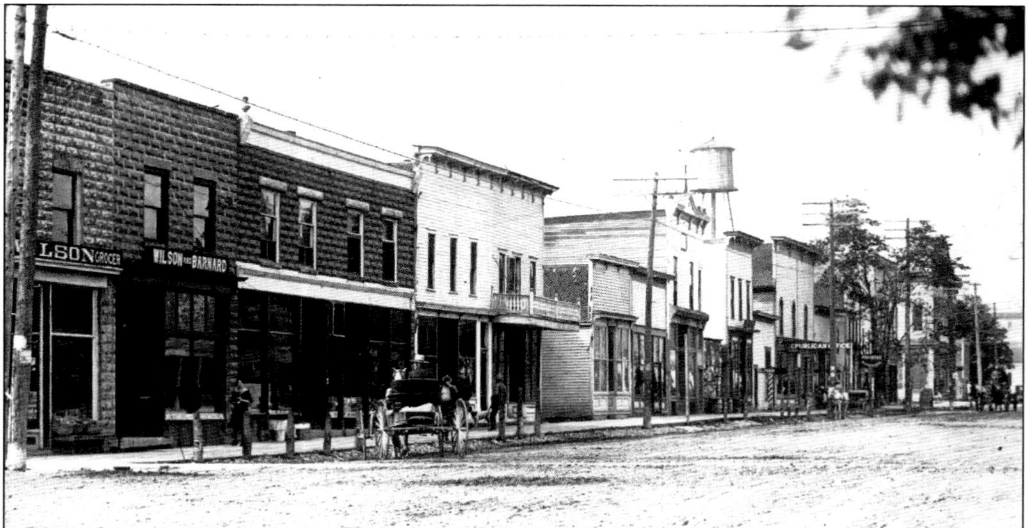

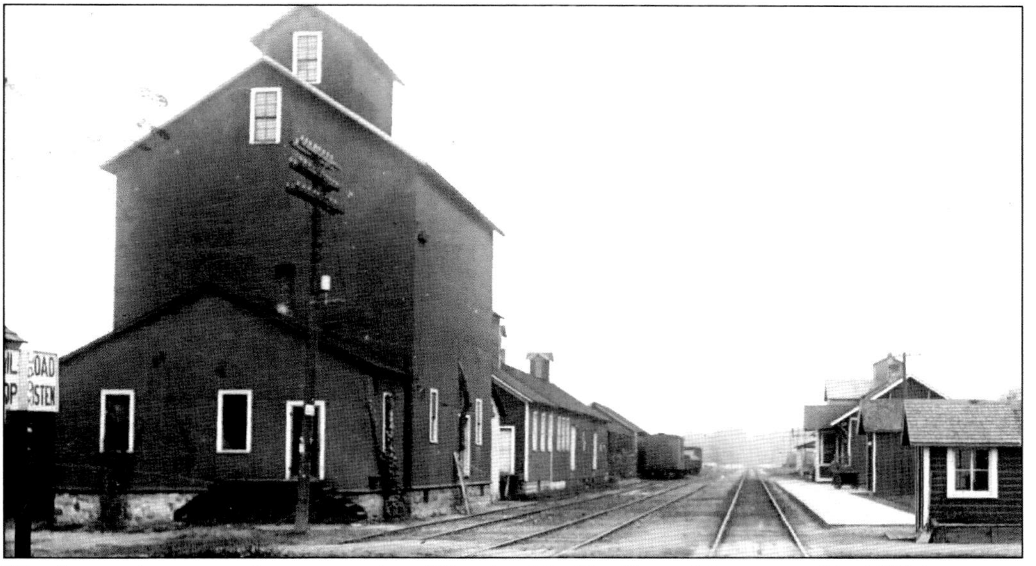

The first settlement at the present site of Shepherd in Coe Township occurred in 1857, known as Salt River. A sawmill and flour mill were built by harnessing the waters of the Salt River at "the Corners." The first United States post office in Isabella County was established in the William Robbins home in 1857. The village was platted in 1866. The Ann Arbor Railroad depot, above with the Estee Grain Elevator, came through west of the original settlement in 1885. Isaac N. Shepherd built an entire block of stone near the railroad, and the village of Shepherd, which encompassed Salt River, was incorporated in 1887. Today the depot, below, serves as a railroad museum, a big attraction during the Shepherd Maple Syrup Festival.

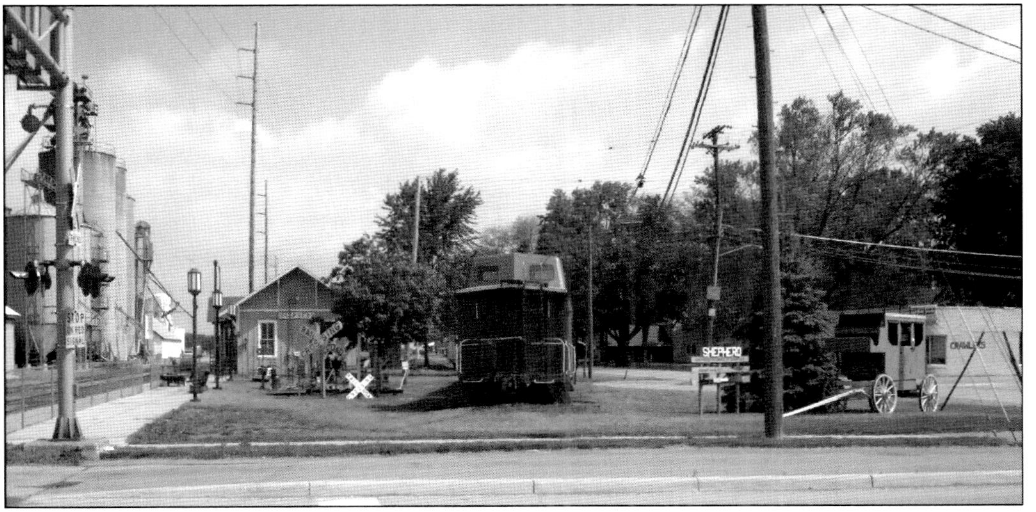

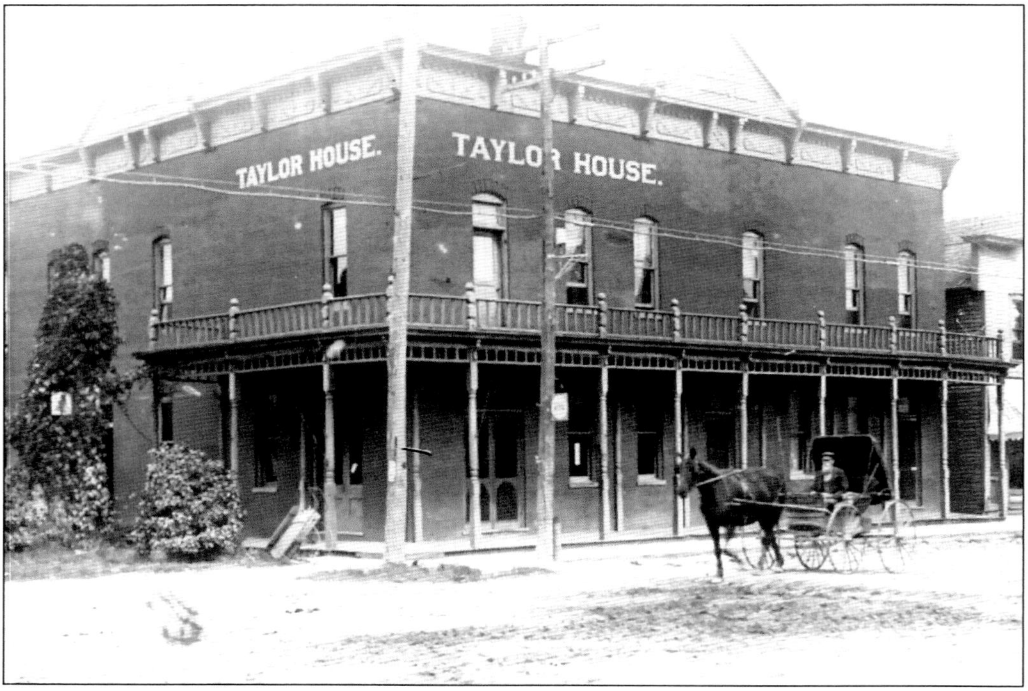

Above is a closer view of the Taylor House hotel, later known as the Calkins House. It is long gone with the improvement of transportation. The processing of sap from Shepherd's abundant maple trees became a community affair in 1958, when the community founded the Shepherd Maple Syrup Festival. The festival saw nearly the total population turn out for tapping the area's maple trees, making the syrup and sausage, operating the kitchens, and directing traffic during the festival weekend. The growing demand for maple syrup as crowds grew to the thousands attending the festival each year long ago surpassed the local trees' ability to produce enough, but the sausage-making work sessions still happen in April each year.

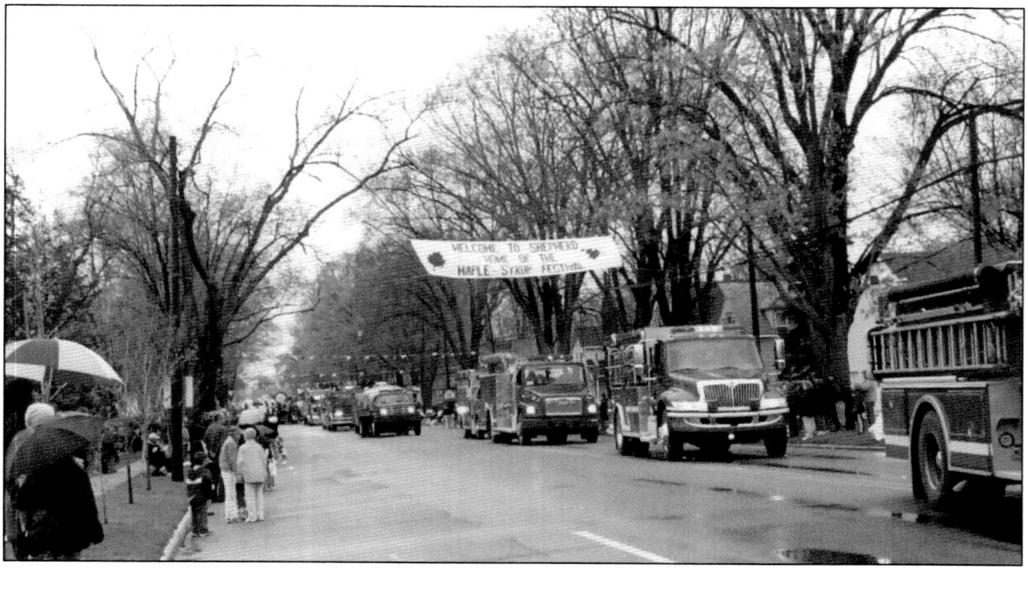

Four

Southwestern Isabella County

Southwestern Isabella County is where Doraville Whitney, among the first African American settlers in central Michigan, was awarded a land grant and became the first settler of Broomfield Township in 1860. By 1873, African Americans owned 1,392 acres in Isabella, Mecosta, and Montcalm Counties. In 1875, there were 60 Isabella County farms owned by African Americans, mostly in Broomfield and Rolland Townships. Broomfield Township was formally established in 1868 and named for pioneer settler William Broomfield, who was township supervisor until 1876.

At the southwest corner of Broomfield Township, the Ionia and Houghton Lake State Road, Michigan's first designated continuous central Michigan road across formerly federal swamplands, enters Isabella County heading northeasterly through Broomfield, Sherman, and Gilmore Townships toward Houghton Lake, then Mackinaw City. The contractor for that road, Detroit businessman Edmund Hall (see page 101), was granted several wooded sections of Broomfield Township in partial payment for building the road, since the State of Michigan was cash-strapped at the time. Hall established a lumbering operation on those granted lands and became wealthy.

Broomfield Township settlements that never incorporated and for the most part are no longer apparent as communities were Broomfield (also Broomfield Center and Coming), with a post office from 1871 to 1879, restored from 1905 to 1907; Bundy (Bondy), a sawmill with a post office from 1894 to 1897 (see page 102); Foster (Foster Siding, Mansfield), which never had a post office but was an active community until about 1905; Hall's Lake, which was named for Edmund Hall and failed to develop into a town; and Stirling, another place with no post office or railroad station, which appeared briefly on railroad maps and was gone by 1917.

Deerfield Township, set up in 1876, so named because it was a great runway for deer and the grassy plains, was a grazing favorite of native whitetail deer. Deerfield Township settlements were Boyden, begun as a post office in the farmhouse owned by the Boydens, 1892–1906, at what is now Deerfield Center; Coomer, a rural post office named for Noah H. Coomer, postmaster from 1892 to 1906; Deerfield Center, an unincorporated settlement served by a one-room school; and Two Rivers (Caldwell), off Broomfield Road at a public access to the Chippewa River and where James C. Caldwell moved from Fremont in 1882 to establish a hotel at the confluence of the Chippewa and Coldwater Rivers (see page 116).

Fremont Township was named for Union army general John C. Fremont in the passionately patriotic Civil War era when it was established in 1863. Fremont Township's only community has had two names, Winn and Dushville (see pages 117–123).

Rolland Township was organized in 1866. The origin of the township name is vague, although in a tract titled *Isabella County*, Charles F. Johnson of Grand Rapids asserts the belief that the name is somehow linked to an Ottawa Indian chief. The township was the 1867 site of one of Michigan's first integrated schools, Oberlin, during the African American settlement movement previously mentioned.

Rolland Township settlements and named places were Blanchard (see pages 107–111); Bristol, with William K. Briggs as the first and only postmaster from February 19, 1872, to November 21, 1873; Mint Mill, with a self-evident name, which never had a post office and has faded to history; Murphy, a railroad flag stop with no post office; Rand, another railroad flag stop; Remick, a railroad station along the Ionia–Big Rapids spur with a post office from 1883 to 1887; Rolland Center, which never had a railroad or a post office; Rowland, with a post office from 1868 to 1905 with William Peterson as the first postmaster and the first Rolland Township supervisor; Rowland Center (Rowland Station), which was a mile south of Blanchard, which does not appear on maps for long and is believed to be the station at Rand; and Shoards, an 1870s site of a sawmill with no permanent development or post office.

The Ionia and Houghton Lake State Road was Michigan's first designated road to be financed by the Swamp Land Act of 1859, which conveyed federal swamplands to the State of Michigan. The road ran diagonally from the southwest corner of Broomfield Township to the northeast to Gilmore Township. Edmund Hall, right, Detroit attorney and founder of Broomfield Township's defunct community of Hall's Lake, was contractor for the project, paid in state-owned lumber land by the cash-poor State of Michigan, making him enormously wealthy in the ensuing lumber-boom years. Below, late-19th-century travelers rest along the "Old State Road" just north of River Road near Rolland Road in Bundy Station.

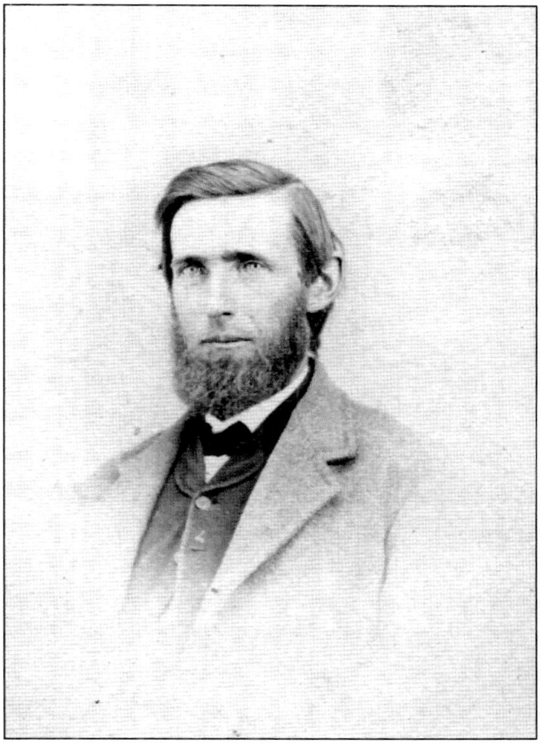

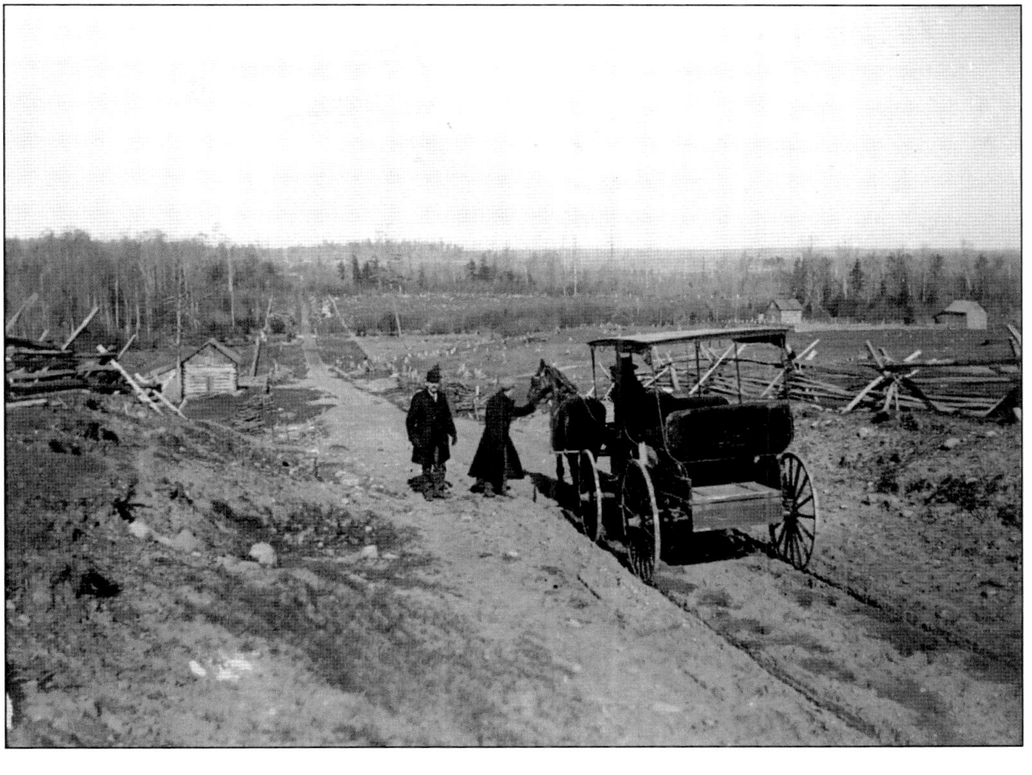

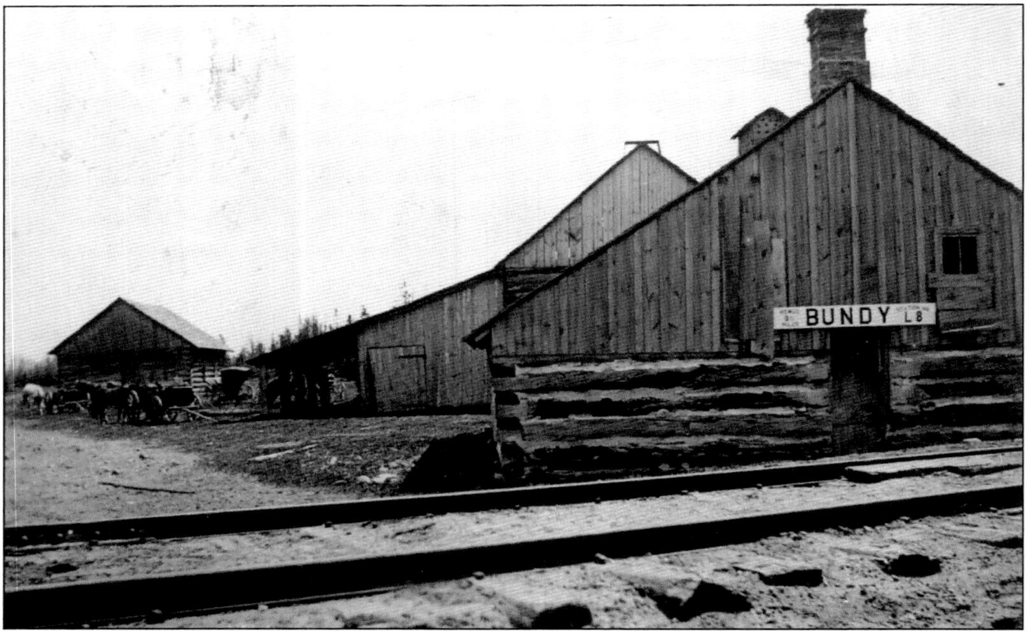

Bundy, known as Bundy Station and, erroneously Bondy, was in section 3, Broomfield Township, on a Pere Marquette spur. Bundy Corporation built a small sawmill there in 1870, above, powered by Squaw Creek. Andrew Acker was postmaster for a post office operating from August 1894 to December 1897.

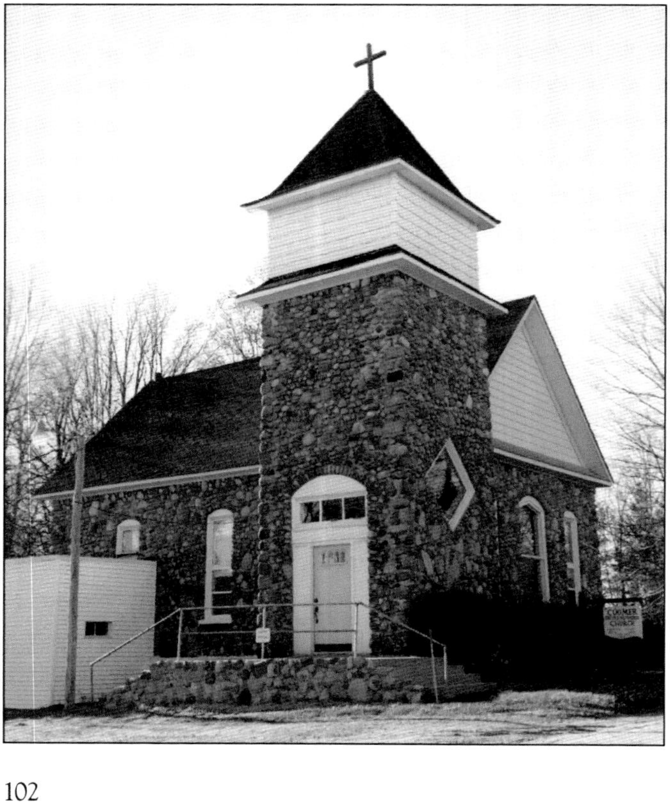

In section 34 of Deerfield Township, Coomer was named for Noah H. Coomer, postmaster from 1892 to 1906. Coomer United Methodist Church began as a frame structure in 1890. In 1908, parishioners gathered cobblestones nearby to be used for the outside of the church, which now looks much the same.

Typifying the "old settlers of Michigan" who settled in Isabella, Mecosta, and Montcalm Counties, the unidentified woman at right is symbolic of the African Americans who settled here in the 1860s from Ontario, Canada, and Ohio, after successfully escaping slavery via the Underground Railroad. The first African American settlers under the Homestead Act of 1862 went into Rolland Township that year. In 1904, 60 Isabella County farms were African American owned. Representing the continued pioneer spirit of old settlers, descendant Carol Norman, below left, is shown in 1993 with Mount Pleasant oil producer Diane Tope and a "skirt" for oil well pumping units invented by Norman.

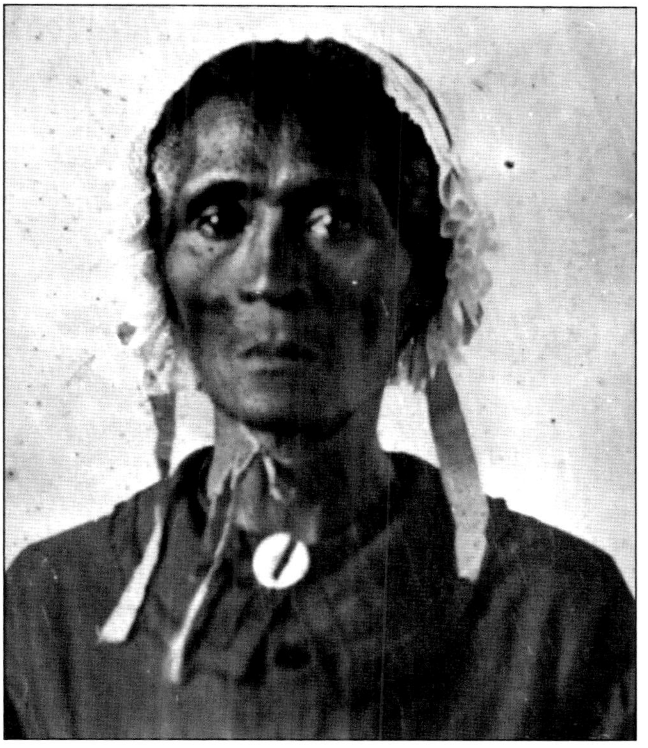

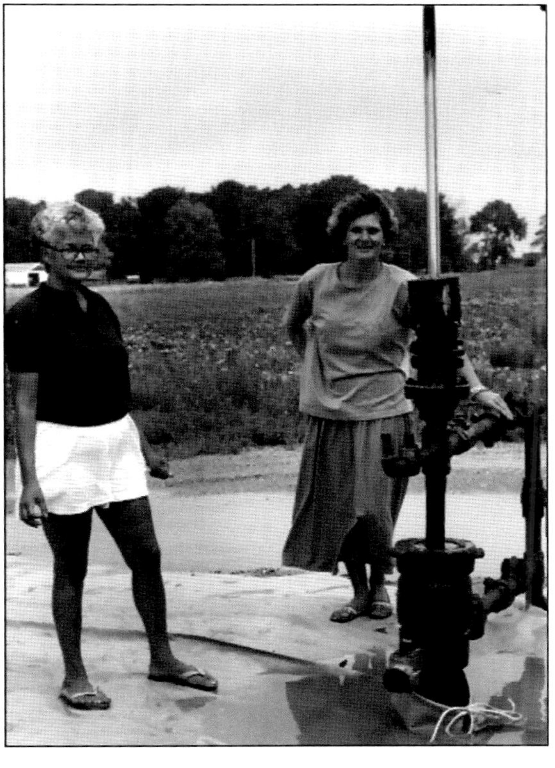

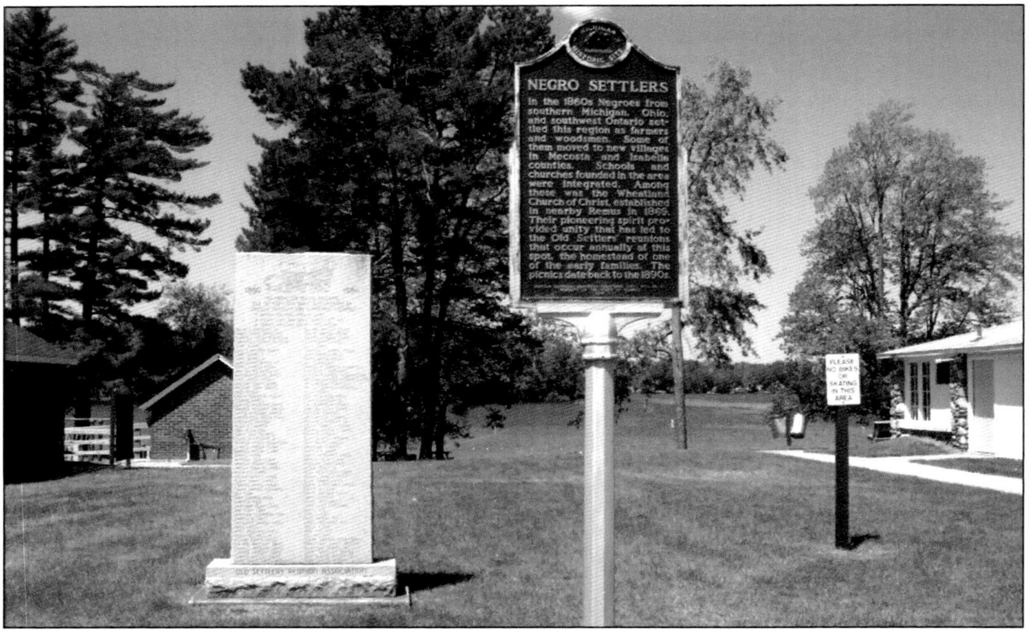

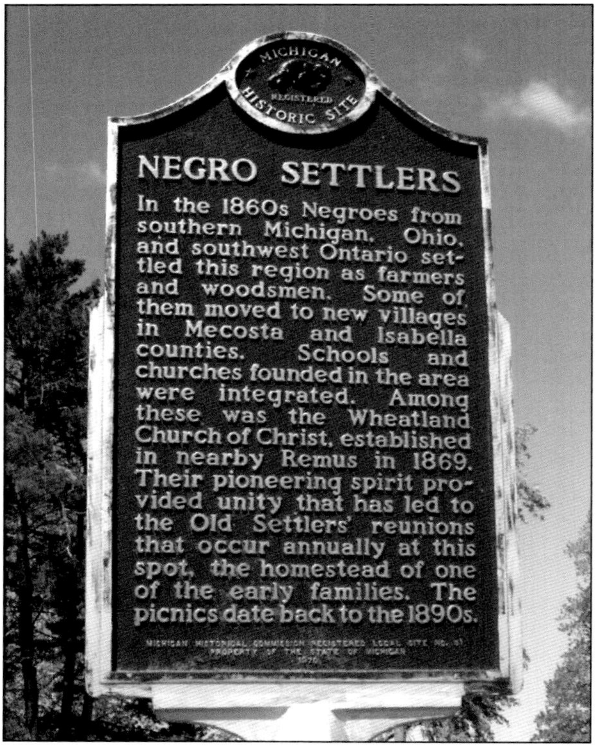

A few miles into Mecosta County from the Isabella County western border, the Old Settlers Monument commemorates the black settlers of Isabella, Montcalm, and Mecosta Counties, who once owned hundreds of acres in those counties, including most of School Section Lake, where the monument stands next to the main building of the School Section Lake County Park. The monument overlooks the beach and public area of the park and includes a stone monument erected in 1984 and engraved with the names of many of the old settler families. Beside the stone monument, the State of Michigan historical marker No. 31 tells the old settlers' story.

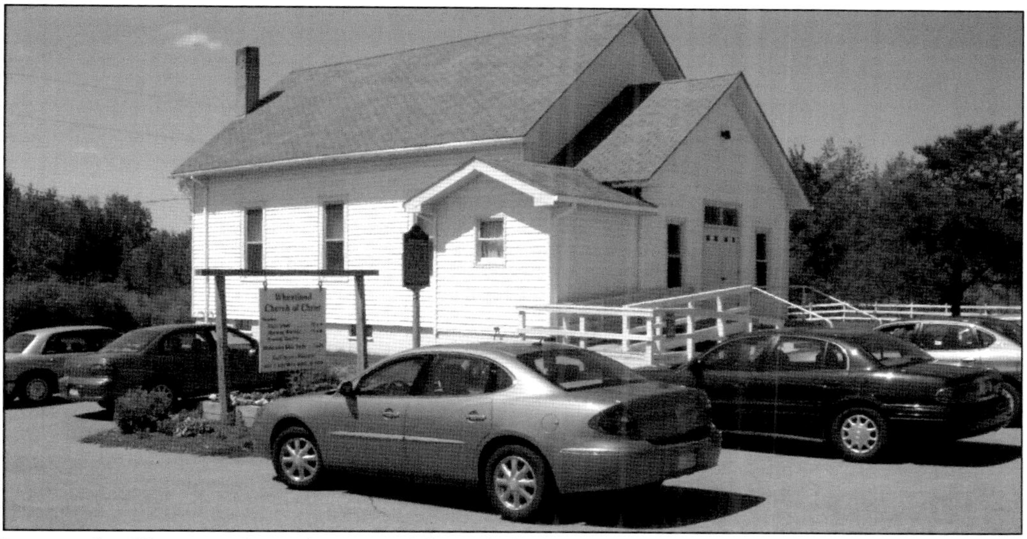

Just north of Remus, a few miles west of the Isabella/Mecosta county line, the Wheatland Church of Christ, mentioned on the Michigan historical marker on the facing page, has been in use as an independent, nondenominational organization since 1968. Old settler and first Wheatland Church elder Thomas Cross (1826–1897) donated land for the church in 1883.

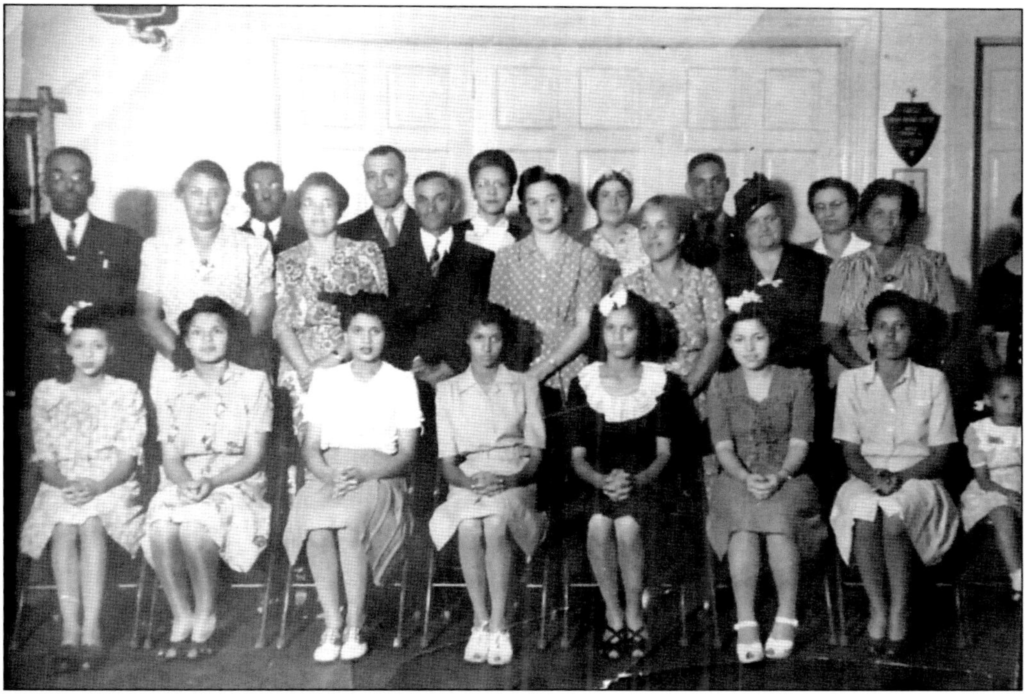

Some descendants of the old settlers of Michigan attending a 1950s reunion are, from left to right, (first row) Lorna Green, Vernice Norman, Dorothy Todd, Lucille Todd, Bernice Todd, Ione Todd, Helen Guy, and Patricia Guy; (second row) Arthur Cross, Irma Guy, Roscoe Cross, Gladys Harper, Lee Mathews, John Todd, Evelyn Cross, Alta Mathews, Fern Cross, Welthy Sawyer, Otis Guy, Lena Newman, Ida Cross, and Elizabeth Cummings.

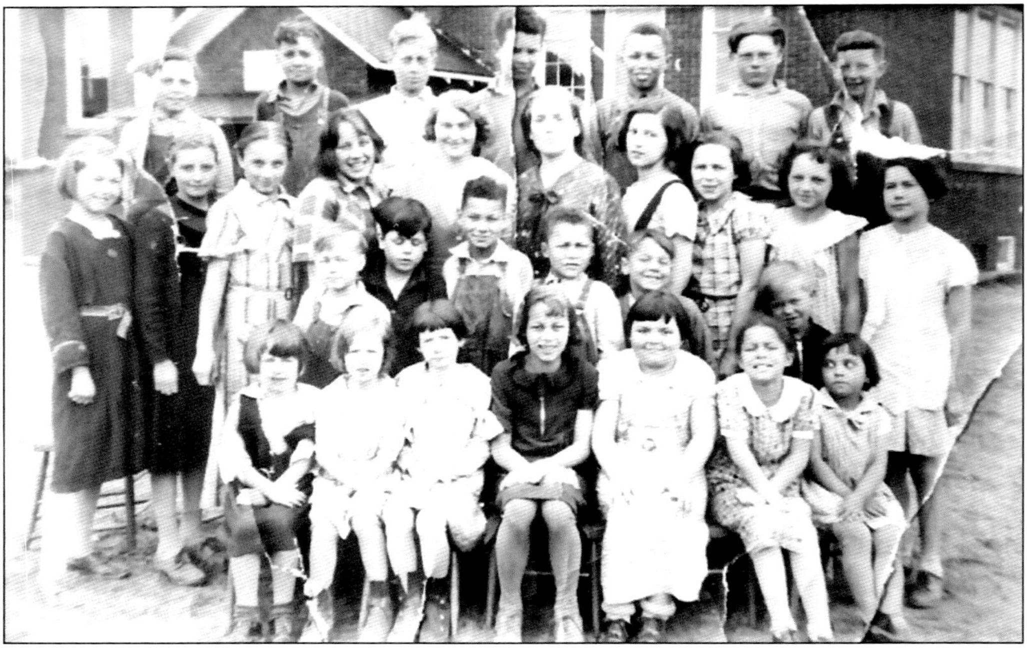

Oberlin School in Rolland Township, above, was among Michigan's first integrated schools. In 1935, Oberlin School's student body includes, from left to right, (first row) Doris Morey, unidentified, unidentified, Donna Sawyer, Lois Taylor, Ione Sawyer, and Betty Jones; (second row) Gerald Vebele, Junior Morey, Junior Norman, Max Sawyer, Dean Taylor, and Orville Hendricks; (third row) Jenny Morey, Francis Murray, Arlene Ward, Loraine Ward, teacher Velma Stout, Florence Murray, Vaneta Jones, Verna Taylor, Donna Jones, and Olga Sagoff; (fourth row) Junior Jones, Duane Norman, Robert Hendricks, another Junior Norman, Worthy Sawyer, Henry Nisonger, and Leo Torpey. Below, the trout fishing was great in southwestern Isabella County in the late 1920s for Harrison (Harry) Francisco, right, and his unidentified grandfather. Harry grew up to be a prominent Mount Pleasant portrait photographer, whose complete files can be found at Central Michigan University's Clarke Historical Library.

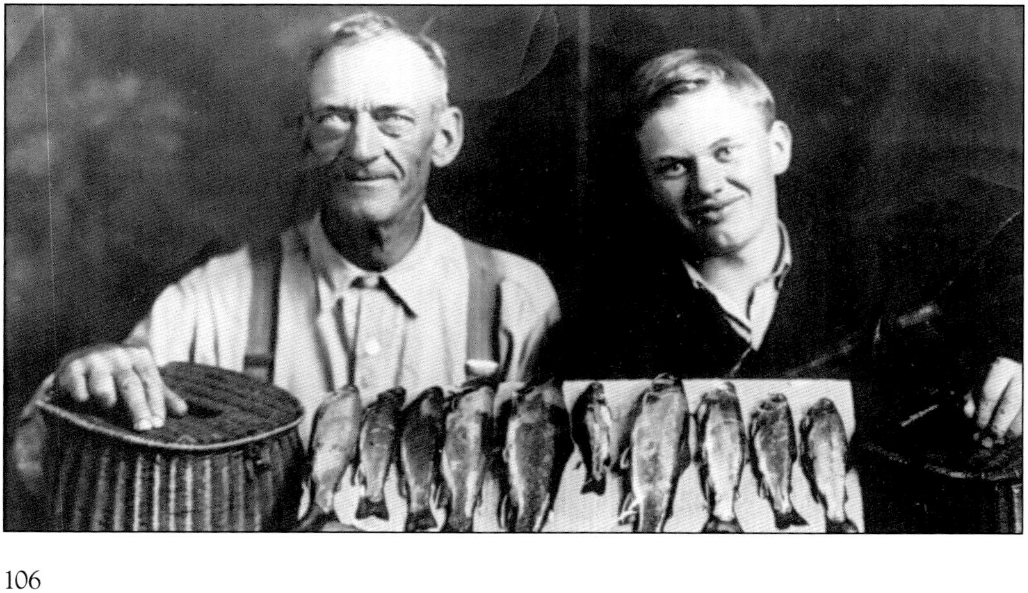

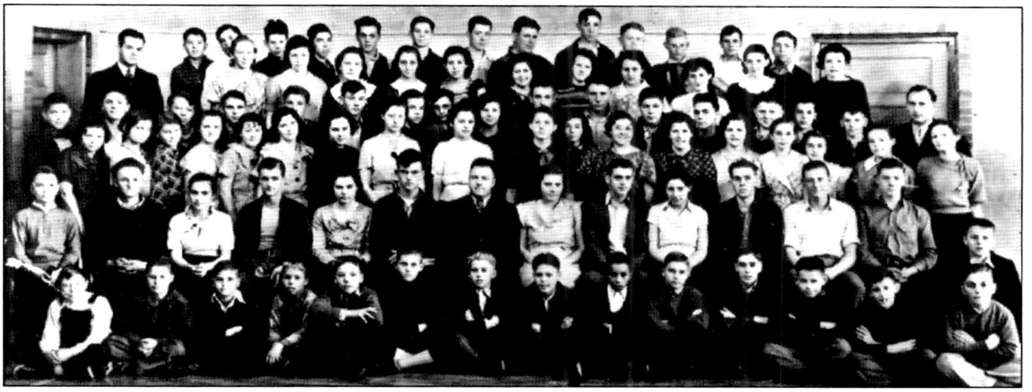

The Blanchard High School, in Rolland Township, graduating class of 1936, with some of the teachers, includes, from left to right, (first row) Ellery Scott, Jim Gibbs, Keith Hoover, Garth Houghton, Wayne Chapman, J. Yager, Hinie Snyder, Paul Corville, Lyle Sawyer, R. J. Nye, Max Robinson, Bill Booth, Jim Swan, and Menzo Chapman; (second row) Wesley Masters, Reubin Ruthruff, Norene Jefferies, Bill Dawson, Minerva Parker, Charles Foster, superintendent Fred Wireck, Ilene Curtiss, Otie McDonald, Mary Curtiss, Bernard Culp, Ray Barker, Edward Curtiss, and Peter Mason; (third row) Doris Young, Eloise Johnson, Adelia Parmalee, Vera Wiley, Leona Banks, Martha Lesky, Hazel Kimble, Leona Metz, Marie Wellhalf, Edith Smith, Grace Raymond, Mildred Morey, Winifred Reynolds, Opal Jones, Jean Jefferies, Donna Snyder, Mary Foster, and English teacher Olivia Kennedy; (fourth row) Molly Dawson, Lyle Walkington, Lawrence Neilson, Leroy Hansen, Lyle Demlow, Roger Sandbrook, Gerald Yager, Chris Fountain, Ruth Coville, Leo Chaney, Donald Sandbrook, Floyd "Junior" Coville, Jack Remmick, Rex Foster, Stan Roomsburg, Max "Pinkie" Decker, and biology teacher Anne Marsa; (fifth row) mathematics teacher Theron Bray, Rose Kimble, Elna Mae Make, Charlotte Nye, Opal Walkington, unidentified, Jewel Nyle, Patty Smith, Betty Mason, Adeline Gibbons, Margaret Robinson, and Myrtle Dewitt; (sixth row) Donald Curtiss, unidentified, Bernard Robinson, L. D. Bush, Judson Jones, Glenn Scott, Wayne Banks, Cleo Cullimore, Leo Walkington, Franklin Foster, J. C. Ray, Ed Kersey, and Stanley "Spud" Briggs.

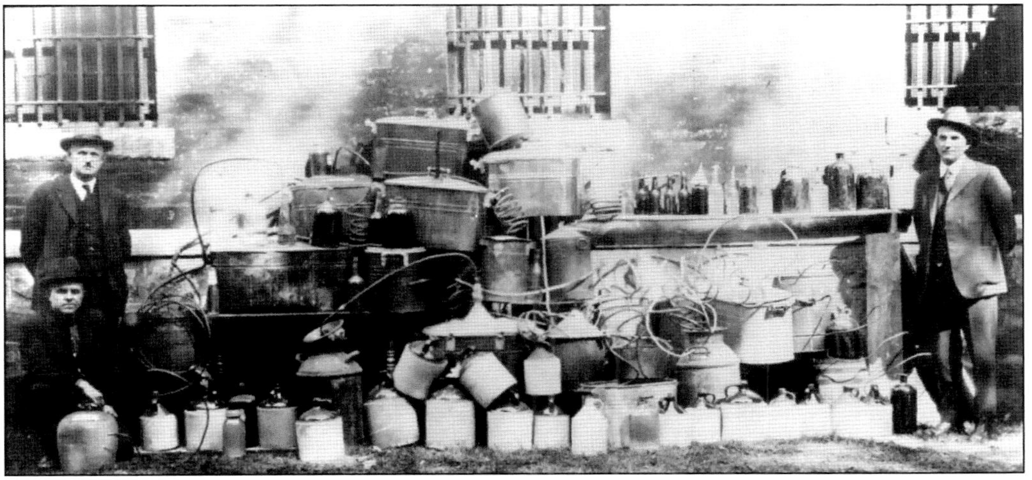

During the United States alcohol prohibition period (1920–1933), as defined by the 18th Amendment to the Constitution, local law enforcement was charged with confiscating and destroying paraphernalia for making alcohol. Isabella County sheriff Palmer Landon, standing at left, and deputies pose with boilers, jugs, and moonshine stills seized during a 1920s raid.

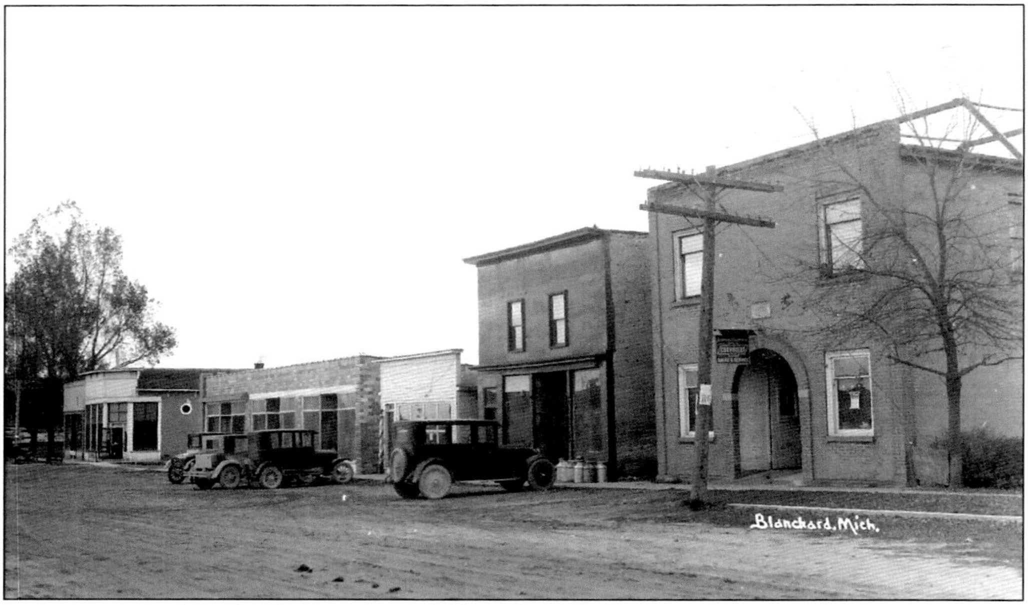

In section 16 of Rolland Township, Phillip Blanchard bought an existing sawmill in 1876, and his P. G. Blanchard mill brought many to the area, prompting him to plat the village of Blanchard in 1879. In 1880, Blanchard sold more than 1,800 acres of timberland and his business to his sons and left the community. The community grew and was rebuilt after an 1884 fire. By 1891, there was no trace of the Blanchard family or its business in the area. For many years, the Dewitt Lumber Company on the millpond was the primary Blanchard business. In modern times, Blanchard is a shopping attraction, pioneered in the 1970s by Loafer's Glory, with several old buildings converted to vintage housewares, sundries, antiques, and dining establishments.

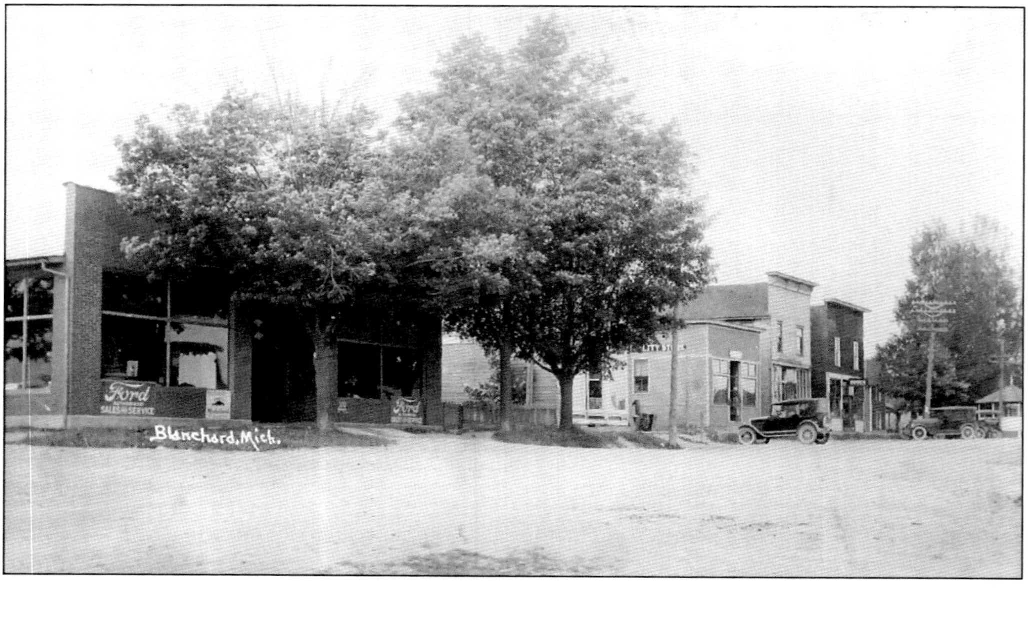

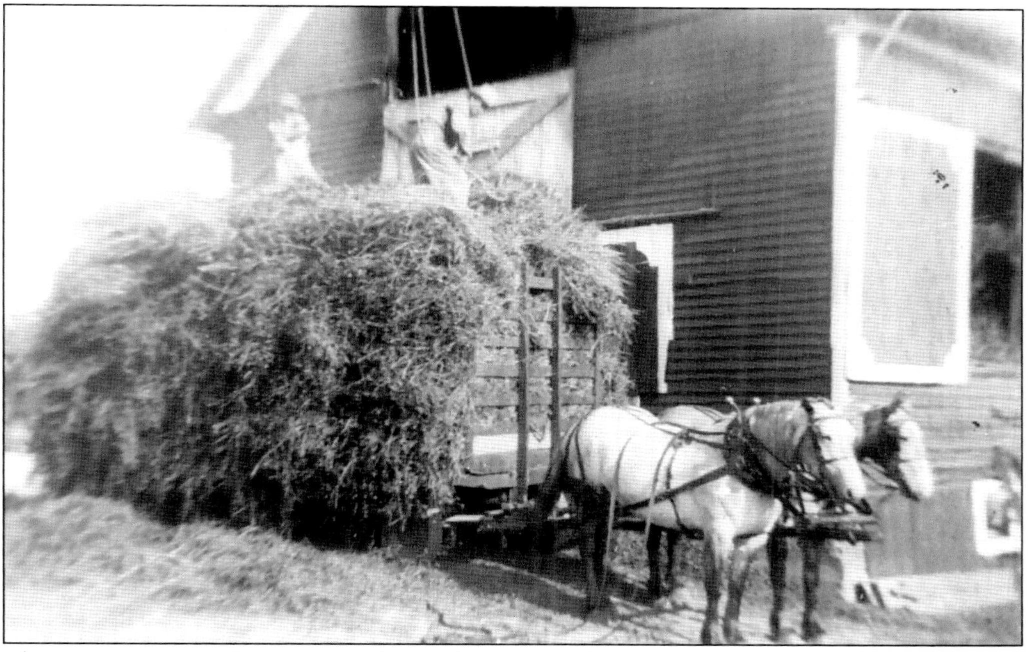

The transition from horse to mechanized power for farm harvesting and hauling equipment is illustrated by the two views, a few years apart, taken on the Peter Gruss farm in Deerfield Township. Above, Joseph and Peter Gruss prepare to load hay into the barn from a horse-drawn wagon. A few years later, Peter, below left, and a larger farm harvest crew prepare to return to the field for more hay after adding to the huge stack, recently transported to the site with greater ease by a wagon drawn by a steam-powered tractor. More information about the Gruss farm appears on page 125.

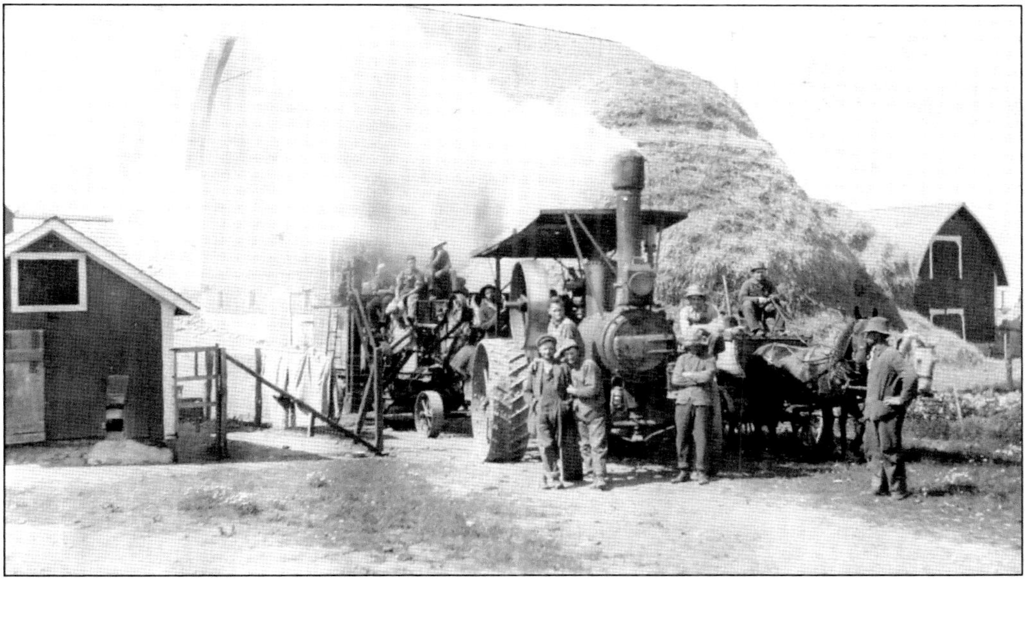

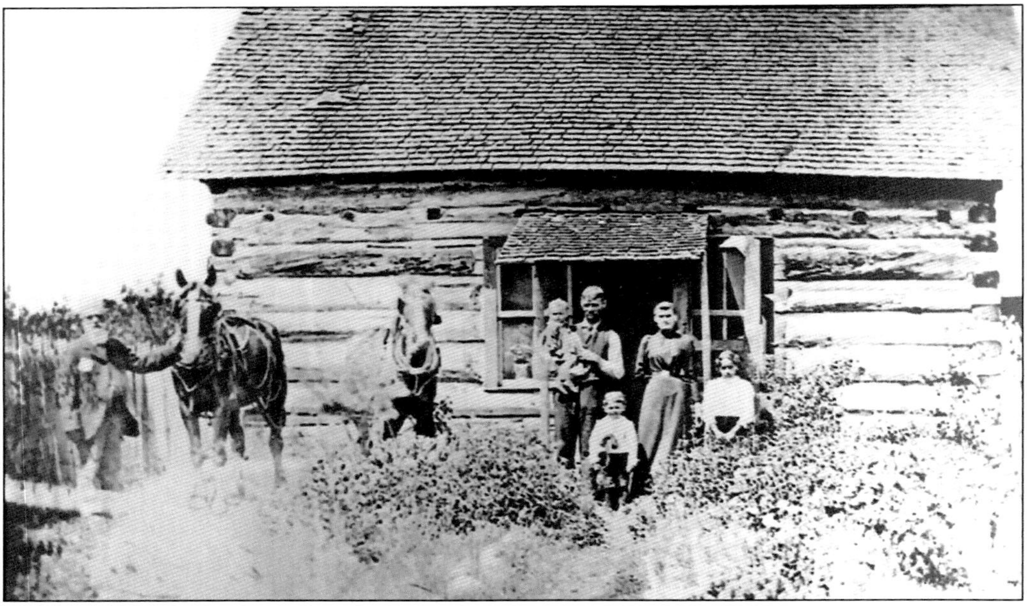

A mini pictorial essay of a typical Isabella County farm begins with the original house on the 40-acre farm of Thomas and Margaret Sandbrook, bought for $750 in September 1895, at 4423 West Fremont Road, Blanchard, above. The house serves as a background for, from left to right, an unidentified horse team driver, Thomas Sandbrook (holding son Wilfred), Willis Sandbrook, Margaret Sandbrook (pregnant with George), and relative Mary Buck.

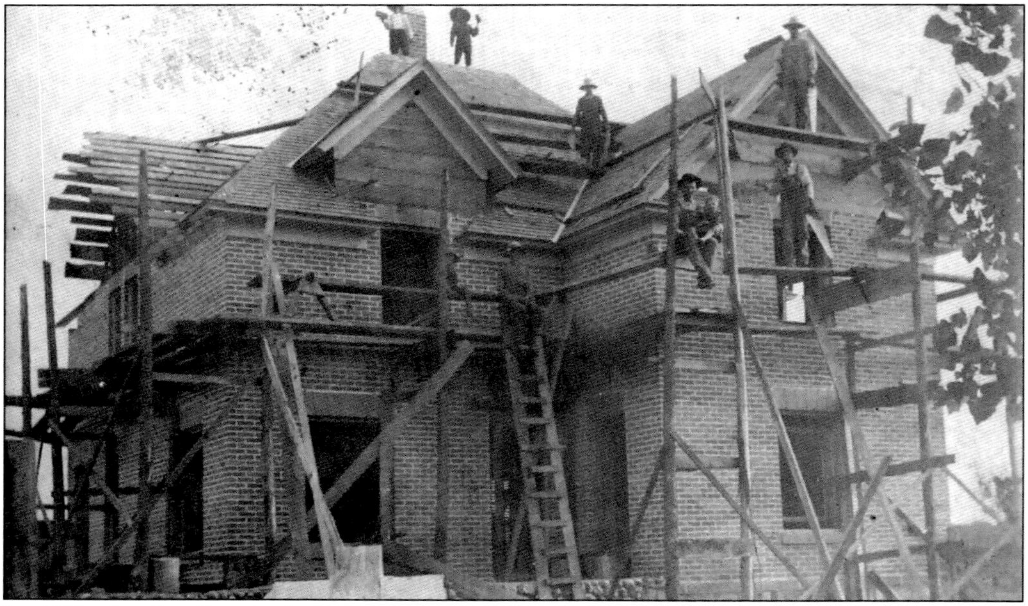

In 1910, the Sandbrooks built a new brick house for a total bricklaying cost of $300. Seen from left to right are Willis Sandbrook (by the chimney), Harry Sandbrook (at the window), Wilfred Sandbrook, Margaret Sandbrook (at the top of the ladder), George Sandbrook, Thomas Sandbrook (at the top of the second ladder holding Ralph Sandbrook), Loren Morey (at the top of the scaffold), and Dewey Lint (at the bottom of the scaffold).

Builders Dewey Lint, left, and Loren Morey work on the cupboard of the new 1910 Sandbrook farmhouse. The cupboards were state of the art for the time, featuring bird's-eye maple (the same as most of the woodwork in the house) and hand-chiseled smoothed-glass panels. Below, Richard Sandbrook (grandson of Thomas and Margaret) and his wife Lois are seen in 1995 with the Michigan Centennial Farm sign at the Sandbrook farm, verifying the ownership by the same family for more than 100 years. (Courtesy of Richard and Lois Sandbrook.)

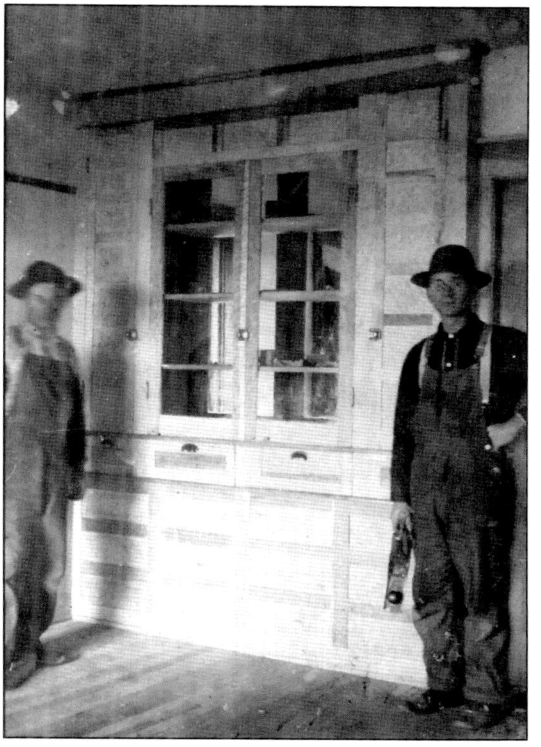

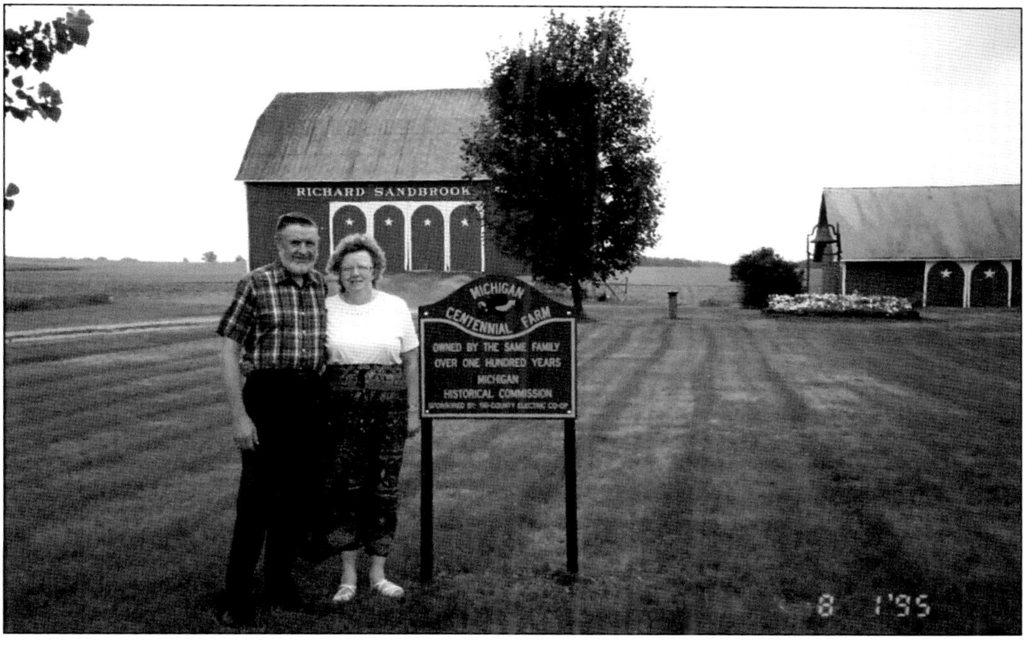

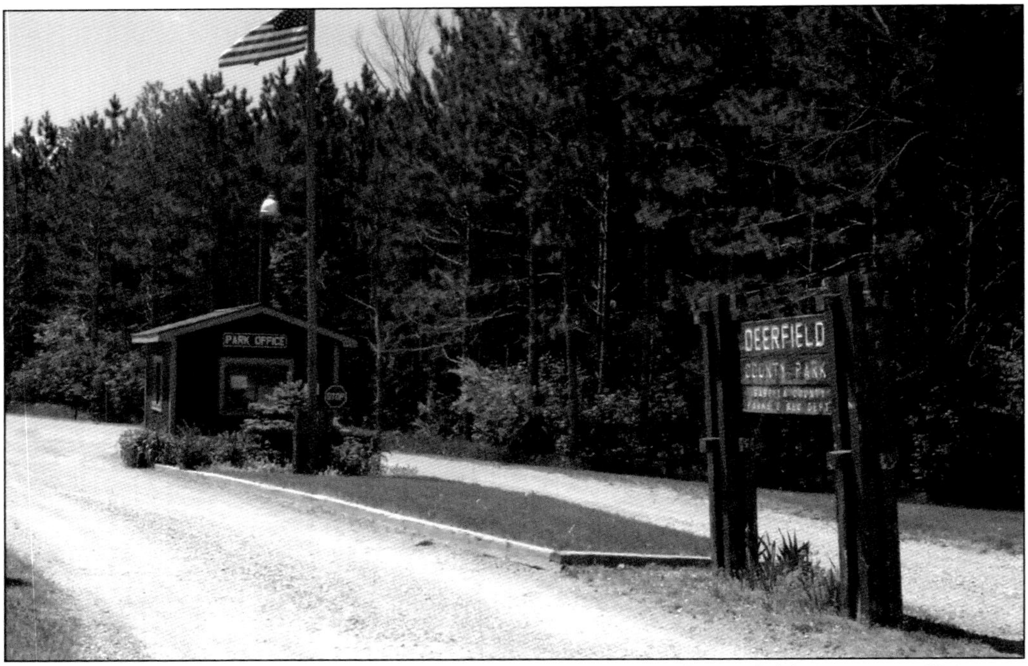

The Deerfield Nature Park on Michigan 20, one mile east of Deerfield Center, is 591 acres with eight miles of hiking and snowmobile trails, two swinging bridges, and the Fisher Covered Bridge. The original covered bridge was destroyed by fire in 1995 and rebuilt as part of a major park improvement in 1996. The park has 10 rustic campsites, two canoe landings, picnic areas, pavilions, and fishing.

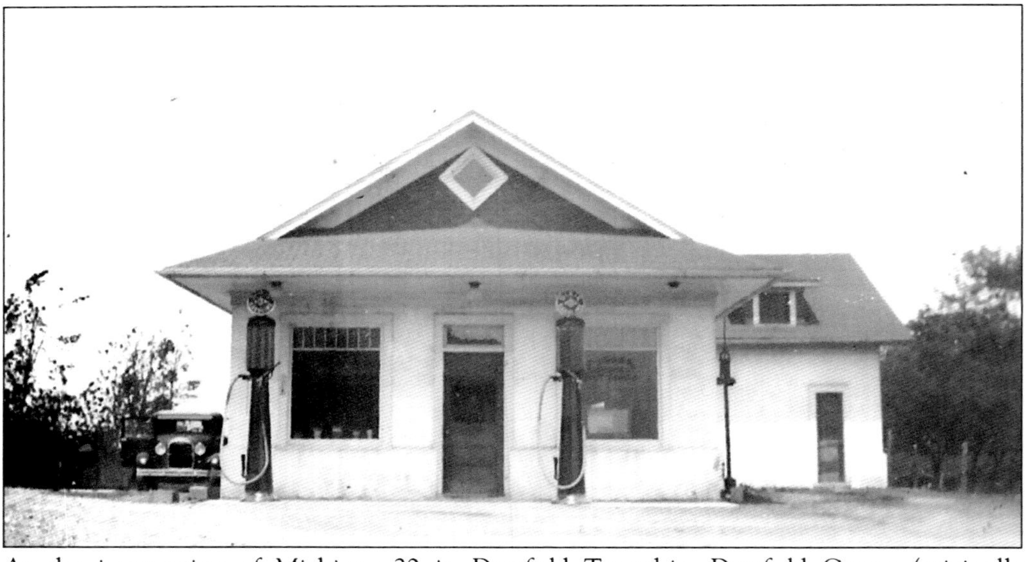

At the intersection of Michigan 20 in Deerfield Township, Deerfield Center (originally named Boyden) was never incorporated but is a busy center. Here is the Deerfield Party Store, the Deerfield Township Fire Department, and, above, the store that served for years on the northwest corner. Once owned by Gerald Rau, the building was expanded many times before being abandoned for a larger store and gasoline station across the road in the early 2000s.

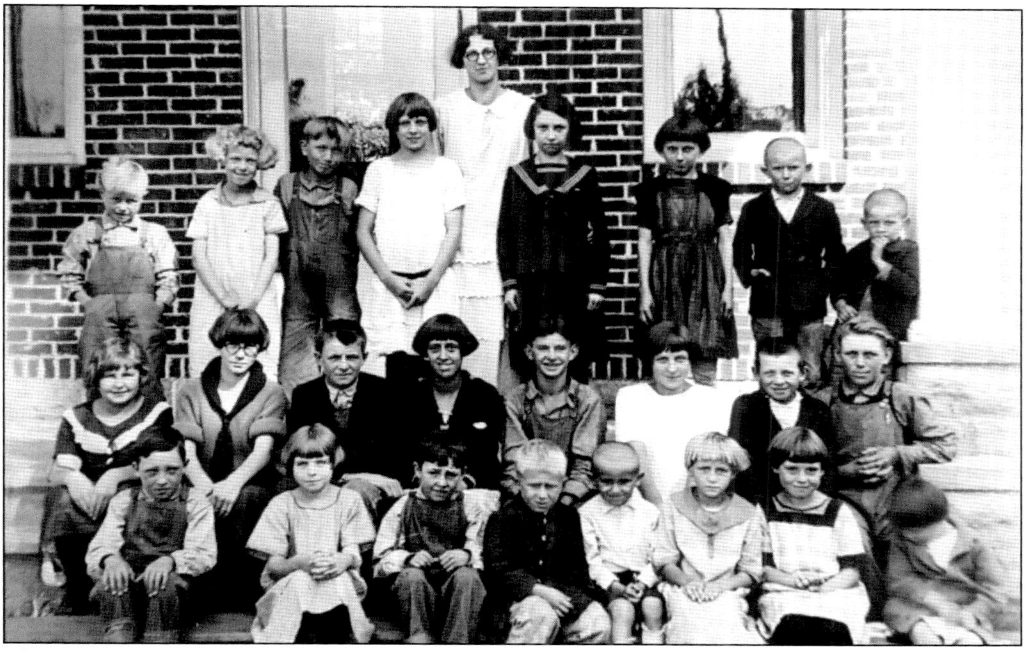

The original Deerfield Center School was a wooden structure built in 1883, and a school served at that location for the next 40 years. The 1924 school body includes, from left to right, (first row) Joe Purtill, Pearlie Campbell, Charlie Purtill, three unidentified students, Florence Russell, and Dollie Coleman; (second row) Neville Young, Reva Campbell, unidentified, Violet Russell, Leslie Adams, Geraldine Jewell, unidentified, and Orlando Bowers; (third row) unidentified, Ruth Dedie, Elton Bowers, Luella Jewell, teacher Margurite Stutting, Francis Purtill, and three unidentified children. In about 1923, the wooden school was replaced by a brick structure that served as a school for another 20 years before being abandoned to private enterprise, below.

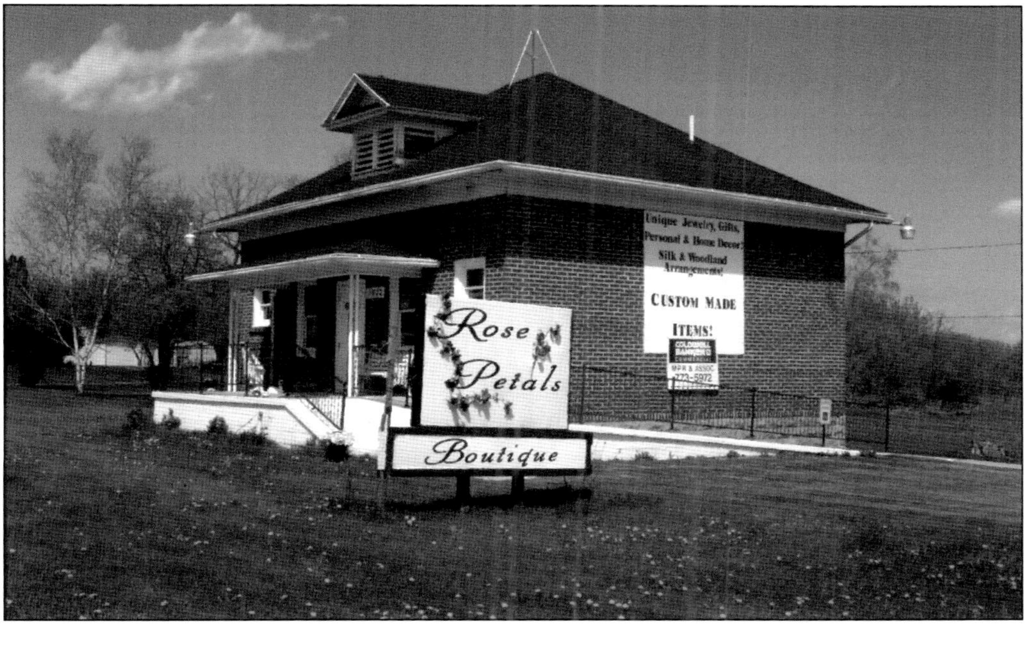

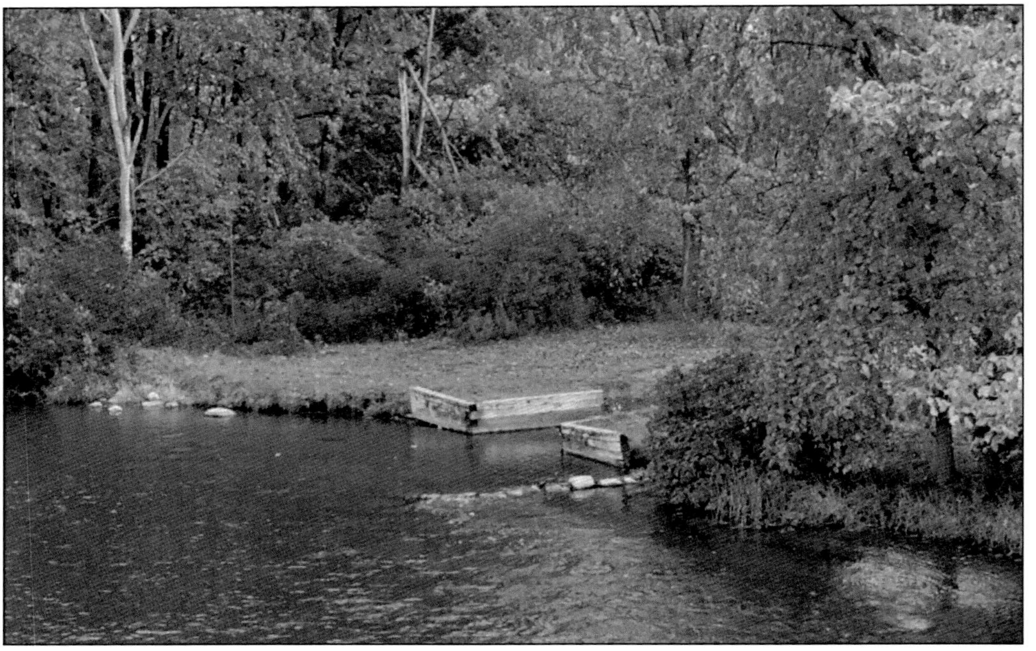

Mount Pleasant petroleum geologist Earl Majeske and his wife Rebecca gave two acres on the Chippewa River, just downstream from Hubscher's gravel pit in section 20 of Deerfield Township, to the county for park use as a canoe landing. The canoe landing comes as a welcome respite for those coming by river from the canoe livery on Michigan 20 headed for Mount Pleasant and other downstream points, since it is just downstream from the Hubscher gravel pit, which must be navigated by river travelers. In 1987, Paul and Grace Hubscher gave the county 100 feet of land just east of Majeske Landing along Broomfield Road, which accommodates a landing access to the road.

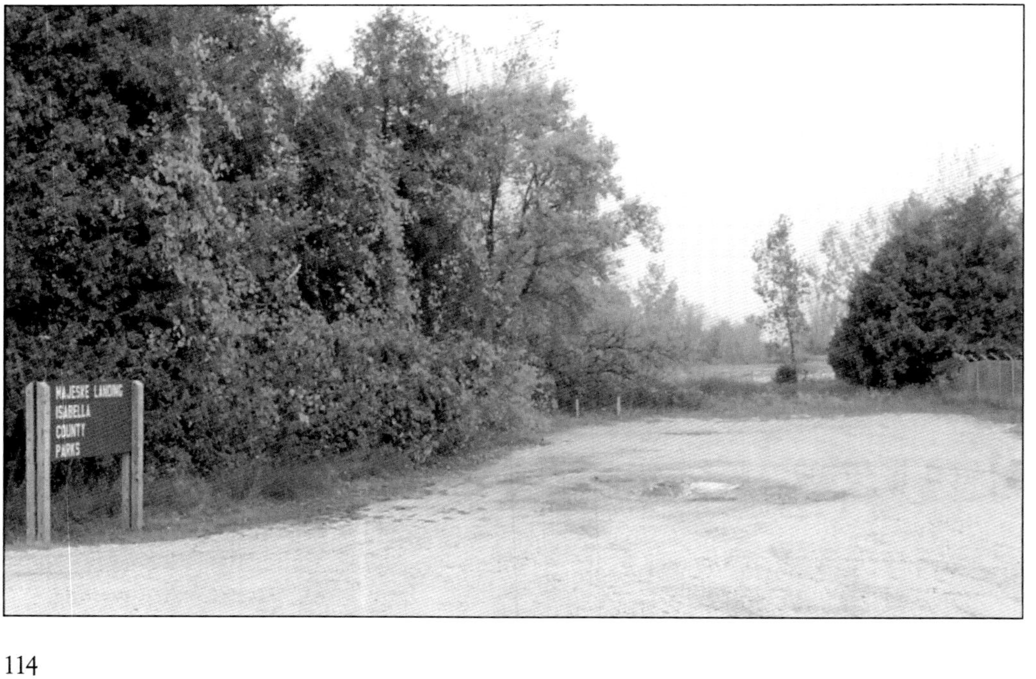

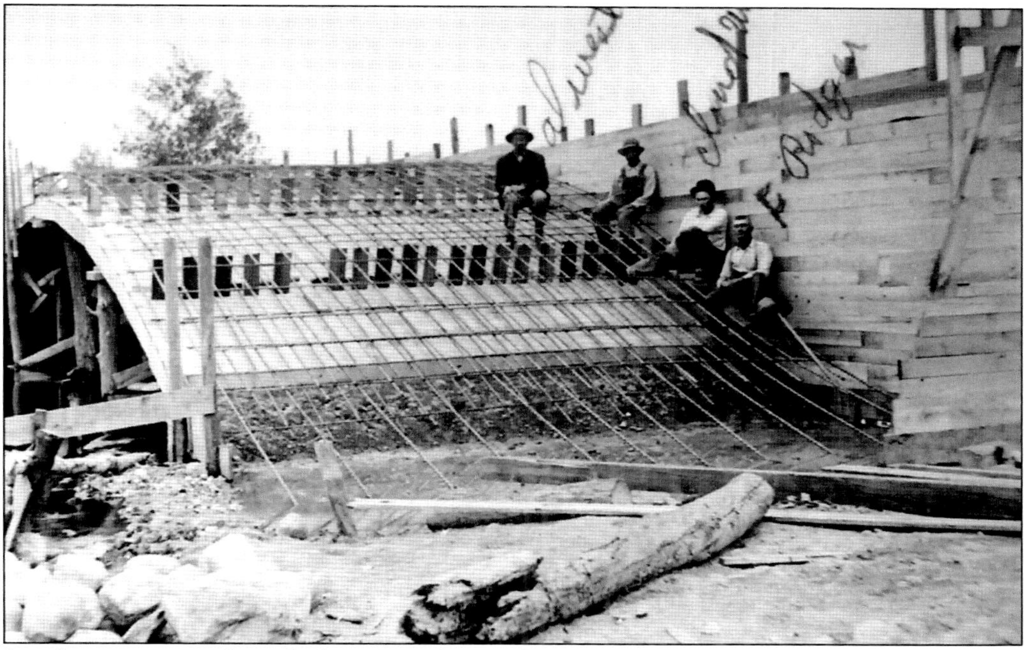

Just downstream and overlooking Majeske Landing, a new 1990s bridge across the Chippewa River on Broomfield Road replaced a "hump back" bridge, built in 1910 by workers, above from left to right, Al West, unidentified, Claude West, and Fred Rogers. Ornate cast concrete guardrails adorned the old Broomfield Road bridge, with the middle of the bridge higher than either approach, which saw heavy use before replacement with a more modern structure. Construction of the modern bridge in the 1990s disrupted not only road but also river traffic and fishing in the pool just below the bridge, well known to local fisherman, including the author, as prime smallmouth bass territory.

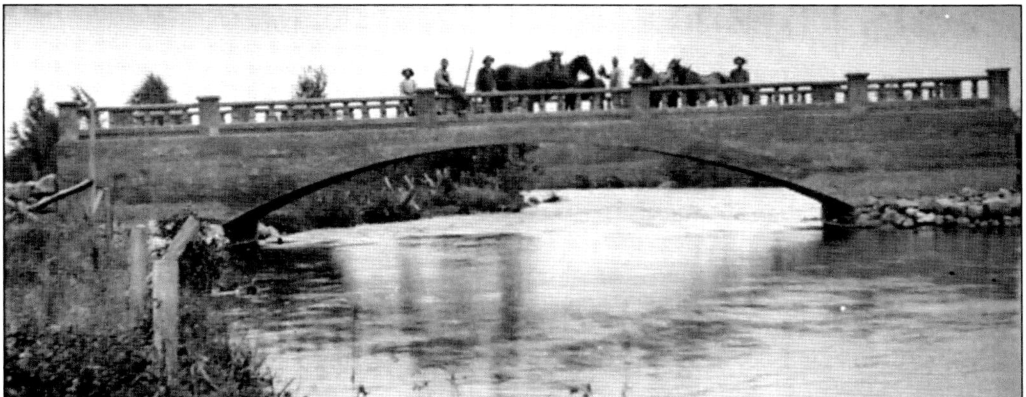

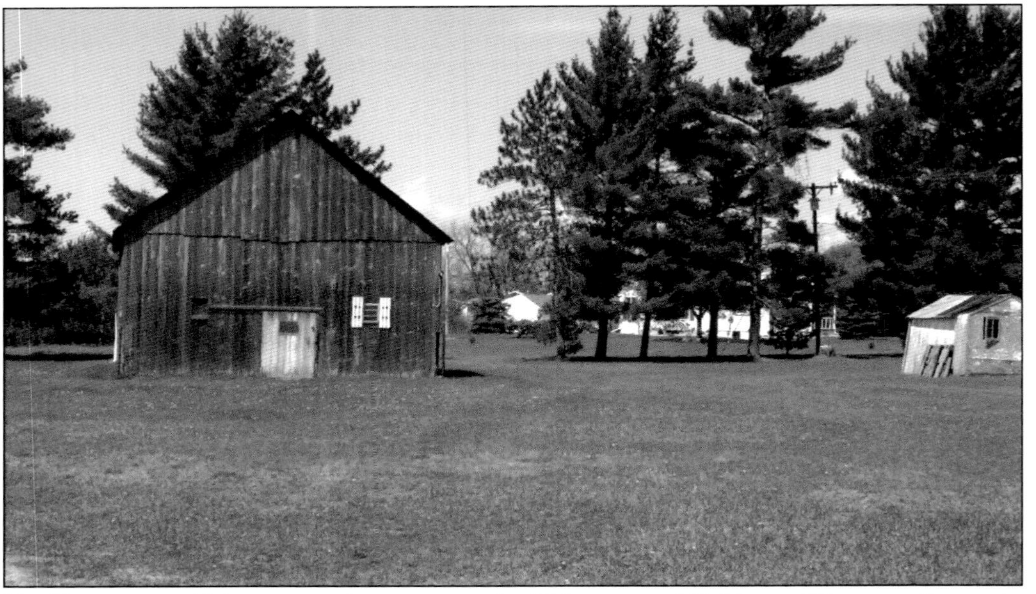

Two Rivers was a 19th-century play spot near the Chippewa and Coldwater Rivers confluence in Deerfield Township. In 1884, the settlement was originally called Caldwell after J. C. Caldwell, owner of the first hotel, which was later the home of S. C. Smiley, who ran a store there. A newer hotel was built by Will Richardson just east of the Smiley's store. Transportation and roads improved, offering wider resort venues, leading to the hotel and the community's decline to today's cluster of residences. Only a rickety barn, above, appears to remain in modern Two Rivers, a thriving residential area where at least three homes display a hanging iron pot with bell on top, below, in a unique apparent tribute to the area's past.

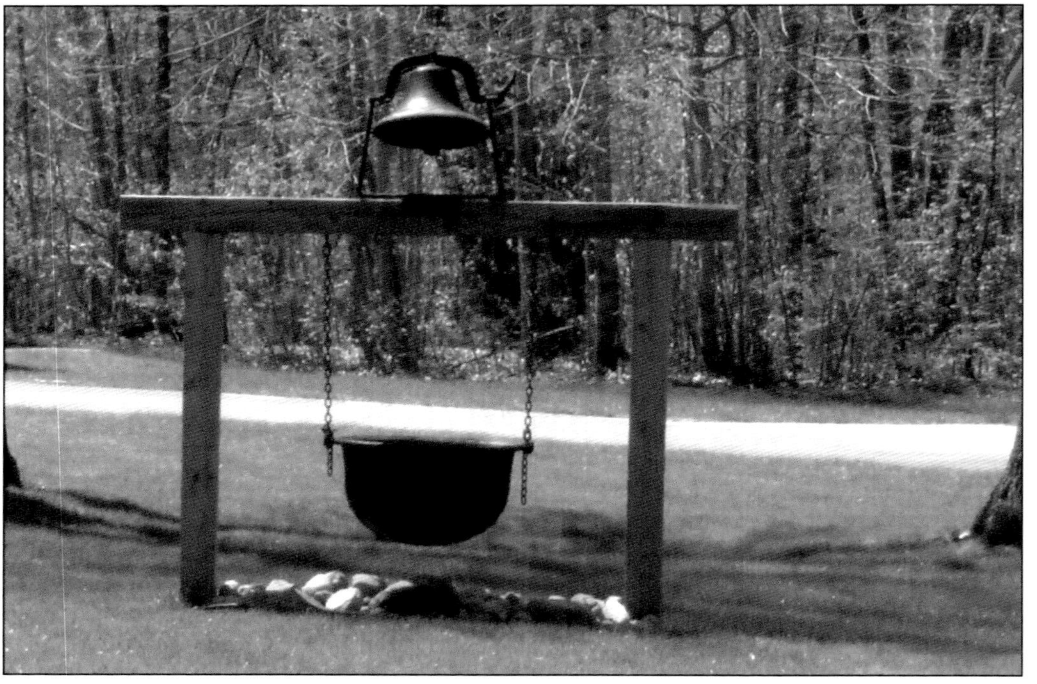

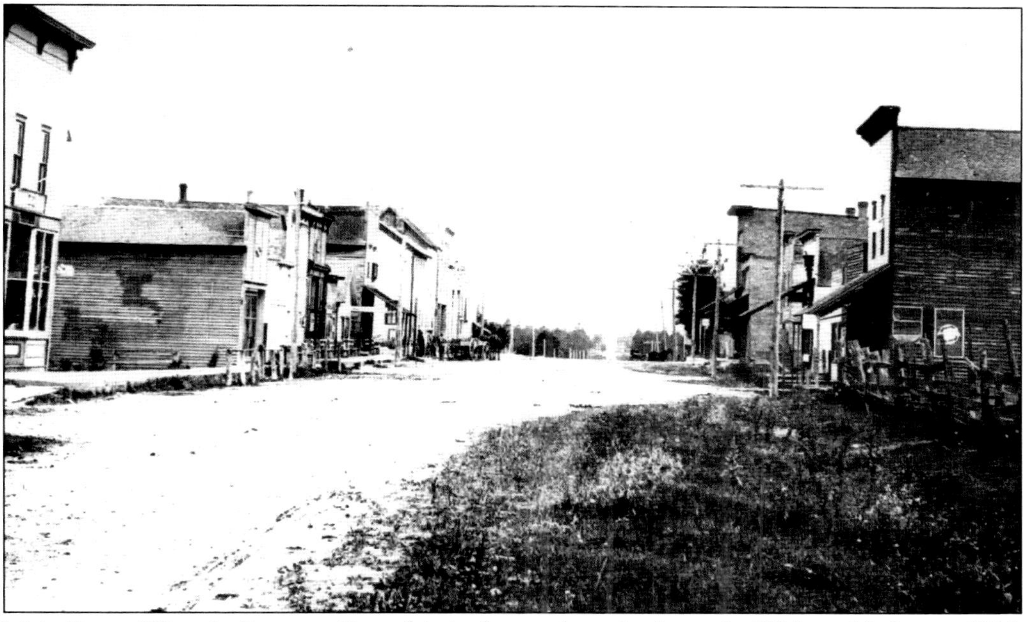

Main Street Winn in Fremont Township is shown above in the early 1900s and below in 1936. The saga of the community's identity switch from Winn to Dushville and back to Winn is an odd tale. Originally an 1867 post office at the corner of Blanchard and Vandecar Roads was named Winn in honor of a pioneer's childhood home, Wynn, England. In 1878, the post office was moved a mile to the west, to the village platted by William Dush, and renamed Dushville. Following Dush's tragic death while cutting ice from nearby Woodruff Lake, the name was changed back to Winn in 1898.

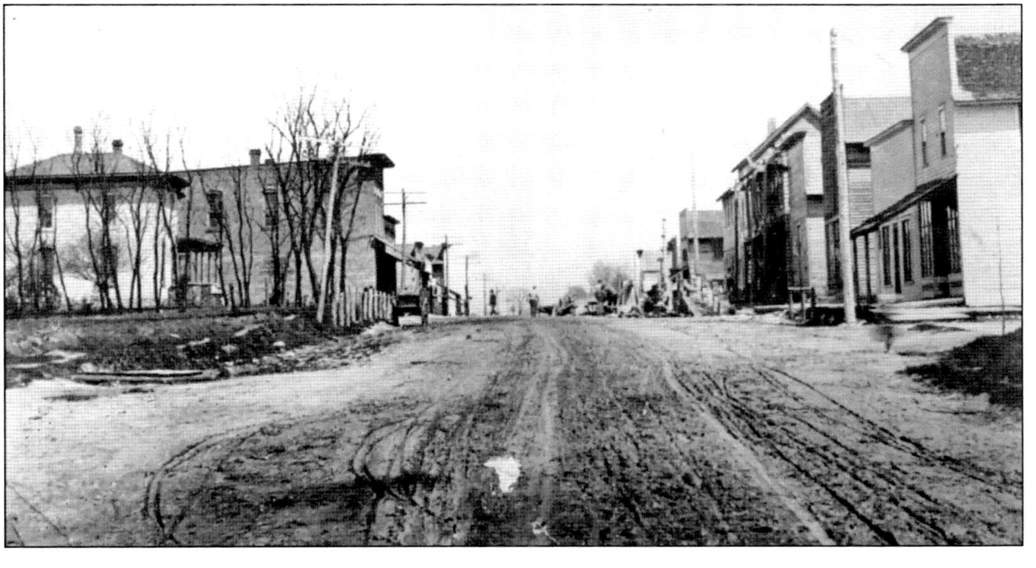

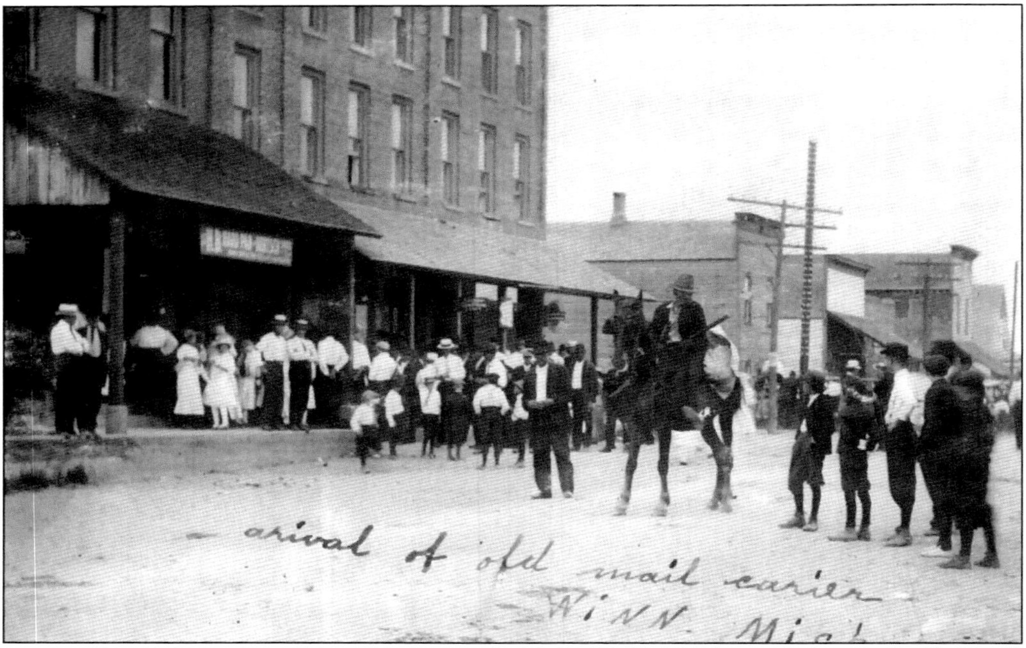

The Winn 50th anniversary celebration in 1917 featured a re-creation, above in front of Starkweather's store on Main Street, of the weekly arrival of the mail courier. The mail carrier rode from Stanton in Montcalm County northeast to Mount Pleasant in Union Township, Isabella County, leaving Winn-area mail in a wood box nailed to a tree a mile west of Winn. Below, Jode Sanderson makes a stop with the Starkweather Grocery egg wagon on his route throughout the Dushville/Winn area buying eggs and selling merchandise.

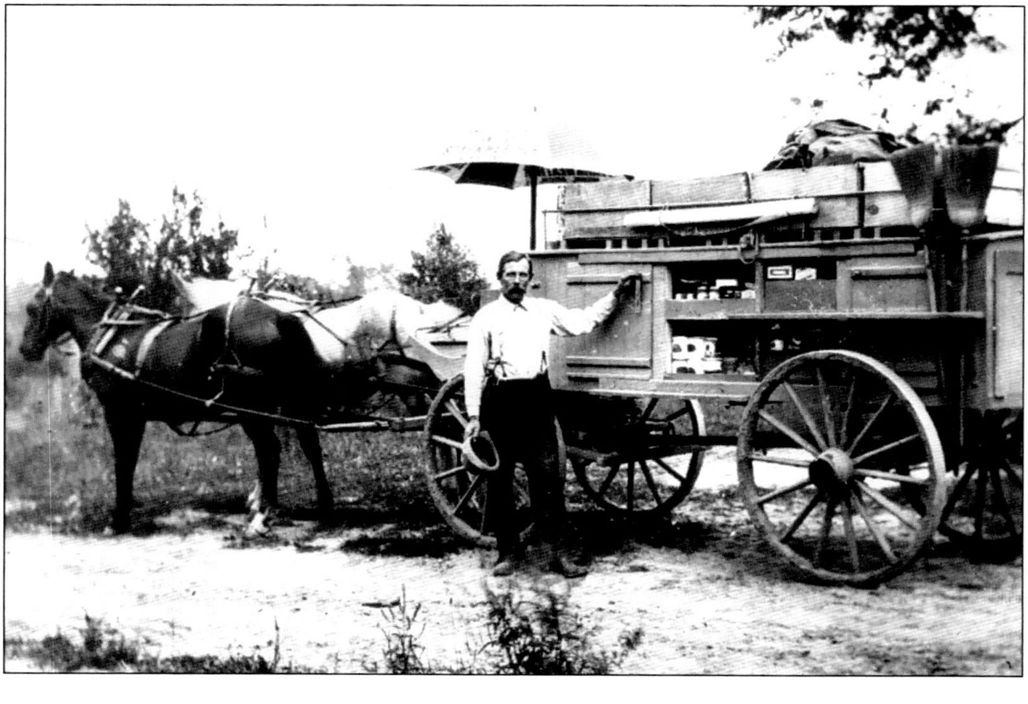

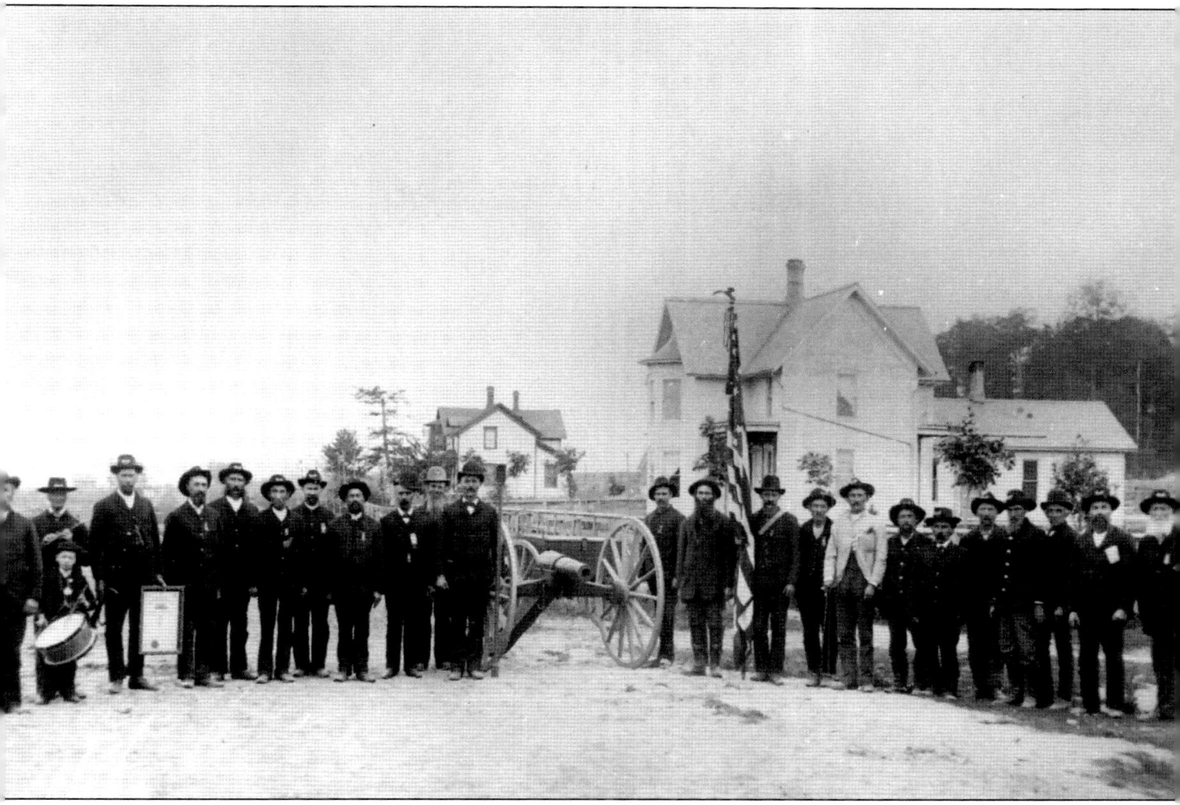

On May 30, 1895, members of Herald Post No. 253, Department of Michigan GAR, pose on Main Street in Dushville (Winn), Fremont Township. From left to right are Berdett Caldwell, an unidentified drummer boy, Theodore Victory, Rev. Edwin R. Coburn, Lewis Priest, Warren Wind, Louis Schroder, George Osborn, Chris Reen, Dr. Mark H. Hillyard, Charlie Delo, Vet Johnson, Harry Brayton, Steve Smith, George Layman, Levi Little, George Doughty, Marshall Batchelder, Theodore Beuch, Elzy E. Dush, Jobe Priest, Thomas Williamson, George W. Foglesong, and George Cullimore.

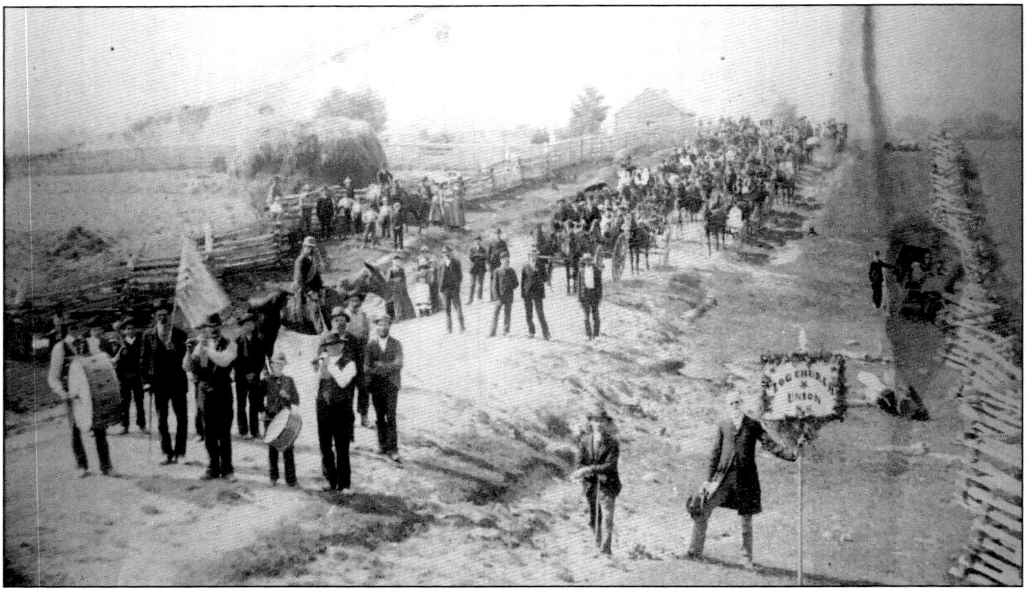

The old log union church just west of Dushville (now Winn) was the scene of a Fremont Township pioneers picnic on Saturday, September 26, 1891, with families tracing their presence in the township to its 1863 formation in attendance, as well as a missionary from Greenville who said he was a missionary in Isabella County in 1866 and therefore had a right to be there. Herb Chapman was there with his camera and lined attendees up in front of the church, below, then went across the ravine to take a picture of the group organized into an impromptu parade, above.

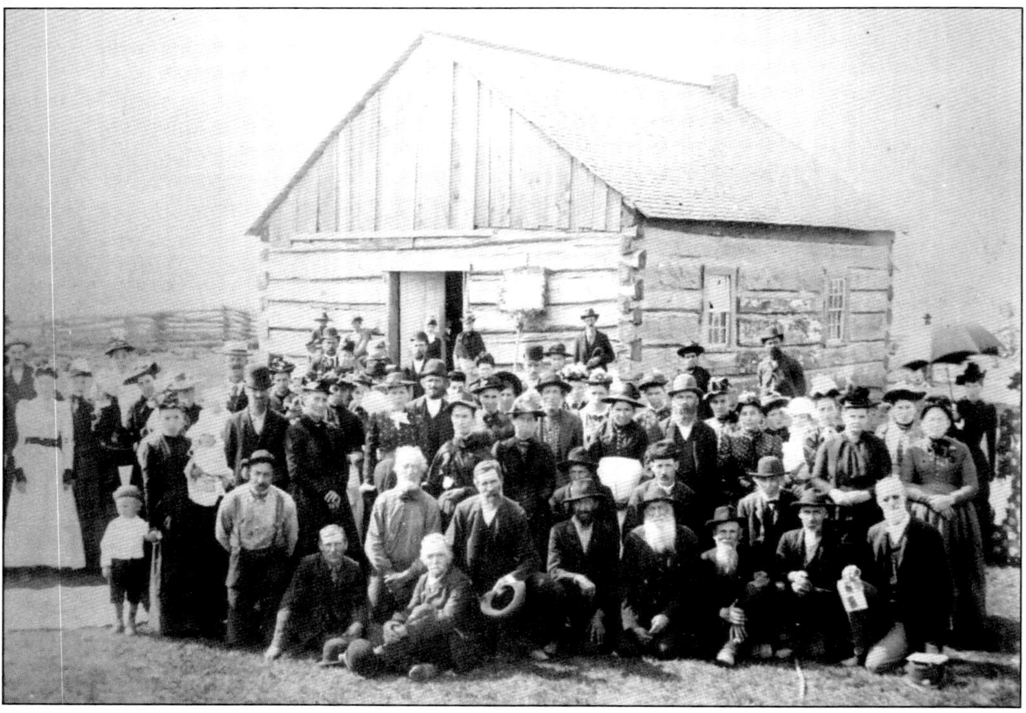

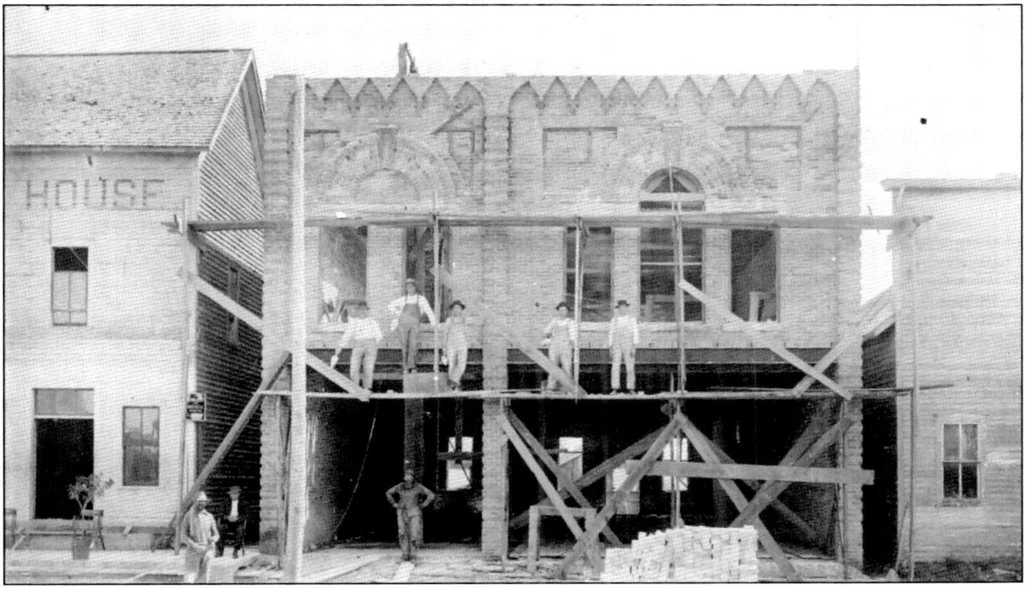

The Cedar Valley Masonic Lodge No. 23 of Dushville (Winn) was officially organized on August 14, 1886. After meeting in a number of buildings in town until the fall of 1907, the decision was reached to build a new building. Lumber was secured from near Campau Lake, inside brick from Mount Pleasant, outside brick from Sebewing, and construction began, above. The new temple was dedicated on December 17, 1908. Posing in front of the new temple are Masons, from left to right below, James Maxwell, David K. Moore, Dr. Allen Keen, John W. Curtiss, John Starkweather, Mark Abbott, Charles Curtiss, and Tom Lowe. The building still stands, now an antique shop owned by Wayne Barrett.

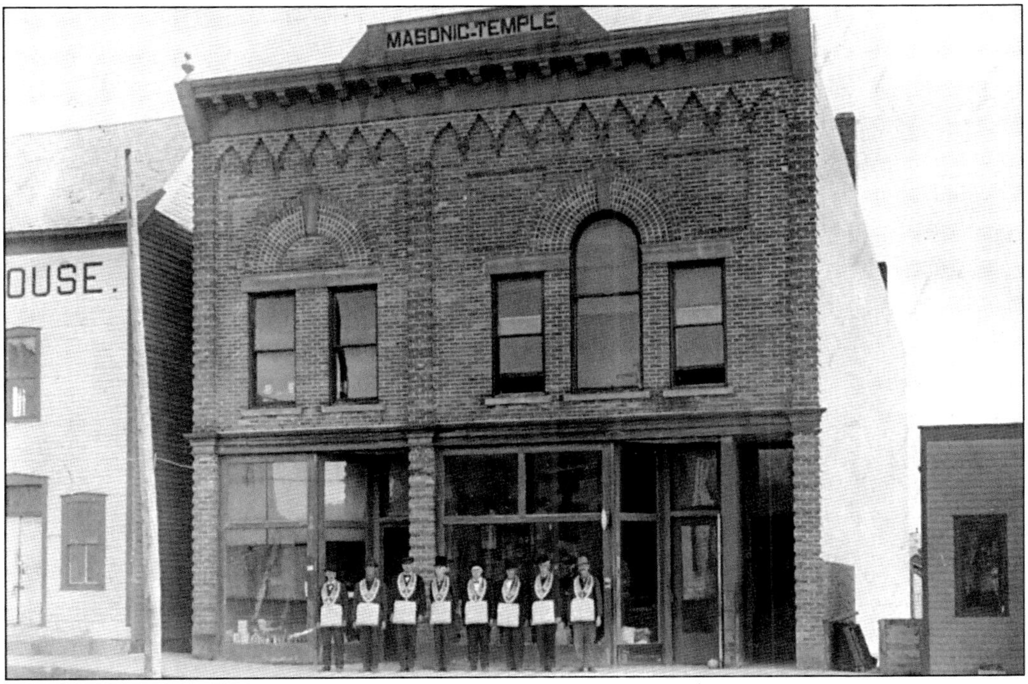

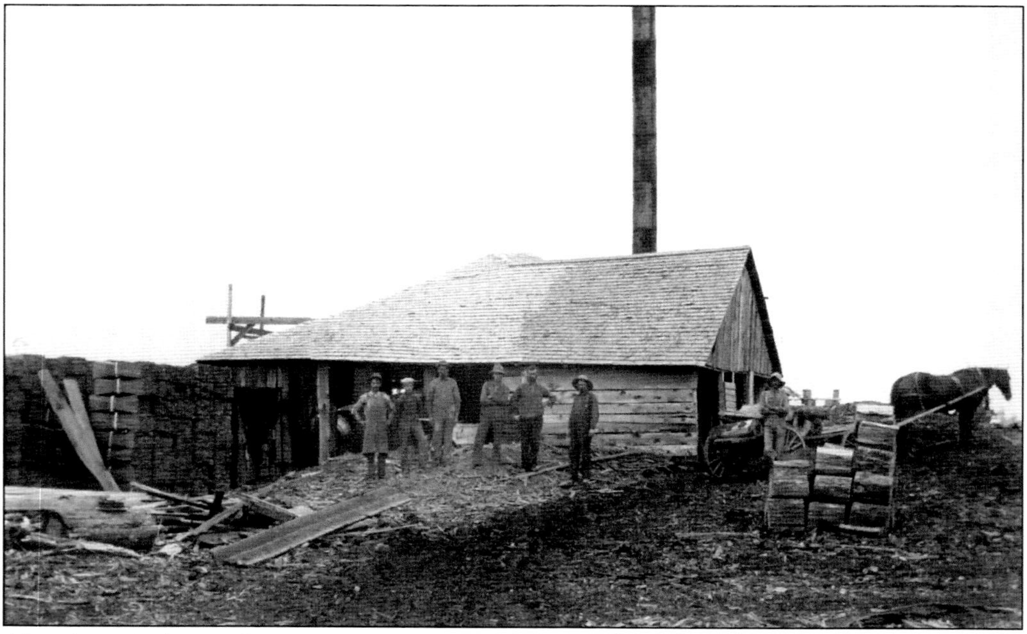

Abundant timber and easy water access to lumber mills and markets via tributaries of the Pine River in Fremont Township caused the Winn area to be settled. Among the many local area lumber-related enterprises was the shingle mill, above, a lumber sawmill, and a planing mill. The rough-and-ready neighborhood north of the platted village of Winn was once called Hardscrabble. As the timber in the area was harvested and lumbering petered out, the land was cleared for agricultural purposes, most commonly using the stump puller. Below, Elmer Moor, left, and his unidentified crew pause for the camera during a Fremont Township clearing project near Dushville/Winn.

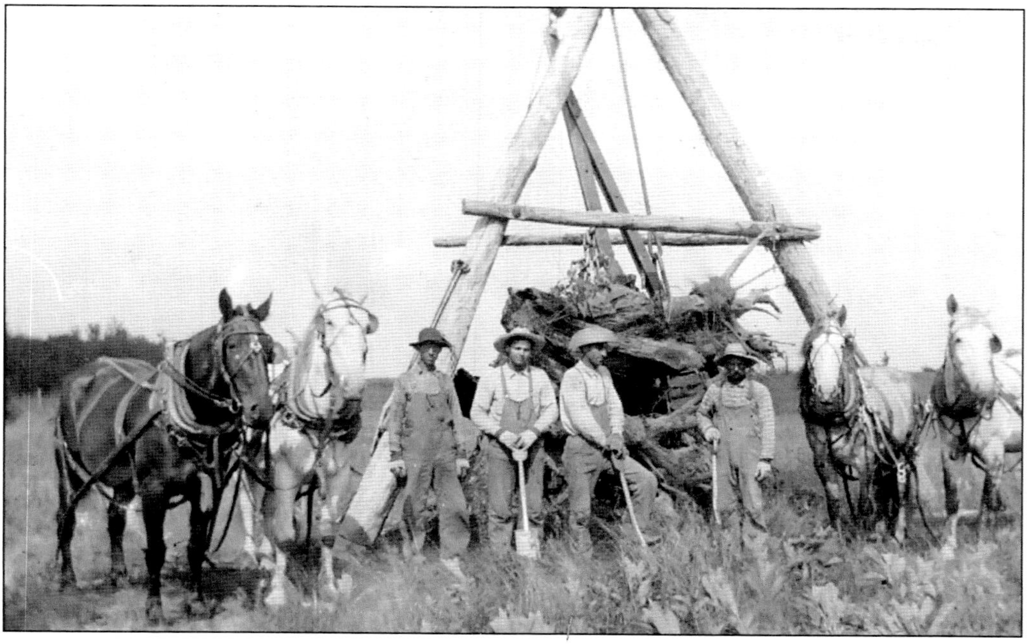

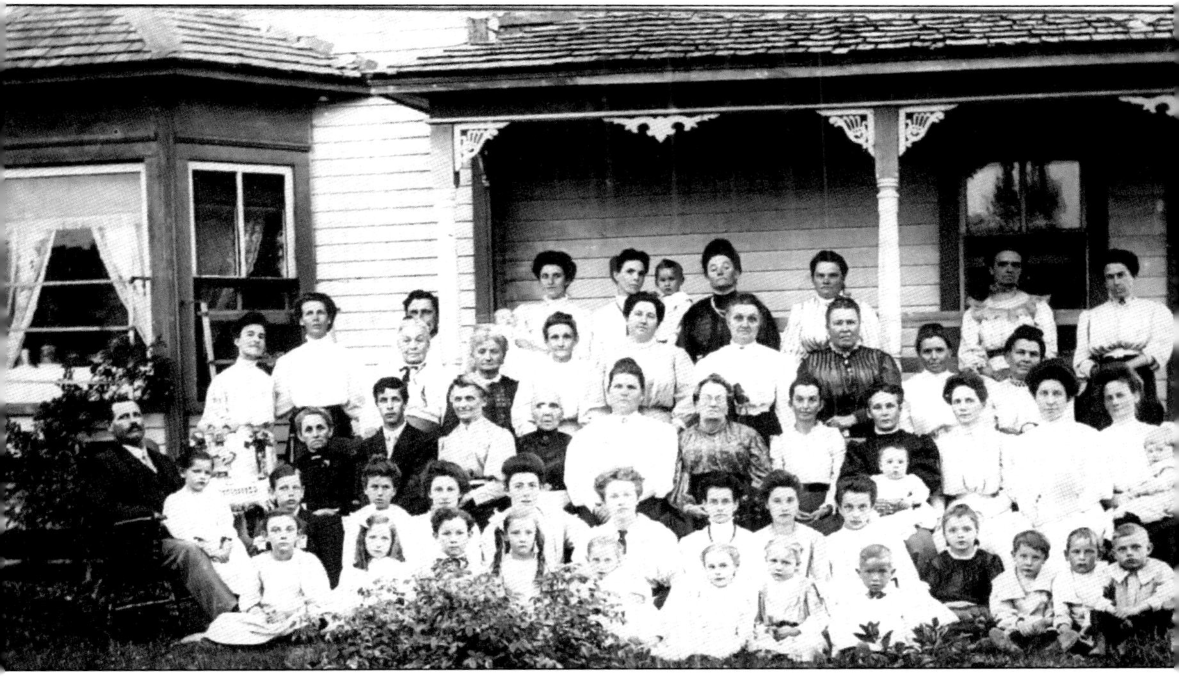

This photograph from the 1967 Winn centennial book shows the 1908 ladies' aid society of Winn posing in front of the parsonage: from left to right, (first row) Marie Morrison, Lucille Adams, Leon Perkins, Kaloe Morrison, Glee Verda Adams, Inez Richardson, Vivian Richardson, Floyd Gifford, Tresa Taylor, Percy Richardson, Lyle Hunt, and Arley Hunt; (second row) Trudy Earl, Esther Osborn, Grace B. Starkweather, Ada Taylor, Arty Reen, Nelly Allen, and Susan Hunt; (third row) Rev. Elmer Vaughn, Bessie Vaughn, Harry Vaughn, Mrs. Vaughn, Vern Vaughn, Mrs. Earl, Grandma Dent, Mrs. Dickerson, Mrs. Vickery, Mrs. Allyn, Maude Richardson, Vada Richardson, Anna Tucker, unidentified, Clara Adams, and Glee Adams; (fourth row) Rachel Sanderson, unidentified, Mrs. Osborn, Rose Priest, Joy Baker, Mrs. Carroll, Clara Sanderson, and Kate Vanalstins; (fifth row) Olive Foglesong, Jen Sullivan, Bert Adamas, Flou Richardson, Sabra Gifford, Lila Gifford, Amina Perkins, Anna Hunt, Mrs. Ryan, and Hannah Foglesong. In the fashion of the time, some married women's first names were not published.

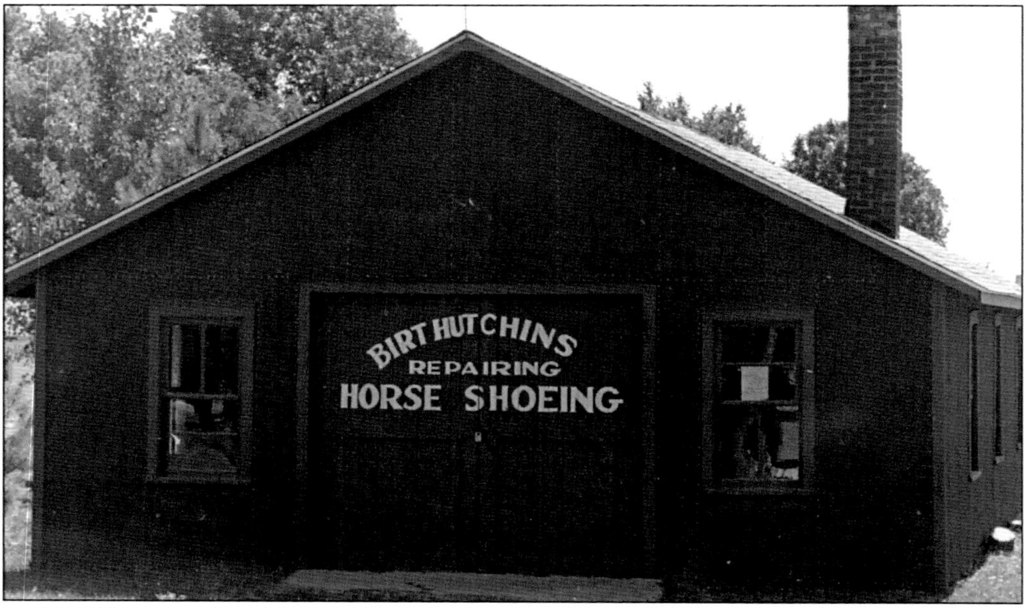

In 1957, Winn resident Norval Morey perfected and patented a tree-debarking machine, and Morbark industries was born, with the early prototypes fabricated in the blacksmith shop at Winn, above. The Morbark name has gained international fame and has an expanding line of forest-harvesting products, combined with a corresponding growth of the headquarters, factory, and offices, just outside Winn in section 15, Fremont Township, below. Morey shared his success in a number of ways with the people of Isabella County; among them, he founded the Morey Cancer Center at Central Michigan Community Hospital, the Morey Foundation, and the Morey Public School Academy.

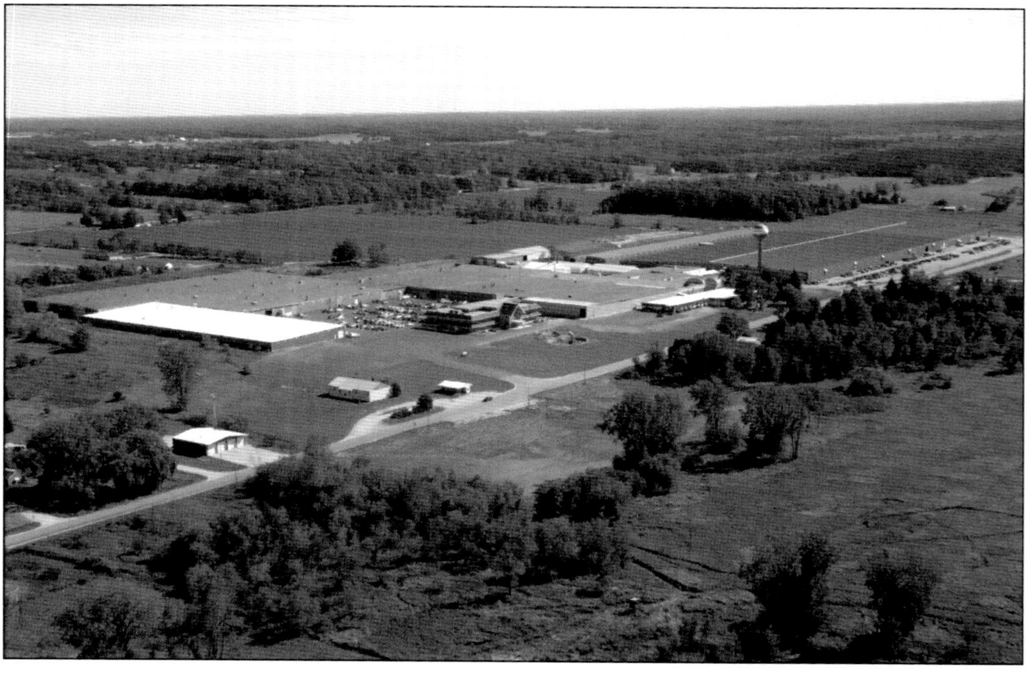

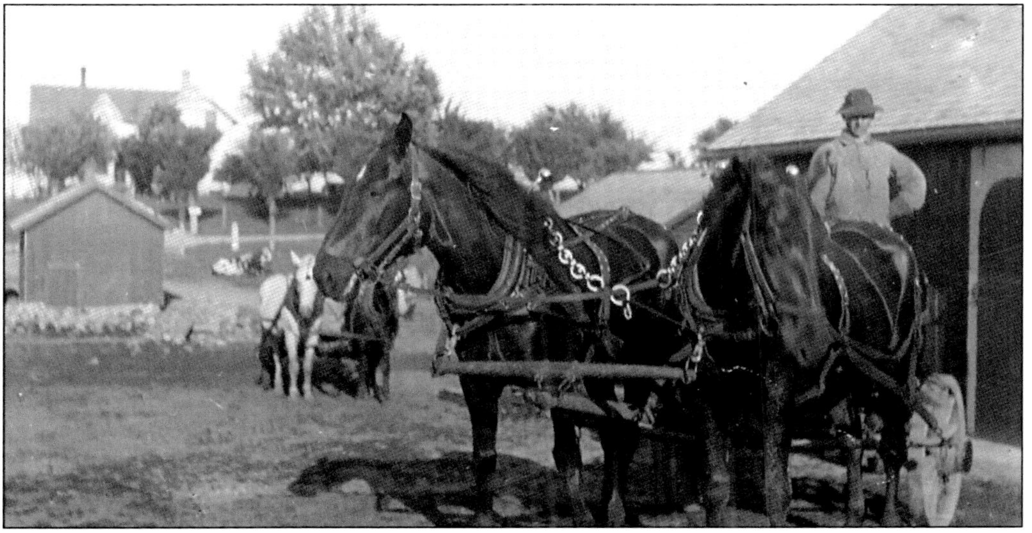

Peter Gruss came from Germany to Grand Rapids in 1879, after serving in the army and learning the butcher trade. Not liking butcher work, in 1885 Peter, above, turned to farming, buying a place on River Road south of Beal City in Deerfield Township. Years later, Peter turned the farm over to his son Joseph. Below, in 1925, a roving photographer was captivated by and took a photograph of Joseph's sons Clarence, Bernard, and Rollen sitting at the roadside in front of the farmhouse.

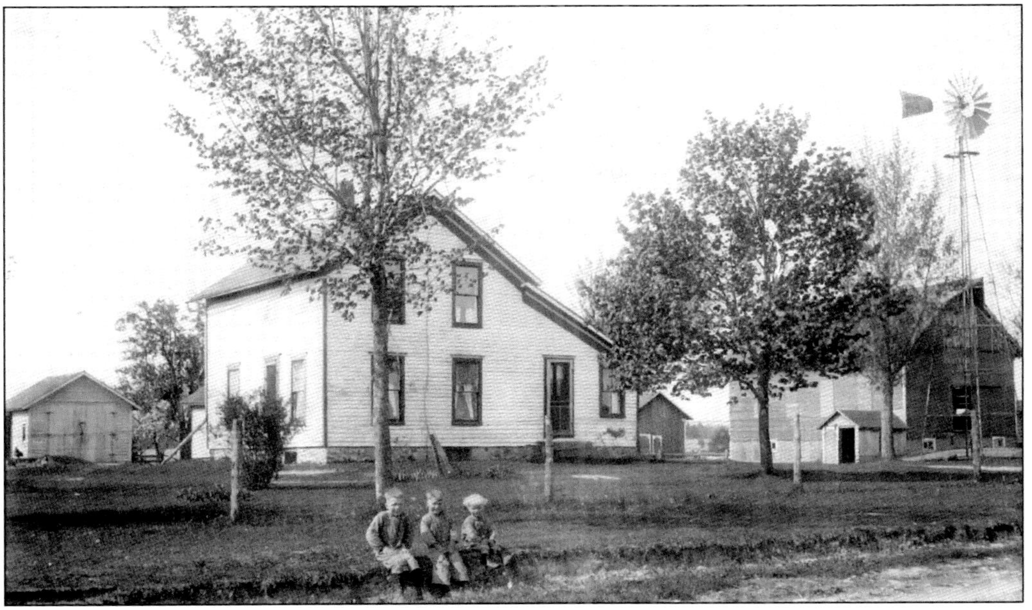

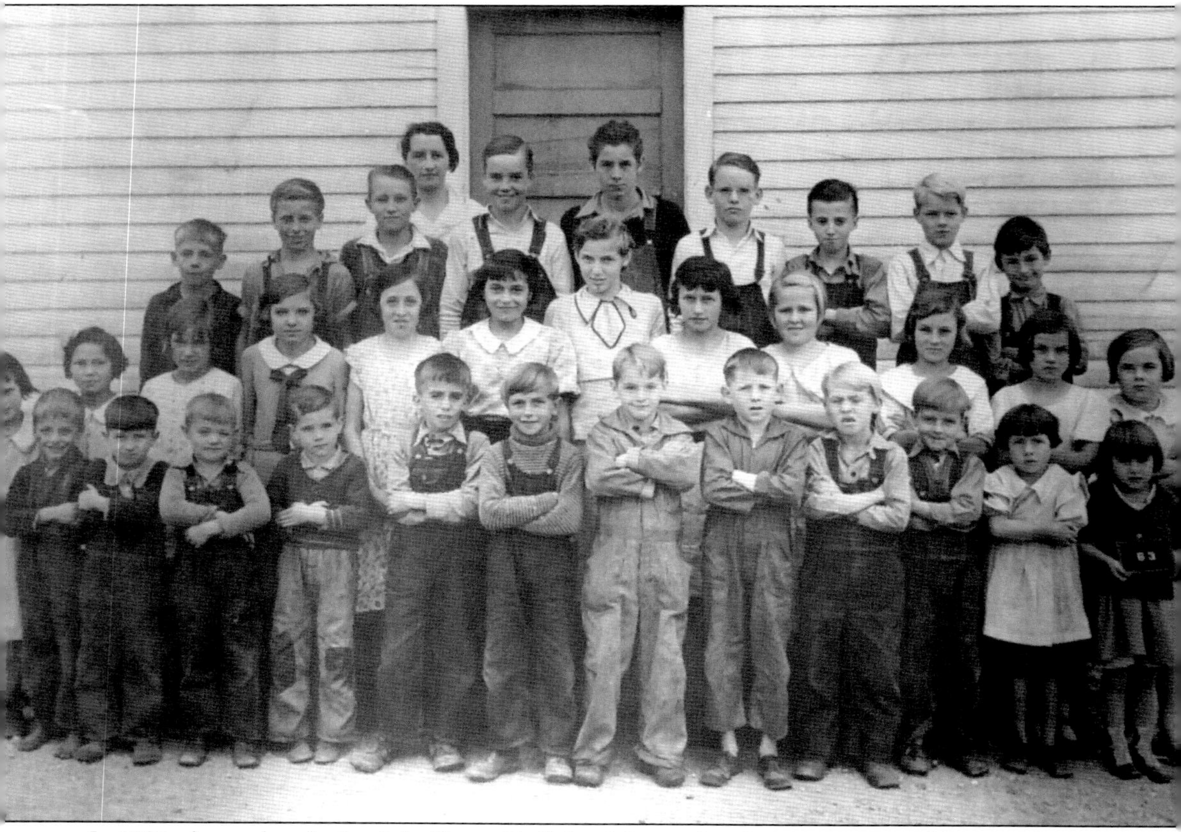

In 1936, the student body of the Reynolds School, located at the intersection of River and Winn Roads in Deerfield Township, included, from left to right, (first row) John Mrazck, Pete Gruss, Jack Boettner, Francis Engler, Robert Fedewa, Charles Mrazck, Henry Kornexel, Junior Rhode, Ed Zuker, Francis Gruss, Donna Rhode, and Rosemary Gruss; (second row) Irene Brever, Ann Brever, unidentified, Emma Esch, Tricia Rhode, unidentified, Russ Kornel, Louise Mrazck, Ovella Rhode, Helen Gruss, Eileen Gruss, and Rosemary Engler; (third row) Matt Engler, Matt Kornel, Gerald Jenning, Vern Fedewa, Robert Rhode, Joe Mrazck, unidentified, Rollen Gruss, and D. Hoisington; (fourth row) teacher Theo Neyer. (Courtesy of Pete Gruss.)

BIBLIOGRAPHY

Beal City Centennial Committee. *Beal City Michigan Area, 1875–1975.* Mount Pleasant, MI: Beal City Centennial Committee, 1975.
Coleman Centennial Committee. *Coleman Area, 1871–1971.* Coleman, MI: self-published, 1971.
Cumming, John. *The First 100 Years: A Portrait of Central Michigan University, 1892–1992*, Mount Pleasant, MI: Central Michigan University Press, 1992.
———. *This Place Mount Pleasant.* Mount Pleasant, MI: Central Michigan University Press, 1989.
Day, J. E. *Sketch of the Settlement and Growth of Isabella County.* Lansing, MI: Michigan Pioneer and Historical Collections, Michigan Pioneer and Historical Society, 1896.
Fancher, Isaac A. *Past and Present of Isabella County Michigan.* Indianapolis. IN: B. F. Bowen and Company, 1911.
Forsburg, Marilyn Geasler. *Brinton! I Used to Go There to Dances.* Mount Pleasant, MI: self-published, 2002.
Isabella County Genealogical Society. *Isabella County, Michigan, Families and History.* Paducah, KY: Turner Publishing, 2003.
Jaquith, Charles E. *Shepherd: An Historical Review.* Shepherd, MI: Grim Printing, 2002.
Johnson, Charles F. *Isabella County.* Grand Rapids, MI: unpublished manuscript, 1991. Clarke Historical Library, Central Michigan University.
Miller, H. A., and Charles J. Seely. *Faces and Places Familiar.* Mount Pleasant, MI: Courier Press, 1906.
Portrait and Biographical Album, Isabella County Michigan. Chicago, IL: Chapman Brothers, 1884.
Shepherd Area Historical Society. *Isabella County 1982.* Dallas, TX: Taylor Publishing Company, 1982.
Shepherd Centennial Committee. *Salt River/Shepherd, 1857–1957.* Shepherd, MI: Grim Printing, 1957.
Weidman Area Centennial Committee. *Weidman Area Centennial Book.* Weidman, MI: 1994.
Winn Centennial Committee. *Winn 1867–1967.* Winn, MI: Winn Centennial Committee, 1967.